A Pearson Custom Publication

Accounting and Finance

MA and MSc Courses

Compiled from:

Finance and Accounting for Non-Specialist Students
by Alan Pizzey

Essential Financial Accounting for Managers
by Leslie Chadwick

Accounting for Non-Accounting Students
Sixth Edition
by J. R. Dyson

Essential Management Accounting for Managers
by Leslie Chadwick

Accounting and Finance for Non-Specialists
Fourth Edition
by Peter Atrill and Eddie McLaney

Pearson Education Limited
Edinburgh Gate
Harlow
Essex CM20 2JE

And associated companies throughout the world

Visit us on the World Wide Web at:
www.pearsoned.co.uk

First published 2006

Taken from:

Finance and Accounting for Non-Specialist Students
by Alan Pizzey
ISBN 0 273 63020 2

Essential Financial Accounting for Managers
by Leslie Chadwick

ISBN 0 27364659 1

Accounting for Non-Accounting Students Sixth Edition
by J. R. Dyson

ISBN 0 273 68385 3

Essential Management Accounting for Managers
by Leslie Chadwick

ISBN 0 273 64654 0

Accounting and Finance for Non-Specialists Fourth Edition
by Peter Atrill and Eddie McLaney

ISBN 0 273 67962 7

ISBN-10 1 84479 582 9
ISBN-13 978 1 84479 582 6

Printed and bound in Great Britain by Henry Ling Limited at the Dorset Press, Dorchester, DT1 1HD

Contents

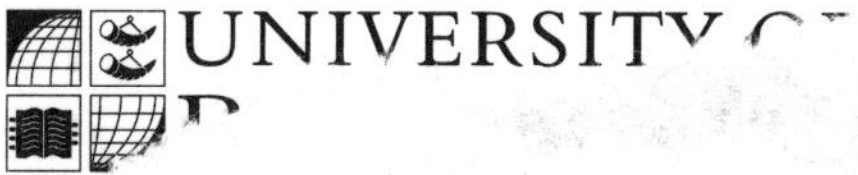

Accounting and Finance

MA and MSc Courses

We work with leading authors to develop the strongest educational materials bringing cutting-edge thinking and best learning practice to a global market.

Under a range of well-known imprints, including Financial Times/Prentice Hall, Addison Wesley and Longman, we craft high quality print and electronic publications which help readers to understand and apply their content, whether studying or at work.

Pearson Custom Publishing enables our customers to access a wide and expanding range of market-leading content from world-renowned authors and develop their own tailor-made book. You choose the content that meets your needs and Pearson Custom Publishing produces a high-quality printed book.

To find out more about custom publishing, visit www.pearsoncustom.co.uk

Preface

This bespoke textbook has been especially designed and compiled by Leslie Chadwick to meet the needs of Bradford University School of Management's MA and MSc students, for their foundation level core module in accounting and finance. *The design should ensure that it is suitable for full time, part-time, distance learning, and action learning study modes.*

Why have a bespoke textbook?

A bespoke book enables us to combine in one book, chapters written by a number of the leading accounting and finance authors. The authors whose work is featured in this text are all FT/Prentice Hall authors, and are:

Peter Atrill
Leslie Chadwick
John Dyson
Eddie McLaney
Alan Pizzey

The objectives

This foundation level text should help you to acquire and develop a knowledge and understanding of the terminology, concepts, principles and the application of the techniques which are used in accounting and finance *e.g. how the figures in the profit and loss account, balance sheet, and cash flow statement have been arrived at; preparing a financial performance analysis; the costing of a product or service; total absorption costing; marginal costing; budgetary control including cash budgets and behavioural aspects; capital investment appraisal;* and to appreciate their limitations.

Teaching and learning features

It is recognised, that for many of you who will be using this text, that English is not your first language, and that many of you have not studied accounting and finance before.

The principal teaching and learning features of this textbook, are:

- You can benefit from the experience of a number of leading authors
- It uses a concise and user friendly writing style, which is both readable and understandable
- The learning objectives are clearly defined at the beginning of each chapter
- Each chapter ends with a chapter summary which provides a useful over-view of the key messages contained within the chapter
- It provides a number of self assessment activities, with suggested answers within the text to encourage self learning

The design, it is hoped should help you to develop your numerical skills, and your discursive and analytical ability.

MA and MSc Accounting and Finance

1 The provision of financial information

OBJECTIVES

The aims of this chapter are to enable students to:

- relate accountancy to the provision of useful financial information;
- appreciate the objectives of the corporate report;
- understand the wide spectrum of stakeholders who have an interest in that report; and
- explain the basic principles on which accounting statements rest.

ACCOUNTING FOR THE BUSINESS

Businesses and other organisations (e.g. hospitals, charities, local authorities) use resources that are under the control of managers. It is appropriate that the managers should report from time to time to those parties who have provided the resources, to inform them of the success of their operations, and the disposition of the resources entrusted to their care. In order to report, it is necessary to account for transactions (i.e. economic events such as sales, purchases, investments) and show their effect on the business during a stated period. Accounting has been defined as the process of identifying, measuring and communicating business information to facilitate judgements and decision making. To do this it covers many different activities and provides a service to a wide spectrum of interested parties both inside and outside the business. The elements of accounting which lead to the provision of financial information are as follows.

■ Accounting system

Setting up and operating an accounting system to recognise and record transactions implies that all economic events in the business, from the payment of wages to the purchase of a subsidiary company, are entered into the system, which is organised to minimise the possibility of resources being misused. Wages sheets, invoices, petty cash vouchers, bank paying-in slips and other prime documents are the means whereby transactions enter the system.

Classification and measurement

Transactions can be classified as creating assets or liabilities, costs or revenues, and these classifications can be further analysed into subgroups. Classification helps to sort out a great mass of transactions and reduce them to order.

TASK 1.1 How many subclassifications can you think of to analyse the costs of a business?

Solution

Your solution could include the following:

- material costs
- labour costs
- production overhead costs
- administration costs
- selling and marketing costs
- financial costs.

If classification produces a set of alternatives, so too does measurement. Judgement is needed to decide on the amount in money terms which will represent a transaction in the system. The value of an asset or the amount of a cost may vary according to the circumstances for which the figure is to be used. It is important to realise at an early stage that financial information is not precisely accurate, and that it may be the outcome of a series of assumptions or judgements, known as accounting policies.

TASK 1.2 A business own a factory building. How many ways can you think of to value the building?

Solution

Some alternatives might be:

- *historical value* (i.e. the amount paid when it was purchased five years ago);
- *replacement value* (i.e. the amount payable if it was bought today);
- *realisable value* (i.e. the amount receivable if it was sold today);
- *economic value* (i.e. the value of the profits to be made from the factory in the future).

Summarisation

Once all the transactions for a period have been recorded and classified they can be summarised into accounting statements. The profit and loss account sets cost against revenue to disclose a profit or loss for the period. The balance sheet lists the assets of the business and the claims against those assets from lenders and owners who have provided the funds used to pay for the assets. This discloses the financial position of the business. Cost statements also summarise a situation for managers entrusted with the resources used by a department.

Communication and interpretation

The provision of financial information is not an end in itself. Accounting statements must be carefully drafted to disclose what users need to know, and what the law (the Companies Act 1985) says they have a right to know. The accountant can also interpret business activity by commenting on the statements, focusing attention on significant items, showing the relationship of one figure to another (e.g. net profit as a percentage of capital employed), and explaining the implications of the financial information for the policy and objectives of the business.

THE CORPORATE REPORT

This is the title of the document which a company, public or private, must produce each year to disclose its performance and financial position. Most companies produce an interim report at the halfway stage, but the annual report, usually published some months after the end of the financial year, is presented to the Annual General Meeting (AGM) for acceptance and confirmation by the shareholders who own the business. Such a report provides a significant opportunity for a public relations exercise and perhaps as much as half of the pages of the report are taken up by a chairman's statement, glossy photographs and other material in order to convince the shareholders that they are right to hold and retain their shares, and make further investments in the company.

The rest of the report concerns the financial statements, which are subject to an independent audit report confirming that they are 'true and fair'. These statements are as follows:

- *The directors' report*, which shows information prescribed by the Companies Act 1985 concerning directors, dividends, share capital, etc.
- *The profit and loss account*, which sets costs against revenue to disclose a profit or loss made during the period, and then shows how the surplus is appropriated to pay tax, and a dividend.
- *The balance sheet*, which analyses the assets as fixed (long-term) and current, and shows the claims against those assets by lenders and shareholders who have provided the funds to purchase them. This statement concerns one point in time – the period end.
- *The cash flow statement*, which analyses cash flowing in to and out of the business during the period.
- *The notes to the accounts*, which explain the figures in the accounting statements, such as an analysis of fixed assets, or debtors, or movements in shareholders' funds. A major note concerns the accounting policies covering the accounting methods, assumptions and judgements used to prepare the accounts.

- *The auditor's report,* which confirms to the shareholders that the accounts presented to them by the directors who manage the company on their behalf show a true and fair view.

Some recent additions to the corporate report have been introduced to meet requirements of the Stock Exchange which, following the Cadbury Report, requires statements covering the corporate governance of the business.

The objectives of the corporate report

Corporate reporting is a costly exercise considering that a copy is sent to every shareholder, and it is expected that these costs will bring associated benefits. The objectives, however, are somewhat in conflict, and doubts remain as to whether the corporate report is worth the cost involved. The objectives of the report are as follows.

Statutory

The Companies Act stipulates that the directors who are elected by the shareholders to manage the business should report on their activities. Statute lays down the minimum amount of information to be disclosed and the format of the balance sheet and profit and loss account. The corporate report is a public document filed with the Registrar of Companies.

Stewardship

The financial information made available, accounts to shareholders for the actions of the directors in terms of profit made in the year, and assets owned at the end of the year. This is a backward-looking assessment commenting on recent past history, with directors reporting as 'stewards' to the owners of the business, whose funds they are elected to manage.

Decision usefulness

This objective is that the financial statements should provide shareholders with information that assists them with decisions which they need to take (i.e. to sell, hold, or buy shares in the business). Such decisions should be based on forward-looking information, so this objective is in conflict with stewardship, which reports on past activity. Directors are not willing to disclose their intentions in budgets, and auditors might find it difficult to report on such figures, so shareholders are left to update historical information with the aid of confident but unaudited public relations statements when they make their decisions.

Confirmatory

The market for investment funds is well served by information about companies as investments opportunities, but not all of this information is reliable. It stems from company announcements, stockbrokers' advice, and the financial columns of newspapers. Some information may be biased and some may be only rumour. The corporate report provides the investor with an opportunity to confirm this 'market information' against audited financial statements.

■ Users of the corporate report

Every business has a wide spectrum of stakeholders with an interest in its operations, and the corporate report provides useful information to all these groups. It must be recognised, however, that the information needs of groups of users differ widely, and the corporate report is subject to considerable conflict to meet these disparate requirements. At the same time, many user groups do not pay for their information, since the cost of the corporate report is borne out profits which belong to the shareholders. The main users can be grouped together as follows.

Shareholders

The legal owners who have invested in the business by buying shares cannot easily be considered as a single group. An individual may hold a few shares, while an investment institution such as a pension fund may own as much as a five per cent stake in the company. Potential shareholders who are considering the purchase of shares, and especially other companies contemplating a take over bid, will also use the corporate report, but with varying degrees of financial sophistication. Some shareholders are interested only in the dividend to be paid, while others need to know about the 'quality' of profits (will they continue into the future), the disposition of assets, the ability of the business to survive and grow, and the risks involved with their investments.

Managers and employees

Most managers will know a great deal about that part of the business under their control, but comparatively little about other parts of the business. People who work for a company have invested their careers rather than their money, and they need an overview to inform them about company performance and the chances of continuing employment and promotion. Trades union representatives also have an interest in the performance of the business.

Lenders

Lenders can be divided into long-term or short-term lenders to the business, but they all have an interest in the security of their loans, and the risk that they will not be repaid. Some long-term loans may be secured on the fixed assets of the business (e.g. plant, property) with interest paid on the loan up to the date of repayment. Such lenders need to know whether the profit made is enough to cover the interest and whether the assets are sufficient security for their loans. Short-term lenders vary from banks which have advanced large amounts of overdraft finance, to trade creditors who need to be paid soon for goods supplied on credit terms. These lenders are interested in the short-term assets of the business (i.e. stocks and debtors) that will soon generate a cash flow from which they are to be repaid.

The Inland Revenue

The published accounts provide the starting point for the tax computation, which works from the accounting profit to the taxable profit on which corporation tax is levied. Some costs are not allowable for tax purposes and must be added back to the profit, while taxation allowances are then deducted. Depreciation is not a tax allowable expense so it is added back to profit, and then capital allowances calculated for the fixed assets are deducted.

Customers and competitors

Customers use financial statements to ensure that they are buying from a reputable business with sufficient resources to perform according to contract. This is particularly important when a subcontractor or component supplier is involved. Competitors use published financial statements to assess the profitability and financial status of rival firms. Competitors are particularly interested to see an analysis of the turnover of another business to compute market share, but managers are keen to preserve the confidentiality of some items, and thus disclose only the legal minimum of information. In some industries it is possible to organise an interfirm comparison scheme whereby accounting ratios computed from corporate reports are compared with the average for a similar group of companies as a measure of performance.

Analysts and advisors

This group comprises stockbrokers, financial advisers and columnists who are among the most financially sophisticated users of the corporate report. They are specialists in 'market information' and use the corporate report to check on other information they have gathered through various channels.

The corporate report has somewhat conflicting goals, and provides information for a wide spectrum of users with disparate levels of financial sophistication and quite different requirements so far as information is required. No single document can cater adequately for all these needs within the parameters of cost/benefit considerations and the needs of managers to preserve confidentiality.

TASK 1.3

As a supplier of raw materials, you sell £50 000 of goods to one customer each month, allowing payment three months after delivery. What items in the corporate report of your customer would be of interest to you?

Solution

Some points in the solution might be:

- the amount of liquid assets – cash and short-term investments in the balance sheet with which to pay the £150 000 you are owed (i.e. 3 months × £50 000);
- the claims of other creditors, including the bank overdraft and unpaid taxation, on the liquid resources of the business;

- the amount of debtors and stocks in the balance sheet which will turn into cash eventually;
- the volume of cash flow in the cash flow statement;
- a profit; remember that losses waste the resources of the business which will then no longer be available to make payment.

MANAGEMENT ACCOUNTING

The corporate report provides information to those outside the business, but management accounting is used to provide financial information that will assist managers with their tasks of planning, decision making, communicating, organising, and controlling the transactions of the business. Management accountants adopt a different attitude from the financial accountants who produce the corporate report, derived from the different situation in which they work. The major differences are as follows.

Users

The corporate report has a wide spectrum of users, but a management accounting statement is tailored to fit the needs of the managers involved, and is often limited to the operations under their control – a department. Management accounting must be cost effective, providing information which will enable managers to control operations, perhaps by a comparison of budgeted cost to actual cost, or will assist them in solving problems and deciding appropriately when alternatives present themselves.

Statutory requirements

The corporate report is confined within a set of disclosure rules contained in the Companies Act 1985, and further accounting rules (i.e. Financial Reporting Standards (FRSs) laid down by the accounting profession. There is no set format for a management accounting statement, which is drafted in a form that will be most helpful to the recipient. While the corporate report is a public document available for all to see, management accounting deals with matters which are confidential to the business.

Periodicity

The corporate report for the year looks back on what has taken place, and appears several months after the end of the period. Management accounting provides more immediate information, since managers cannot wait to learn of the success or failure of their activities and organise remedial action if necessary. The period covered by a management accounting statement might be a week, or a month, or a quarter, but to be of interest to forward-looking managers the statement must be completed very soon after the end of the accounting period. This creates a tension, since the need for speed in reporting is often achieved by forgoing accuracy, and the management accountant must establish tolerances with the managers to whom the information is provided.

Analysis

The corporate report gives an overview of the whole business, with comparative figures for the previous year, but management accounting analyses transactions to show the contribution made by the constituent parts to the overall profit. Management accounting can compare performance with a previous period, but it is more likely to make a comparison of actual with the budget or planned performance in order to identify remedial action required at an early stage.

Technique

Management accountants use the financial accounting system, but that is only a part of their activities. Forecasting and budgeting will need the skills of the mathematician and economist to deal with risk and uncertainty, while the application of behavioural theories assists when control reports are made. Above all management accounting is forward looking.

Audit

A further statutory requirement is that the corporate report should be subject to an audit in order to confirm the reliability of the statements submitted by the directors to the shareholders. With management accounting there is no such formal audit, but the system of internal control will build in checks and balances to ensure the reliability of the figures. The management accountant will need to explain to the recipient of the statement, the assumptions and techniques applied to produce forward-looking management information. The internal audit department, which checks the operation of the accounting system and protects the assets from misuse, is an important part of management accounting. Managerial information is expensive to produce and, accordingly, is subjected to a different type of audit based on cost/benefit principles, whereby the worth of financial information must be proved and its use optimised if its production is to be maintained.

THE CHARACTERISTICS OF USEFUL FINANCIAL INFORMATION

Whether in the corporate report, or as part of management accounting, the design and provision of financial information must conform to certain principles.

Relevance

The accountant must accept the discipline of selecting information that is of interest to the user. The statement gains focus by highlighting significant points, and adapts the format of the information to meet user needs. This characteristic is more important for management accounting than financial reporting, where statute prescribes what is to be disclosed and user needs are spread over a wide spectrum of stakeholders. Non-relevant information supplied to a manager may complicate performance evaluation or the issue on which a decision is to be made, and can lead to mistakes in the absence of clear focused thought.

Reliability

Financial information must be reliable if it is to be used with confidence. An audit report, verifying the system used and confirming the methods and assumptions applied, will increase user confidence. Accounts should be complete and free of bias, showing all aspects of the situation. There is a tension here between the need for relevant figures (e.g. the current value of property) and reliable figures, when valuation can produce widely different amounts for the same asset depending on the individual valuer and the method used.

Understandability

A useful financial statement will present its information as simply as possible and in a format which is easy to assimilate. A complicated mass of detail will confuse users, but the oversimplification of complex business affairs will not communicate adequately with users. As in the corporate report, a brief statement accentuating certain figures will need to be supported by notes to the accounts that give a more detailed explanation to those users who can appreciate further analysis.

Perspective

Financial information may be confusing to users unless it is set in context by the disclosure of 'comparative' figures. The corporate report always places last year's figures alongside current information. Good management accounting will show figures for the same month last year, or for the budget this month, or will quote costs as a percentage of the total, or per unit. The consistent use of accounting rules and assumptions enables comparison to be made with other firms, both within and outside a group of companies.

Timeliness

Information which is out of date has lost much of its usefulness for control, appraisal, or decision-making purposes. Good managers are by nature forward looking and thinking of the next set of transactions to be organised, so delayed cost information may be seen as an irritant rather than a cost-effective management tool.

THE BASIC PRINCIPLES ON WHICH ACCOUNTING STATEMENTS REST

Some assumptions are so fundamental to the accountant that it is assumed that they are followed when accounts are drafted, and a note to the accounts must warn users if this is not the case. There are *four* important principles which are enshrined in most financial information.

The going concern

When the accounts of a business are drafted it is assumed that the business is going to continue in operation in the future. Without this assumption, assets would have to be valued at what they would realise if sold, and this amount is very different from their 'book value' (i.e. historic cost less depreciation to date) or 'value to the business' (i.e. if they are held to be used in profit-making operations rather than for immediate sale). The auditor must be satisfied that the business is a going concern.

TASK 1.4 What items do you consider to be significant when judgement is exercised to test the going concern assumption for a business?

Solution

Some points worthy of consideration are as follows:

- Short-term financial viability – Can the business pay its way in the future? Are its liquid resources (e.g. cash) insufficient to meet known liabilities, in which case trade creditors and the bank will no longer have confidence to lend short-term finance?
- Capital structure – Has the business balanced its long-term capital requirements between owner and lenders, and can it recruit additional funds to finance future operations? Is profit large enough to give confidence to investors to risk their funds?
- Competitive condition – Is the business efficient in terms of costs, and can it acquire sufficient materials, labour, and new plant to continue in the future?

Matching, or the 'accruals' principle

When a profit is measured it is important to match the cost of earning sales revenue with that revenue, so that cost and revenue represent the same goods and time period. The cost of goods purchased but not yet used is carried forward to next year as the closing stock, a short-term asset in the balance sheet. It would be wrong to charge the cost of materials not used against the revenue earned by the sale of other products.

Prudence, or 'conservatism'

Uncertainty exists in most business transactions until the deal is complete, so a prudent approach is needed to avoid counting a profit before the transaction is finalised. The accountant will select the lower asset value, or profit, when alternatives are available in order to avoid overstating a profit and paying a dividend out of a surplus which later proves to be illusory. This rule can be summarised as: 'Anticipate no profit and provide for all possible future losses'.

Matching prompts accountants to carry forward unused cost items as assets, but prudence demands that those assets are valued at realistic/conservative amounts.

Hence the rule for the valuation of stock in the balance sheet at the lower of cost or net realisable value, to take no profit made because stock values have increased since their purchase, but to account for any loss made if stocks are worth less than their cost at the balance sheet date.

Prudence can be misused by accountants who make provisions against profit in a good year to release in a bad year, thus smoothing out the fluctuation of business income and disclosing a false picture to users. Bias in accounts caused by understating asset value departs from the need for correct reliable figures.

■ Consistency

Judgement in the selection of appropriate values and methods to use when drafting financial statements is an essential part of accounting. Once the choice is made, the same method must be used in future years if comparability over time is to be achieved. To change methods in order to increase the profit disclosed is to introduce an unacceptable element of bias into the accounts. Change is only allowed to improve the true and fair view disclosed in the statements.

OTHER CONVENTIONS OF ACCOUNTING

Accounting principles depend for their authority on their acceptance by accountants as the best way to operate. Accordingly change is slow as the accounting profession reacts to new situations. Important principles are as follows:

- *Objectivity* (as opposed to subjectivity), which seeks to verify the value accorded to transactions by evidence (an invoice), rather than by valuations which may be biased;
- *Materiality*, which holds that unimportant items should not be allowed to confuse the message contained in a financial statement and need not thus be disclosed. Unfortunately, a good definition of what is 'material' has not yet been agreed;
- *Substance over form* – a relatively new principle – suggests that the strict legal form of a transaction can be ignored if it impedes the disclosure of a true and fair view, and can be substituted by the economic substance or commercial effect of the transaction. If a company leases a machine from a bank, the asset belongs to the bank, and if the rentals are paid up to date then there is no amount owing. Thus the legal form of this situation is that no asset or liability exists in the company accounts at the balance sheet date. However, if, as part of the leasing contract, the company has a right to control the use of the machine throughout its working life, the machine may be considered as an asset of the company, rather than of the bank. If future rentals are agreed as payable by a contract, then they too should appear in the balance sheet as a long-term loan. In this and similar situations most accountants now agree that economic substance requires the balance sheet to show the asset and the liability.

CONCLUSION

In this chapter, we have demonstrated the great variety of financial information provided by organisations, and the very real differences between information for users outside the business and for managers. A further problem is the disparity of financial sophistication between user groups and the tensions which this places on providers of financial information. Statute and principles have evolved to ensure that a minimum of useful information is adequately presented, but inevitably, accounting statements cannot fully meet the needs of all users. Good accounting is not an end in itself, but must be judged on the usefulness of its product, and depends also for its value on the skill and judgement employed and on the methods selected for application when transactions are processed.

DISCUSSION TOPICS

Thirty-minute essay questions

1 'Accountancy is not only concerned with recording transactions, it provides a service to a wide spectrum of interested parties.' Discuss.

2 'Corporate reporting is a costly exercise, but the objectives of the exercise are far from clear.' Explain.

3 The information needs of the various groups of users of the corporate report vary widely. Who are these users and how far do their needs for financial information differ?

4 Relate the characteristics of useful financial information to the information needs of a manager.

4

The profit and loss account

Objectives

When you have worked through all the material contained in this chapter, you should be able to do the following:

- ☐ Calculate the:
  - cost of sales;
  - gross profit;
  - net profit;
  - retained profit (profit and loss account balance) carried forward.
- ☐ Have a good working knowledge of the format and purpose of the profit and loss account and the appropriation account, as used by a company for internal accounting purposes.

The profit and loss account (P&L)

This can be described as the account in which the profit or loss is computed. It is concerned with the measurement of business income for an accounting period, for example one year. The economic activity of the accounting period is measured according to the rules, such as accounting concepts, accounting standards and the relevant legislation. It provides the answer to the question 'how much have we made?'

You have probably encountered a type of profit and loss account in your social life. The income and expenditure account used by clubs and non-profit-making societies is really a profit and loss account under another name. The illustration in Figure 4.1 could have been

Profit and loss account for the period ended . . .
Income less Expenditure equals **Profit or loss**

Figure 4.1 The calculation of the profit or loss

called an income and expenditure account. If that were the case, the profit would probably be described as a surplus and a loss as a deficiency.

The profit and loss account is often **referred to as the P&L account P&L or the income statement**. Thus, the income for the period has to be compared with, or matched against, the expenditure for that period involved in generating the income. This provides the profit figure, as illustrated in Figure 4.2.

However, for limited companies the picture is a little more complex. They produce an additional section to the profit and loss account called a profit and loss appropriation account or the appropriation account. They also have to produce accounts for internal and external reporting purposes. For the time being we will concern ourselves with their internal accounts, as illustrated by Figure 4.3. The external accounts (i.e. the published report and accounts) of limited companies will be examined in Chapter 8.

The appropriation account shows how the profit for the period is shared between the following categories:

- ☐ taxation;
- ☐ dividends;
- ☐ transfers to reserves;
- ☐ retained profits/earnings.

From our 'loaf of bread' diagram (Figure 4.4) you can see that after dividing the profit for the period between tax, dividends for shareholders and transfers to reserves, the final

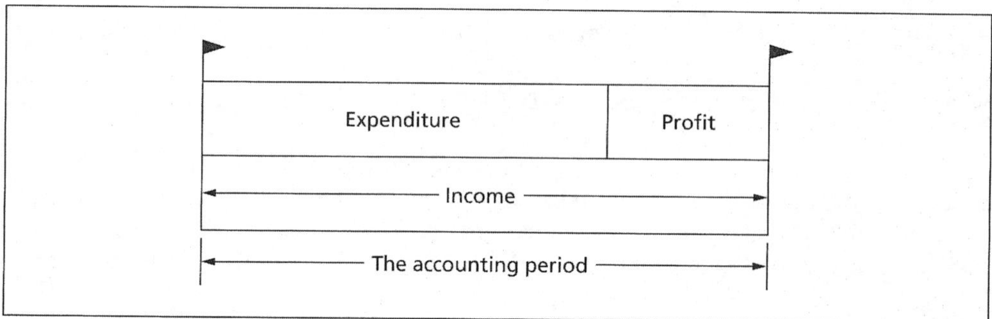

Figure 4.2 The accounting period

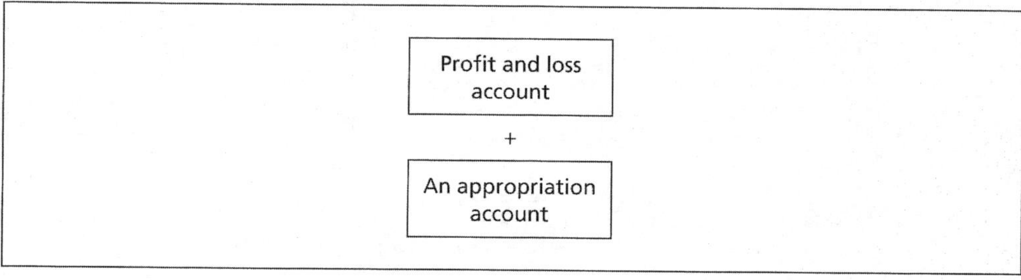

Figure 4.3 Internal company accounts – income measurement

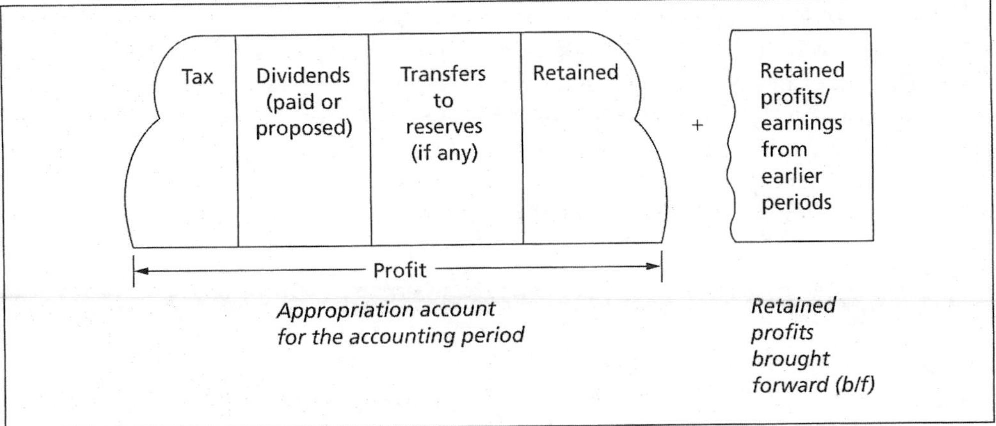

Figure 4.4 The appropriation account of a limited company

portion remaining represents the retained earnings which will be added to the retained earnings brought forward from earlier periods. The cumulative figure for these retained earnings, i.e. ploughed back profits, will be shown as a reserve in the balance sheet, and may also be described as P&L account balance.

We will now take a look at the component parts of Figure 4.3 in greater depth. The first part of the profit and loss account is called the trading account, and is used to calculate the gross profit (gross margin or mark-up), see Figure 4.5. Sales represents the revenue received from trading or the provision of a service.

Trading account
Sales
less
Cost of sales
equals
Gross profit

Figure 4.5 The trading account

The calculation of the cost of sales will depend upon the type of product or service which is being marketed, be it retailing, manufacturing, or a service, etc. The cost of sales in terms of materials can be computed as shown in Example 4.1.

Example 4.1 The cost of sales

	Abbreviated to:
Opening stock of materials	Opening stock
Add Materials purchased during the period	*Add* Purchases
Less The closing stock of materials	*Less* Closing stock
= Cost price of goods sold	= Cost of sales

If the business concerned was involved in manufacturing, then manufacturing wages and associated overheads would be included in the cost of sales figure. The costs of production, i.e. materials consumed, manufacturing labour and factory overheads, would be calculated in a manufacturing account. This information would then be used in the trading account, as shown in Example 4.2.

In a manufacturing environment, the stocks of raw materials and work-in-progress would be dealt with in the manufacturing account.

Example 4.2 The costs of production

Opening stock of finished goods
Add Factory cost of production for the period (as computed in the manufacturing account)
Less Closing stock of finished goods

= Cost of sales

The purpose of the profit and loss account is to compute the net profit or loss for the period, and this is illustrated by Figure 4.6.

Profit and loss account
Gross profit plus Other income less Expenses equals **Net profit or loss**

Figure 4.6 The profit and loss account

The other income, i.e. the non-trading income which is added to the gross profit, could consist of items such as rent received, discounts received for prompt payment of amounts owing, investment income, etc.

The expenses could be grouped into administration expenses, selling expenses and distribution expenses. The expenses would include the wages and salaries of employees and directors (other than those which were dealt with in the trading/manufacturing accounts), loan interest and debenture interest paid, various overhead expenses and the depreciation for the period charged for the use of fixed assets such as plant, machinery, fixtures, fittings, equipment, motor vehicles, etc. All the expenses which are not dealt with in the trading/manufacturing account and appropriation account are dealt with in the profit and loss account.

The first calculation in Figure 4.7 simply states that net profit less tax equals the net profit after tax. From this figure the appropriations are deducted and could consist of the following:

	Profit and loss appropriation account
	Net profit (per the profit and loss account) *Less* Tax
equals	Net profit (loss) after tax *Less* dividends and transfers to reserves
equals	Retained profits (loss) for the current period *Add* Retained profits brought forward from last year
equals	Retained profits (P&L account balance) carried forward to next year

Figure 4.7 The profit and loss appropriation account

- ☐ transfers to reserves, and/or
- ☐ dividends for the period which have been paid or proposed on ordinary shares (and, preference shares if any).

When produced in statement form the three component parts of the profit and loss account, as illustrated in Figures 4.5, 4.6 and 4.7 tend to merge into each other. We will now look at a typical profit and loss account, as set out in Figure 4.8. While working through it, note the following:

- ☐ Layout and presentation are important.
- ☐ Key figures are highlighted, e.g. sales, cost of sales, gross profit, net profit, etc.
- ☐ Directors' fees, loan interest and debenture interest are regarded as charges against income and are therefore included in the profit and loss section of the statement. They are **not** treated as appropriations of profit.
- ☐ The appropriation section shows how the profit earned is shared between the stakeholders, e.g. the tax authorities, the shareholders, and the amount ploughed back by the company, i.e. reserves and retained earnings (P&L account balance).

Having studied Figure 4.8 and referring back to it as and when necessary, now see if you can complete the following self-assessment activity to ensure that you understand what we have covered in this chapter so far.

Self-assessment

The profit and loss account

1. Which two words describe the period of time covered by the profit and loss account?
2. What name is usually given to the profit and loss account produced for a club or non-profit-making organization?
3. Which rules dictate/advise on how business income (i.e. the profit or loss) should be measured?

Scotgate Ltd

Profit and loss account for the year ended 30 June 20X4
(for internal use)

	£000	£000
Sales		800
Less **Cost of sales**		
Opening stock	14	
Add Purchases	165	
	179	
Less Closing stock	29	150
Gross profit		650
Add Rent received		20
		670
Less **Expenses**		
Salaries and wages	252	
Directors' fees	123	
Motor expenses	40	
Light and heat	16	
Stationery and telephone	10	
Rent and rates	14	
Loan interest and charges	50	
Repairs and renewals	7	
Sundries	4	
Audit and accountancy	3	
Depreciation:		
Motor vehicles	16	
Equipment	33	568
Net profit		102
Less Corporation tax		33
Net profit after tax		69
	£000	
Transfer to general reserve	40	
Ordinary share dividend paid and proposed	14	54
Retained earnings (for the year ended 30 June 20X4)		15
Add Retained earnings (i.e. P&L balance) b/f		227
Retained earnings c/f		242

Figure 4.8 A typical profit and loss account

4 Which one of the following statements do you consider to be correct? The appropriation account of a limited company deals with:
(a) Tax, dividends, transfers to reserves, retained earnings.
(b) Tax, dividends, directors' fees, transfers to reserves.
(c) Tax, dividends, debenture interest, retained earnings.
(d) Tax, dividends, directors' fees, debenture interest.

5 From the following information calculate the cost of sales and the gross profit:

	Opening stock	Closing stock	Purchases	Sales
	£000	£000	£000	£000
Materials	12	18	100	150

6 Which account would be used to compute the factory cost of production?

7 From the data provided, see if you can work out the net profit before tax:

	£000
Gross profit	184
Expenses	63
Depreciation	18
Dividends paid	6
Loan interest	4
Directors' fees	24
Tax	9
Proposed dividends	8

8 What other terms are used to describe the gross profit?

9 Calculate the retained profit figure which will be carried forward to the next accounting period from the following information:

	£000
Net profit before tax	164
Taxation	32
Dividends paid	8
Dividends proposed	10
Retained earnings b/f	38
Directors' fees	26
Loan interest	14
Transfers to general reserve	50

10 What other description did we use for retained profits/retained earnings?

You will find the answers to these self-assessment questions on pages 114–15.

The connection with the recording system

How does the profit and loss account tie up with the double-entry system? You will recall that the recording system stores and accumulates the financial information which is needed to produce the final accounts. In the United Kingdom the expenses are recorded in the ledger accounts as debits and income is recorded as a credit.

Summary: the profit and loss account

The profit and loss account is the financial statement which attempts to measure the economic activity/business income of an accounting period in accordance with accepted accounting concepts, accounting standards and relevant legislation, etc.

The internal profit and loss account of a company really consists of three sections and this is illustrated in Figure 4.9.

Section	Format	Purpose
Trading account	Sales *Less* Cost of sales* equals **Gross profit**	To calculate the gross profit
Profit and loss account	Gross profit *Plus* Other income (if any) *Less* Expenses (including directors' fees, loan interest, debenture interest and depreciation) equals **Net profit (or loss)**	To calculate the net profit (or loss)
Appropriation account (See also Figures 4.4 and 4.7)	Net profit (or loss) before tax *Less* Tax, transfers to reserves and dividends *Add* Retained earnings brought forward (b/f) equals **Retained earnings** c/f	To show how the net profit (or loss) before tax for the period is distributed between taxation, dividends and retentions and to calculate the retained earnings carried forward

*The cost of sales calculation in its simplest form is: opening stock *add* purchases *less* closing stock for a manufacturing/retailing concern or the direct costs of providing a service.

Figure 4.9 The form and purpose of an internal company profit and loss account

Profit and Loss Account

		This year		**Last year**
	£000	£000	£000	£000
Sales		54,000		43,000
Cost of sales		36,000		34,000
Gross profit		18,000		9,000
Administration costs	3,000		2,000	
Selling costs	4,000		2,000	
Distribution costs	5,000	12,000	3,000	7,000
Operating profit		6,000		2,000
Interest payable		500		500
Profit before taxation		5,500		1,500
Taxation		1,500		400
Profit after taxation		4,000		1,100
Dividends paid and proposed		1,600		800
Retained profit for the year		2,400		300

Figure 4.10 An internal profit and loss account in summary format

Note

You should also note that, in practice, in the UK and certain other countries the tax figure is not a percentage of the profit before tax. It has to be computed in accordance with tax law e.g. certain expenditure may not be allowed as a deduction for tax purposes, and taxation capital allowances for fixed assets would have to be computed.

It should be noted that directors' fees, loan interest, debenture interest and depreciation are used to calculate the net profit or loss in the profit and loss account. They are not appropriations of profit, but charges which should be deducted in measuring the profit. Also, note that the dividends which have to be included in the appropriation account are the dividends which have been paid or proposed for the accounting period which is under review. Note also, that the profit and loss account can also be called the P&L account or the P&L, or the income statement.

Finally, an example of the profit and loss account of a company (for internal purposes) was illustrated by Figure 4.8 for Scotgate Ltd. For another example of an internal profit and loss format please review Figure 4.10.

Further reading

Dyson, J., *Accounting for Non-Accounting Students*, Financial Times Pitman Publishing, 2000.
Mott, G., *Accounting for Non-Accountants*, Kogan Page, 1999.
Wood, F. and Sangster, A., *Business Accounting 1*, Financial Times Pitman Publishing, 1999.

5

The balance sheet

Objectives

The aim of this chapter is simply to ensure that you become familiar with the language of balance sheets, i.e. the terminology which is used to describe the various constituent parts, and, in particular, the following:

- ☐ The balance sheet equation.
- ☐ Capital employed.
- ☐ Share capital.
- ☐ Authorized share capital.
- ☐ Ordinary shares.
- ☐ Calls.
- ☐ Preference shares.
- ☐ Share premium.
- ☐ Capital reserves.
- ☐ Revenue reserves.
- ☐ Long-term debt.
- ☐ The employment of capital.
- ☐ Fixed assets.
- ☐ Investments.
- ☐ Working capital.
- ☐ Current assets.
- ☐ Current liabilities.
- ☐ Window dressing.

You should also appreciate the following:

- ☐ That the book value of an asset can be significantly different from its resale value.
- ☐ How the balance sheet is affected by the cost concept, the money measurement concept and materiality.
- ☐ Why capital is shown alongside certain liabilities.
- ☐ The characteristics of ordinary shares and preference shares.
- ☐ The limitations of the balance sheet.

What is a balance sheet?

In order to answer this question fully, we also need to specify what a balance sheet is not, and to identify its limitations.

A balance sheet is a statement of the financial position, in terms of the capital, assets and liabilities, of a business entity. It is not an account and not part of the double-entry system. Figure 5.1 illustrates that the balance sheet shows where the capital of the business has come from and how it has been used in terms of providing assets, such as buildings, equipment, stocks of raw materials, balances in the bank, etc., after taking into account the liabilities, i.e. amounts owing to creditors for raw materials bought on credit, shareholders for dividends, etc. Another way of looking at a balance sheet is shown in Figure 5.2.

In short, the balance sheet shows where all the finance comes from, for example ordinary share capital, loans, creditors, etc., and how this has been used, for instance how this finance is represented by the various assets.

You should have noticed in Figure 5.1 that the balance sheet is prepared as at a specific date. This is frequently described **as a moment frozen in time**. It is not prepared to cover a period of time – it is, in fact, rather like a photograph. A balance sheet prepared

Balance sheet as at 31 December 20X5
Assets less Liabilities equals **Capital**

Figure 5.1 The balance sheet equation

Balance Sheet as at 31st March, 20X7
EMPLOYMENT OF CAPITAL (Uses): Fixed Assets plus Investments plus Working Capital **CAPITAL EMPLOYED (Sources):** Share Capital plus Reserves plus Long Term Loans

Figure 5.2 What a balance sheet shows

now may reveal a picture of health, but one prepared tomorrow, or in a week's or a month's time, may reveal a completely different picture. Thus, the balance sheet has also been described as a position statement.

The figures reported in the balance sheet may have been affected by 'window dressing', (i.e. creative accounting) which means that the position which is being reported is either better (or worse) than it should be! For example, the stock level at the year end may have been run down, so that it is totally unrepresentative of the value of stock which was held throughout the year. The same goes for the debtors' and creditors' figures. This is important, because the balance sheet figures are used for interpretation and analytical purposes. For example, a lower stock figure will produce a higher rate of stock turnover figure, a lower debtors' figure will make the credit control ratios look better, and so on.

The balance sheet can be affected by the concept of materiality, i.e. the decision as to what is significant in terms of value. For example, certain inexpensive items of equipment could be charged as an expense in the profit and loss account, i.e. written off, and not treated as a fixed asset, i.e. capitalized, in the balance sheet.

Although balance sheets can be adjusted for **inflation**, the majority of balance sheets which you are likely to encounter will have been prepared using 'historic cost' (i.e. the cost concept), for example certain assets are shown at their cost or cost less depreciation. Also, the money measurement concept is applied to the construction of balance sheets. Only those items which can be measured in monetary terms are included. Thus, important factors such as good industrial relations, the quality of the management and morale cannot be shown in the balance sheet. This is illustrated in Figure 5.3.

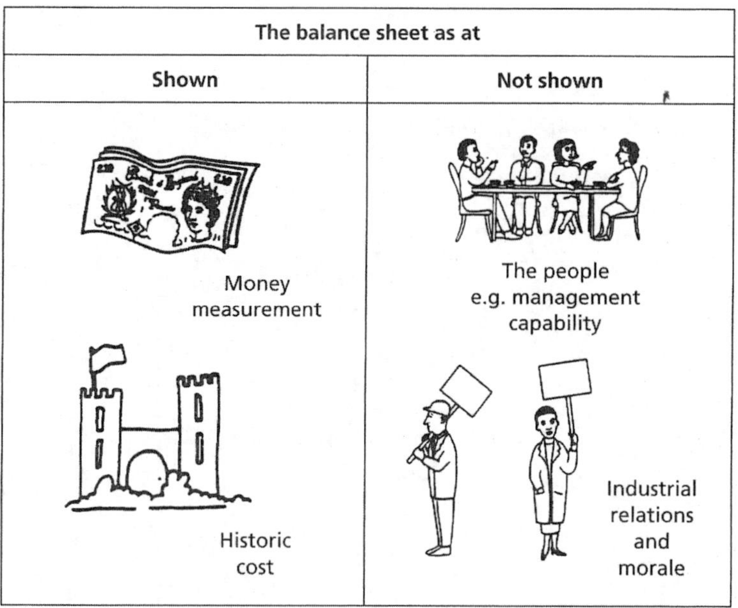

Figure 5.3 Balance sheet limitations

Self-assessment

The balance sheet 1

From what we have looked at so far, plus a commonsense approach, see how well you can do with the following self-assessment activity:

1 Provide the missing words to complete the following sentences:

(a) The balance sheet is not an account and not part of the double-entry system, it is simply a .... of the financial position as at a certain date.

(b) The balance sheet equation is capital = ...

(c) The capital and liabilities in a balance sheet show where the finance .... and the assets show where the finance ....

(d) A balance sheet is prepared .... a certain date. This is rather like a moment .... in time.

2 List three factors which place limitations on the information provided in a balance sheet.

3 The value of the equipment shown in a balance sheet was arrived at, as follows:

Cost	Depreciation to date	Net (Book value)
£000	£000	£000
600	200	400

Explain briefly whether or not you consider that the company would be able to sell this equipment for £400,000.

4 Give one example of how window dressing (or creative accounting) can affect a balance sheet.

5 Name two concepts which we said particularly affect the figures which are reported in the balance sheet?

You will find the answers to these self-assessment problems on pages 115–16.

The internal balance sheet of a company

We will now have a look at the internal balance sheet of a company in pictorial format, Figure 5.4, to illustrate the layout and to help you understand the terminology.

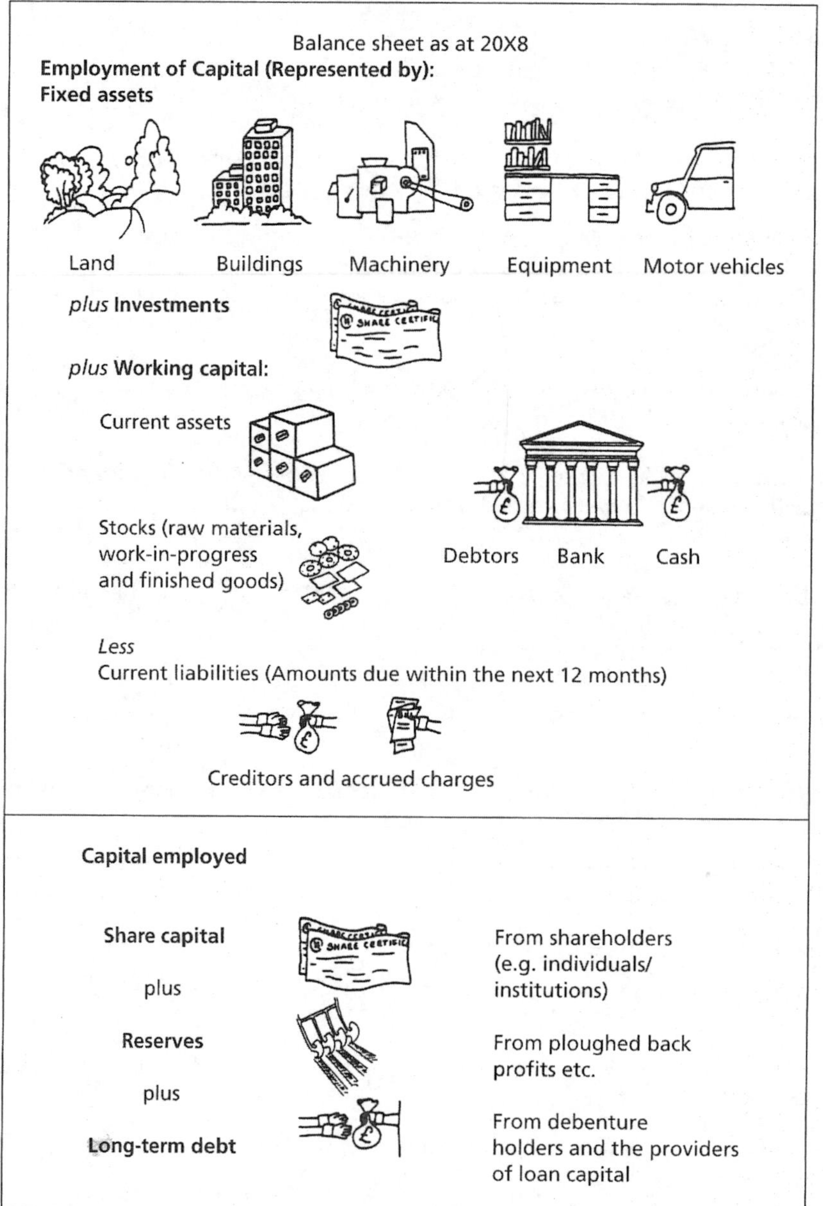

Figure 5.4 Pictorial balance sheet

Employment of capital (represented by)

This major heading of the pictorial balance sheet in Figure 5.4 shows how the funds invested in the business have been deployed. Hence examples of other descriptions which are sometimes used include the employment of capital or uses.

Fixed assets

These are items which are bought for *use* in the business and not for resale, for example land, buildings, leasehold property, plant and machinery, office equipment, fixtures and fittings, motor vehicles, etc. Note that fixed assets (other than leasehold property) which are hired, leased or rented are not shown in the balance sheet because the company does not own them and has not bought them outright. However, details of such **'off-balance-sheet financing'** will appear in a company's published accounts but only if it is a significant amount.

Investments

Investments refer to where a company has used its own funds to invest in stocks and shares of other companies.

Working capital

Working capital is sometimes called the circulating capital. It represents the difference between the current assets and the current liabilities. In effect, it keeps the wheels of business turning by financing the everyday type of operating expenses.

Current assets

Current assets consist of the following:

- ☐ *Stocks*
  These can be stocks of fuels, raw materials, work-in-progress and finished goods.
- ☐ *Debtors*
  Debtors are customers who have not yet paid for goods supplied to them on credit. The figure in the balance sheet may, however, be reduced by the accumulated provision for bad and doubtful debts – an accounting process which is very similar to the way in which depreciation of fixed assets is dealt with.
- ☐ *Prepayments*
  These can be goods or services already paid for, but which will not be used up until the next (or a future) accounting period.

- *Bank balance.*
- *Cash balance.*

Current liabilities

Current liabilities are amounts owing which will tend to be settled within the next twelve months. Some examples of current liabilities are as follows:

- *Creditors*
  The suppliers of goods to the business on credit which have not yet been paid for.
- *Accrued expenses*
  The expenses for the current period which have not been paid.
- *Taxation*
  The amount owing for taxation.
- *Proposed dividend*
  This is the amount owing to the shareholders for dividends.
- *Bank overdraft*
  The bank overdraft is usually considered as a current liability unless it is being used as a long-term source of funds.

You should note that the format of internal company balance sheets can and does vary. Examples of other formats are shown in Figures 5.5 and 5.6.

You may also have come across double-sided balance sheets. However, in an attempt to provide greater clarity the practice nowadays is to prepare vertical balance sheets; after all, the balance sheet is a statement and not an account!

Balance sheet as at
Capital employed
Employment of capital (i.e. represented by:)

Figure 5.5 An alternative format of the balance sheet

Balance sheet as at	
Sources:	**Capital** and **Liabilities**
Uses:	**Assets**

Figure 5.6 Another possible format of the balance sheet

Intangible assets

In addition to the assets already mentioned there are also intangible assets. These are non-physical long-term assets such as the following:

- ☐ patents;
- ☐ copyrights;
- ☐ trade marks;
- ☐ brand names;
- ☐ goodwill;
- ☐ certain research and development expenditure.

Capital employed

This section of the balance sheet shows the sources from which the capital invested in the business has been provided, such as share capital, reserves and long-term debt. All of these may be described as amounts owing because they are owing to the individuals or institutions which have provided them.

Share capital

This can be subdivided into two, as follows:

- ☐ *Authorized share capital*
  This will only appear as a note on the balance sheet and refers to the maximum number of shares that can be issued by the company. The shares may be ordinary shares or preference shares – a contrast of their usual characteristics is shown in Figure 5.7. From Figure 5.7 it can be seen that the ordinary shareholders (frequently referred to as the equity shareholders) are the real entrepreneurs of company, i.e. the real risk-bearers, because they are paid out last on a winding-up.

- ☐ *Issued share capital*
  The amounts shown represent the proportion of the **nominal (or par, or face) value of shares** (ordinary or preference) which have been received to date. It can be observed from the three examples shown in Figure 5.8 that the nominal value per share is £1 and the amount which has been received in excess of this value is called the **share premium.** The balance, if any, which is to be paid at some future date for the shares is referred to as **calls.** Once shares have been issued and are fully paid and then sold on the open market, the company does not receive any more money, apart from a very small transfer fee.

Characteristics	Ordinary shares	Preference shares
Voting rights	Yes, usually one vote per share	Not usually, unless their dividends are in arrears
Dividends	Variable, according to the company's dividend policy	Usually a fixed percentage but some types may include participating rights
Winding-up	Paid out last, i.e. they bear the greatest risk	Paid out before the ordinary shareholders
Repayable	Not usually except in the event of a winding-up or special circumstances, e.g. redemption by the company of their own shares. This is why they are classed as permanent financing. However, they can be sold to third parties	They tend to be repayable between certain future dates
Rights	The rights of each class of share are laid down in the company's Memorandum and Articles of Association	

Figure 5.7 Characteristics of ordinary and preference shares

Example A: Issued 500,000 £1 ordinary shares for £1.50 per share (all monies received)

Balance sheet (extract)	
Issued share capital	£000
500,000 £1 ordinary shares (fully paid)	500
Reserves	
Share premium (500,000 × 50p)	250

Example B: Issued 500,000 £1 ordinary shares at £1.50 but only £1.25 per share received to date

Balance sheet (extract)	
Issued share capital	£000
500,000 £1 ordinary shares	500
Reserves	
Share premium (500,000 × 25p)	125

Example C: Issued 500,000 £1 ordinary shares at £1.50, but only 75p per share called up and received to date

Balance sheet (extract)	
Issued share capital	£000
500,000 £1 ordinary shares (75p per share called up)	375

Figure 5.8 Shares and share premium

Reserves

Reserves can consist of the following:

- ☐ *Share premium*
  A kind of capital reserve representing the amount received from an issue of shares, over and above the nominal value of the shares. It may also be described as a statutory reserve, i.e. it can only be used for certain specific purposes laid down by company law, for example to provide the premium on the redemption of shares or debentures. It cannot be distributed as dividends.
- ☐ *Capital reserves*
  These may be caused by:
  - the revaluation of fixed assets;
  - the acquisition of shares in a subsidiary company;
  - the redemption of own shares.
- ☐ *Revenue reserves*
  These represent the profits which have been ploughed back into the company, i.e. retained profits or undistributed profits, and tend to comprise:
  - general reserve – a reserve to which transfers are made from the profit and loss appropriation account;
  - profit and loss account/retained earnings – the cumulative balance of profits ploughed back into the business since it commenced trading.

Many non-accountants have differing perceptions of what the balance sheet figure of reserves means. They tend to think of a reserve as being cash and/or bank balances which are kept on one side for emergencies. This is not so. The reason for this is that reserves are liabilities and not assets. They represent profits which have been retained and reinvested in the business on behalf of the ordinary shareholders. Thus, the stake of the ordinary shareholders in a company (sometimes called ordinary shareholders' interest or equity) is their ordinary share capital plus reserves. However, the reserves will be represented by a variety of assets, which could be cash, stock or fixed assets or investments (see Figure 5.9).

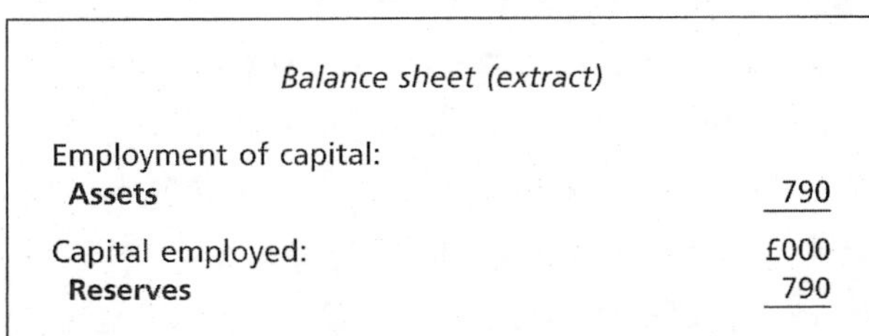
Balance sheet (extract)

Employment of capital:	
Assets	790
Capital employed:	£000
Reserves	790

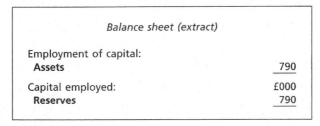

Figure 5.9 What are reserves used for?

Long-term debt

Types of long-term debt include the following:

- ☐ *Debentures*
  A special type of loan, usually secured on an asset or assets belonging to the borrower. A debenture carries with it a legal obligation to pay interest by certain dates and to repay the capital.
- ☐ *Long-term loans*
  Obtained from banks and other financial institutions.

Before going any further see how you are getting on by attempting to answer the questions in the following self-assessment, and then compare your answers with the suggested answers on pages 116–17.

Self-assessment

The balance sheet 2

Please attempt the following 20 questions:

1. Why is capital shown with the liabilities?
2. Which three groups of items, when taken together, can be described as capital employed?
3. Under which heading should debentures be shown?
4. How should the authorized share capital be shown?
5. Which class of shares normally has the voting rights?
6. Which class of shareholders has to bear the greatest risk?
7. Which class of shares tends to receive a fixed dividend?
8. Give another name which is used to mean the nominal value of a share.
9. What is the amount called which is received from an issue of shares over and above their nominal value?
10. What do revenue reserves represent?
11. Why are revenue reserves shown as liabilities?
12. What does the equity shareholders' interest in a company consist of?
13. Give two examples of items which are classed as long-term debt.
14. When should a bank overdraft not be shown as a current liability?
15. Why don't we show rented fixed assets in the balance sheet?
16. How is the working capital calculated?
17. In which section will the company's own proposed dividends be shown?

18 Where will a prepaid expense be shown?

19 In relation to ordinary shares, what are calls?

20 Give two causes of capital reserves.

How much is a business worth?

It has been said that a balance sheet will answer the question 'How much is the business worth?' But does it? The balance sheet does provide *a* valuation – it tells us what the net worth (or net assets) amounts to. Figure 5.10 shows that the net worth can be calculated by either of the two methods illustrated.

However, we would only really know how much the business was worth if it was sold. The assets would no doubt fetch a lot more or a lot less than their balance sheet values, i.e. book values. The amounts received would also depend upon whether or not the business was being sold as a going concern. If it was, an additional amount may be received which represents the goodwill. **Goodwill** purchased represents the right to take over the orders, customers, organization and profit-earning capacity, etc. of the business which has been acquired. If the business was simply being liquidated, the assets would be sold at their break-up values, which are likely to be much lower than their going-concern values.

Example 5.1 Internal balance sheet

To conclude your study of this chapter we will now take a look at a more detailed balance sheet which has been prepared for internal reporting purposes as shown in Figure 5.11. As you work through this balance sheet, refer back to the appropriate reference in this chapter for any of the items which you are not clear about.

While studying the balance sheet in Figure 5.11 you should have noticed the following:

- ☐ The freehold property is quite likely to be worth far more than its original cost, especially if it was acquired several years ago.
- ☐ The investments could be subdivided into different classes, e.g. quoted and unquoted.

Method 1	Method 2
Total assets *less* **Current liabilities** **e.g. Creditors, etc.** **= Net assets** (net worth)	**Capital** *plus* **Reserves** *plus* **Long-term debt** **= Net assets** (net worth)

Figure 5.10 The calculation of net worth (net assets)

Balance Sheet as at 20X9 of a limited company

	Cost	Depreciation to date	Net
Employment of capital:			
Fixed assets	£000	£000	£000
Freehold property	600	—	600
Plant and machinery	240	140	100
Office equipment	110	50	60
Motor vehicles	100	60	40
	1,050	250	800
Investments			120
Working capital:			
Current assets			
Stock and work-in-progress	220		
Debtors less provision for bad debts	180		
Prepayments	30		
Bank	40		
Cash	10	480	
Less Current liabilities (falling due within one year)			
Creditors	110		
Accrued charges	30		
Taxation	25		
Proposed dividends	50	215	265
			£1,185

Capital employed:	£000	£000	£000
Authorized share capital			
£750,000 £1 ordinary shares		750	
£200,000 9% preference shares at £1 each		200	
		950	
Issued share capital			
£500,000 £1 ordinary shares (fully paid)		500	
£200,000 £1 9% preference shares (fully paid)		200	700
Reserves			
Share premium account		100	
General reserve		60	
Profit and loss account (retained earnings)		75	235
Capital plus reserves			935
Long-term debt			
10% debentures		100	
Long-term loans		150	250
			£1,185

Figure 5.11 An internal balance sheet of a limited company

- ☐ The company has not yet issued the whole of its ordinary share capital, i.e. £750,000 authorized and only £500,000 issued.
- ☐ There are no calls, i.e. instalments due, on the ordinary or preference shares as indicated. The shares which have been issued are fully paid.
- ☐ The company did issue the shares at a premium.
- ☐ To date, the company has ploughed back into the business £60,000 by way of a general reserve and £75,000 retained earnings.
- ☐ The rate of dividend on the preference shares and the rate of interest on the debentures reflect the going rate at the time of issue.

Summary: the balance sheet

The balance sheet is an accounting statement of assets, liabilities and capital prepared as at a specific date, i.e. a moment frozen in time. It is not an account and not part of the double-entry bookkeeping/recording system. Figure 5.12 spells out what a balance sheet is and what it is not.

Other things to remember when dealing with the balance sheet are the balance sheet equation, which states that capital equals assets less liabilities, and also window dressing creative accounting. Window dressing means making the balance sheet portray an untypical picture of the business, e.g. running down stocks or having a special effort on collecting money from debtors in the period leading up to the year end.

The language of the balance sheet

The employment of capital

The employment of capital, i.e. the uses to which the capital employed has been applied, is made up of the following:

- ☐ *Fixed assets*

  Assets owned by the company, which have been bought for use in the business and not for resale, e.g. land and buildings, machinery and plant, fixtures and fittings, office equipment, and motor vehicles.

A balance sheet	
Is: • a statement • prepared as at a certain date • usually based on historic cost or historic cost less depreciation	**Is not:** • an account • drawn up to cover a period of time • always a very good guide as to the value of the assets

Figure 5.12 What a balance sheet is and what a balance sheet is not

☐ *Investments*
For example shares in other companies which have been purchased.

☐ *Working capital*
Current assets less current liabilities. This is the circulating capital of the business which is used to finance the everyday-type operating expenditure.

☐ *Current assets*
These are made up of the following:
- stocks of raw materials, fuels, work-in-progress and finished goods;
- debtors, representing amounts owing from customers who have bought goods from the company on credit. To give a more realistic indication of this figure, the debtors may be reduced by a provision for bad and doubtful debts;
- prepayments, deferred expenditure, i.e. paid out in the current accounting period but not yet consumed. The benefit of the expenditure extends beyond the current accounting period;
- bank balance;
- cash balance.

☐ *Current liabilities*
These are simply amounts due to be paid within the next twelve months which are owing to:
- creditors and accrued expenses, for goods and services which have been supplied to the business/organization on credit;
- the tax authorities, for taxation;
- the shareholders, for proposed dividends which have not been paid.

Capital employed
The capital employed consists of the following:

☐ *Issued share capital*
The amount invested in the company by the shareholders by way of ordinary shares/ preference shares.

☐ *Reserves*
There are several types of reserves, as follows:
- share premium – the amount which is received from an issue of shares over and above the nominal (par or face) value of the shares;
- capital reserves – which may result from a revaluation of fixed assets; the acquisition of shares in a subsidiary company or the redemption of the company's own shares;
- revenue reserves – usually a general reserve and profit and loss account balance, both of which represent profits which have been ploughed back and retained in the business, i.e. the undistributed/retained earnings.

☐ *Long-term debt (or long-term liability)*
The following are examples of long-term debt:
- debentures – a specialized type of loan usually secured by a charge on the assets of the company;
- long-term loans – from banks/financial institutions.

Limitations

The usefulness of the balance sheet is limited because of the following:

☐ The time factor, i.e. the fact that it only shows the position at a particular moment in time, rather like a photograph.
☐ The application of the materiality concept, the cost concept and the money measurement concept, i.e. items tend to be shown at their historic cost or historic cost less depreciation. Also items which cannot be measured in monetary terms cannot be shown, such as morale, good industrial relations, management expertise, etc.
☐ Valuation – the book value of the assets shown in the balance sheet may be much less or much more than their re-sale values. Thus, it is dangerous to say that a balance sheet will show us how much the assets are worth!

Further reading

Mott, G., *Accounting for Non-Accountants*, Kogan Page, 1999.
Waterston, C. and Britton, A., *Financial Accounting*, Longman, 1999.
Wood, F. and Sangster, A., *Business Accounting 1*, Financial Times Pitman Publishing, 1999.

6

Cash flow statements

Objectives

The principal objectives of this chapter are that by the time you have worked carefully through it, you should be able to do the following:

- ☐ Appreciate why it is necessary to produce a cash flow statement.
- ☐ Understand the flow of business funds as illustrated in Figure 6.1.
- ☐ Prepare a cash flow statement in line with FRS 1.
- ☐ Deal with problems involving the sale of a fixed asset.

Why a cash flow statement?

The profit and loss account of a business shows how much profit or loss was earned during an accounting period and how it has been arrived at. However, it does not show what has happened to it. The balance sheet shows the resources of the business at the beginning and end of the accounting period, but it cannot clearly show the movements in capital, reserves, long-term debt, assets and liabilities.

In order to answer the questions 'what has happened to cash, or profits?' and 'what has happened to working capital?' we need to draw up a cash flow statement (funds flow statement).

The objectives of the cash flow statement are to show what has happened to the following over an accounting period:

- ☐ The way in which the business has financed its operations.
- ☐ The sources from which funds have been derived, for example share capital, loans, profits, etc.
- ☐ The way in which the funds have been used, for instance to buy stocks of raw materials or fixed assets.

In short, a cash flow (funds flow) statement shows how a business has financed its assets, for example from long-term sources or out of working capital.

In addition to a profit and loss account and the balance sheet, the published accounts of UK companies also include a cash flow statement. However, the information which is used to produce it is in fact a selection or a reclassification and summary of the information contained in the profit and loss account and the balance sheet.

The flow of business funds

A study of Figure 6.1 shows that finance can come into a business from a number of sources.

It can come from the following external sources:

☐ *Share capital*

- Ordinary shares. The holders of the ordinary shares usually have voting rights and receive dividends. They bear the greatest risk in that they are paid out last on a winding-up. They also attract capital gains (or capital losses) if they sell their shares and determine who controls the company.
- Preference shares. These usually tend to have a fixed dividend and have no votes unless their dividend is in arrears. They can be redeemable or irredeemable.

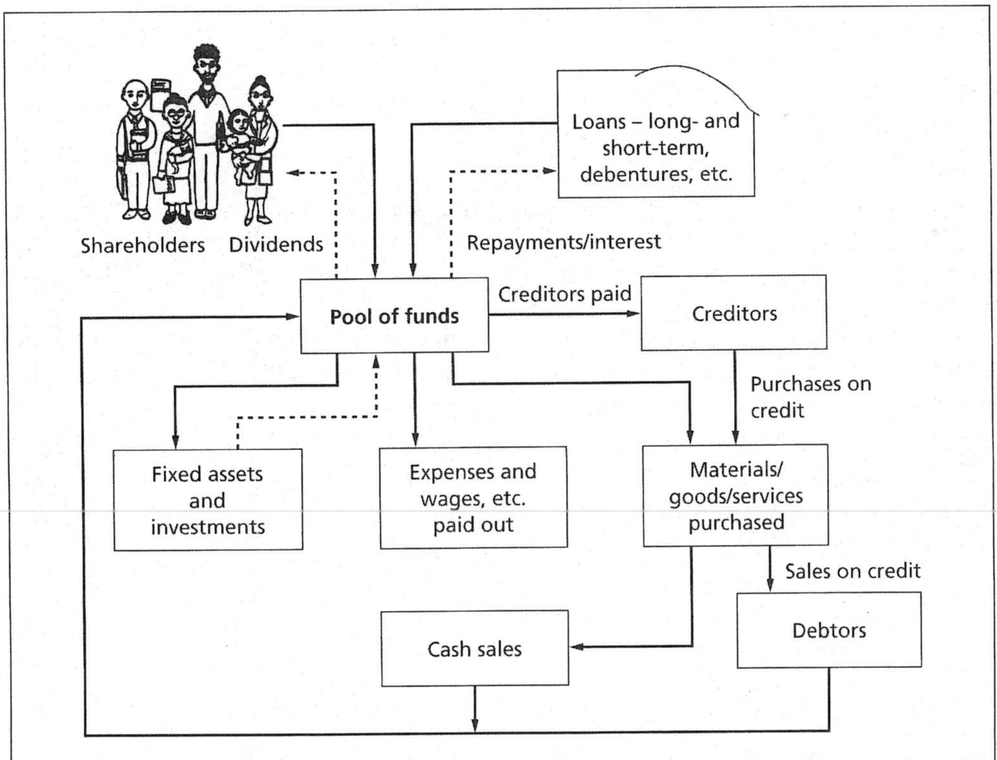

Figure 6.1 The flow of business funds

- *Debentures*
  Debentures are a special type of long-term loan: they are usually fixed-interest, repayable at a future date and are secured on assets via a deed of trust. If the company defaults in paying the interest, the trustees for the debenture holders have to act in accordance with the provisions of the deed of trust, e.g. to start winding up proceedings.
- *Long-term loans*
  They may be secured or unsecured and attract fixed or variable rates of interest. In the event of the company being unable to meet its interest payments it may be possible to reach an agreement with the provider to re-schedule the debt. The risk to the company is not therefore as high as it is for debentures, as it will not be lawful to arrange a compromise with the trustees for the debenture holders.
- *Convertible loan stock (or convertible debentures)*
  The holders tend to receive a fixed rate of interest but have the option to convert into ordinary shares between specified future dates. This frees the company from having to provide a lump sum to repay the capital. When the holders convert there could be a reduction in the earnings per share (EPS); this is called a dilution of earnings.
- *The bank overdraft*
  Although it is described as being repayable on demand quite a large number of companies/organizations treat it as a long-term source of finance. It may be secured or unsecured.
- Other external sources which may be used include: sale and lease back, hire purchase, mortgages, and the period of credit received from creditors.

There are also quite a number of internal sources of finance, the most important of which is that which is **self-generated, i.e. the ploughed-back profits** (the profit and loss account balance and general reserve which is shown in the reserves section of the balance sheet). Additional cash flow can also be generated by selling off unwanted assets, e.g. land, buildings, equipment and stocks of raw materials, etc.

You should note that there are other ways of financing assets. In addition to outright purchase certain fixed assets can be **rented or leased**, e.g. plant, machinery and equipment, motor vehicles, etc. This frees the company/organization from having to find a lump sum and then having to pay interest on it. Another available option is to use **sub-contractors**, for example, using them rather than providing every fixed asset and employing every single person to complete a construction contract.

The finance received can be used to pay:

- Dividends to shareholders.
- Interest on loans and also the repay existing loans.
- Creditors and expenses.
- For materials.
- For fixed assets.

The longer-term funds from share capital and loans tend to be used to finance the purchase of fixed assets and provide a certain portion of the working capital.

The working capital shown in Figure 6.1, i.e. the current assets and current liabilities, tends to be used to finance the everyday-type operating expenses, such as wages and various overheads. Thus, you can see why it is also called the circulating capital. As transactions take place its form changes, for example if materials are bought on credit, stock goes up and creditors go up.

The cash flow statement (FRS 1)

The cash flow statement should help you understand the reasons for the movement of cash during an accounting period. The formats adopted for reporting purposes (i.e. the published accounts) in the United Kingdom are prescribed by FRS 1 (Financial Reporting Standard) and cover the following major headings:

- ☐ net cash in/outflow from operating activities;
- ☐ returns on investments and the servicing of finance;
- ☐ taxation;
- ☐ investing activities;
- ☐ financing.

The final figure is the *increase/decrease in cash and cash equivalents*, e.g. an increase or decrease in the bank balance (Figure 6.2).

Cash flow statement for year ended 31 December 20X7	£	£
Net cash flow from operating activities		
Returns on investments, and the servicing of finance:		
Dividends received		
Dividends paid		
Interest paid	———	———
Taxation:		
Tax paid		———
Investing activities:		
Purchase of tangible fixed assets		
Sale of tangible fixed assets		
Proceeds from sale of trade investments	———	———
Financing:		
Proceeds from new share capital		
Repayment of borrowings	———	———
Increase (or decrease) in cash and cash equivalents		———

Figure 6.2 An FRS 1 cash flow statement

The net cash flow from operating activities may have to be computed by taking into account the increase/decrease in retained earnings, depreciation charged for the period, and profits/losses on the sale of fixed assets, interest paid, tax appropriated, dividends appropriated and movements in stocks, debtors and creditors.

A much quicker way of computing it, provided the information is available is to take the net profit before interest and tax (NPBIT) and add back depreciation and losses on sales of fixed assets (less any profits on the sale of fixed assets) and then adjust for the movements in stocks, debtors and creditors.

From your observations of Figure 6.2 of the statement, you should be able to see how much cash went out during the period on dividends, taxation, new fixed assets and the repayment of borrowings and how these were financed, e.g. from ploughed-back profits, the sale of fixed assets and new borrowings.

You should be able to see how cash is moving through the organization and the net impact on the cash balance at the year end. It informs the user where the cash came from and where it went to. It should help investors, creditors, and other users to determine the relationship between income and cash flows and provide an indication of the availability of each for dividends and long-term investment; it should also help users and managers to demonstrate the firm's ability to finance growth from internal sources.

We will now, using the information provided in Example 6.1 Jean Ltd, prepare a cash flow statement in the FRS 1 format, via a step-by-step illustration with a commentary.

Example 6.1 Cash flow statement for Jean Ltd

Jean Ltd
Balance sheet as at 31 December 20X8

Capital employed		This year 20X8			Last year 20X7	
	£000	£000	£000	£000	£000	£000
Authorized share capital –						
Ordinary shares			600			600
Issued share capital						
Ordinary shares of £1 each			450			300
Reserves						
Undistributed profits						
(i.e. P&L balance)			30			14
Capital plus reserves			480			314
Long-term debts						
11% debentures			50			120
			£530			£434

Represented by						
Fixed assets	Cost	Depreciation to date	Net	Cost	Depreciation to date	Net
	£000	£000	£000	£000	£000	£
Land and buildings	320	Nil	320	280	Nil	280
Plant and machinery	152	50	102	130	24	106
	472	50	422	410	24	386
Working capital						
Current assets						
Stock	90			50		
Debtors	50			35		
Cash at bank	20	160		14	99	
Less **Current liabilities**						
Creditors	30			36		
Proposed dividend	10			7		
Taxation	12	52	108	8	51	48
			530			£434

Profit and loss appropriation account (extract) for the year ended 31 December 20X8 (this year)

	£000s
Net profit before taxation*	38
Less Corporation tax based on this year's profits	12
	26
Less Proposed dividend	10
Undistributed profit for this year	16
Add Balance brought forward (from last year)	14
	30

*After depreciation £26,000 and interest on debentures £9,000.

☐ *Step 1*

Compute the net cash flow from operating activities, as follows:

	£000
Retained profits (*this is taken from the profit and loss account* but could be calculated from the Balance Sheet, (i.e. 30 – 14))	16
Depreciation (this is given, but could be calculated, see W1 below)	26
Profit and loss on sale of fixed assets	nil
Interest paid (given)	9
Tax appropriated (given in the P&L A/c)	12
Dividend appropriated (given in the P&L A/c)	10
	73

Movements in current assets and current liabilities

	£000	
Stocks (up), i.e. more cash tied up	40	
Debtors (up)	15	
Creditors (down)	6	61
		12

You should note that the £73,000 figure above is the net profit before interest and tax (NPBIT) plus the depreciation added back, which could be computed as follows:

	£000
Net profit before tax (given)	38
Add Debenture interest (given)	9
Net profit before interest and tax	47
Add Depreciation	26
	73

☐ *Step 2*

Next, compute the amount which has been spent on the purchase of new fixed assets, as follows:

	Cost of land and buildings		Cost of plant and machinery
	£000		£000
This year 20X8	320		152
Less Last year 20X7	280		130
	40		22
	Total	62	

☐ *Step 3*

You then pick up the whole of the sale proceeds for any fixed assets or investments which have been sold during the period, if any. In this example there weren't any.

☐ *Step 4*

Then you pick up any new finance coming in such as share capital, loans or debentures, and borrowings repaid:

	This year 20X8	Last year 20X7	+ or –
	£000	£000	£000
Ordinary share capital	450	300	**150**
11% debentures	50	120	**(70)**

☐ *Step 5*

Finally ensure that your calculations agree with the increase (or decrease) in the cash and bank balances:

	This year 20X8	Last year 20X7	+ or –
	£000	£000	£000
Cash at bank	20	14	**6**

This will provide you with an arithmetic check on the accuracy of your other figures.

W1 The calculation of the depreciation charge for the year

This was given as £26,000. However, if it is not given we compare the depreciation to date figures, as follows:

	Depreciation of plant and machinery
	£000
This year 20X8	50
Less Last year 20X7	24
= Charged in this year's P&L account	**£26**

However, this particular calculation will only suffice in cases where no sales of fixed assets have taken place, e.g. as in this example. We will look at how the sale of a fixed asset affects the figures which go into the funds flow shortly.

Example 6.2 Cash flow statement (FRS 1 format)

Jean Ltd
Cash Flow Statement for the Year Ended 31 December 20X8

	£000	£000
Net cash flow from operating activities		12
Returns on investments, and the servicing of finance:		
Dividends received	—	
Dividends paid	(7)	
Interest paid	(9)	(16)
		(4)
Taxation:		
Tax paid		(8)
		(12)
Investing activities:		
Purchase of tangible fixed assets	(62)	
Sale of tangible fixed assets	—	
Proceeds from sale of trade investments	—	(62)
		(74)
Financing:		
Proceeds from new share capital	150	
Repayment of borrowings	(70)	80
Increase in cash and cash equivalents		6

The sale of fixed assets

The sale of fixed assets makes the picture a little more complex and will be dealt with in the cash flow as follows:

- ☐ The profit or loss on sale will be adjusted for in the computation of the net cash flow from operating activities:
  - **a profit on sale**, which could also be described as an overprovision for depreciation, must be deducted. This, in effect, takes the net profit before taxation back to what it was before the profit on sale was added;
  - **a loss on sale**, i.e. an underprovision for depreciation, will be added back.
- ☐ The whole of the sale proceeds received must then be included in the investing activities section of the cash flow as illustrated in Figure 6.2.
- ☐ Care must be exercised when computing the cost of new fixed assets purchased during the period under review and when computing the depreciation for the period.

Example 6.3 Sale of fixed assets

Plant and machinery	Cost	Depreciation to date	Net
	£000	£000	£000
20X3	300	70	230
20X4	440	86	354

During 20X4 a machine which cost £28,000 on which £17,000 depreciation had been charged, was sold for £12,000, thus:

	£000
Machine cost	28
Less depreciation	17
Book value	11
Sale proceeds	12
Profit on sale	1

The profit on sale of £1,000 would be deducted in the computation of the net cash flow from operating activities and the £12,000 sale proceeds would be included as a source of funds in the investing activities section. The new fixed assets purchased and the depreciation for the period can be calculated, as follows:

Plant and machinery	Cost	Depreciation to date
	£000	£000
Brought forward from 20X3	300	70
Less Applicable to machine sold	28	17
= Plant and machinery b/f but not disposed of	272	53
Carried forward 20X4	440	86
Cost of new plant and machinery =	**£168** **Depreciation charged in 20X4 =**	**£33**

Self-assessment

Festiclyn plc (Cash flow statement)

Now see if you can prepare a cash flow statement in the FRS 1 format from the information provided for Festiclyn plc.

Festiclyn plc
Balance sheet summary

	20X7 31 December	20X8 31 December
Capital employed:	£000	£000
Ordinary shares, £1 each	200	350
9% preference shares, £1 each	120	nil
P&L account	40	55
Bank loan	nil	60
Trade creditors	25	29
Dividends payable	16	22
Taxation	64	78
	£465	£594
Represented by:		
Plant and machinery		
Cost	490	563
Aggregate depreciation	76	90
	414	473
Stock	21	75
Debtors	19	27
Bank	11	19
	£465	£594

You are also given the following summarized profit and loss appropriation account for the year ended 31 December 20X8:

	£000
Profit before tax (after depreciation)	109
Taxation:	
Corporation tax for the year	72
	37
Proposed dividend (ordinary shares)	22
	15
Balance b/f	40
	55

You are also informed that during the year ended 31 December 20X8 plant costing £24,000 on which £4,000 depreciation had been provided was sold for £17,000.

The profit before tax was after charging bank loan interest of £5,000. You will find the answer to this self-check assessment on pages 118–19.

Summary: cash flow statements

A knowledge of cash flow statements will help answer questions such as:

- ☐ What has happened to cash?
- ☐ Why has profit gone up and cash gone down?
- ☐ Where have the profits gone?
- ☐ What has happened to the working capital?

In addition to showing the funds generated from operating activities during the period, a cash flow (funds flow) statement will also show the other funds which were received during the period and what has become of them, i.e. the uses to which they have been put.

The FRS 1 cash flow statement

The cash flow statement which is currently being used for external reporting purposes in the United Kingdom, i.e. it forms part of the published accounts/company's annual report, is the FRS 1 cash flow statement.

As with other cash flows it is a re-classification and re-ordering of profit and loss account and balance sheet data. It shows:

- ☐ *The net cash flow from operating activities*
  You should note that this is made up of the net profit before interest and tax, plus depreciation of fixed assets, plus losses on the sale of fixed assets (or less profit), and then adjusted for movements in stocks, debtors and creditors (see Example 6.1).
- ☐ *Returns on investments (if any), and the cost of servicing the financing*
  E.g. dividends paid to ordinary and preference shareholders, loan and debenture interest, etc.
- ☐ *Taxation*
  You should note the way in which we calculated the tax-paid figure, see below.
- ☐ *Investing activities*
  The purchase and sale of fixed assets, etc.
- ☐ *Financing*
  Details of new finance, e.g. more ordinary share capital and also details of repayments of loans and debentures, etc.

The final figure should then be equal to the increase or decrease in the cash and bank balances.

Certain figures which are needed for this cash flow may have to be calculated as follows, for example, dividends paid and tax paid (from the Jean Ltd example):

	Dividend	Taxation
	£000	£000
Balance b/f (20X7) i.e. owing at start of year	7	8
Add P&L account appropriation (for 20X8)	10	12
	17	20
Less Balance c/f (20X8) i.e. owing at year end	10	12
= **Amount paid**	£7	£8

The sale of fixed assets

If a fixed asset (or an investment) is sold during the period under review note the treatment for cash flow/funds flow purposes, in computing the net cash flows from operating activities:

- a profit on sale is deducted, and
- a loss on sale is added back.

Please note that a cash flow forecast (cash budget) is a different kind of financial statement and is not another name for a cash flow statement or a funds flow.

Thus, a cash flow statement is a statement which is prepared in addition to the profit and loss account and the balance sheet, showing the manner in which a business has financed its operations, over the last financial year/period.

Further reading

Dyson, J., *Accounting for Non-Accounting Students*, Financial Times Pitman Publishing, 2000.
Gillespie, I., Lewis, R. and Hamilton, K., *Principles of Financial Accounting*, Prentice Hall, 1997.
Mott, G., *Accounting for Non-Accountants*, Kogan Page, 1999.
Waterston, C. and Britton, A., *Financial Accounting*, Longman, 1999.

CHAPTER 10 The annual report

A plea for narrative reporting . . .

Company annual reports need to consider user's needs, report says

A lack of focus on the user in the process of setting reporting standards is undermining quality in business reporting, according to a research report published by ICAS. "Voluntary Annual Report Disclosures: What Users Want", aims to seek out users' views in relation to a comprehensive set of disclosure items.

During the last decade, the importance of narrative reporting in corporate annual reports has increased significantly. This is due to the rapid pace of change in business, which has meant that past performance has become a less useful guide to future prospects. It is also due to the growth of intangible assets, including those generated from intellectual capital, that are not recognised in the traditional financial statements.

This growth in importance of narrative reporting is currently being recognised in the UK in the Company Law Review proposal for a statutory Operating and Financial Review (OFR), which has been endorsed by the draft Companies Bill, and in the revision to the OFR Statement being developed by the Accounting Standards Board.

ICAS Director of Research and co-author of the report, Professor Vivien Beattie says: "The findings of this report should be of value both to preparers seeking to improve the usefulness of their disclosures and to regulators whose decisions are influenced by the preferences of their constituencies."

To assist in the research, a questionnaire was sent to 1,645 interested parties representing finance directors, audit partners, private shareholders and expert users.

CA Magazine, January 2003.

Questions relating to this news story may be found on page 222 ▸▸

About this chapter

We explained in the previous chapter that a limited liability company usually publishes an annual report and accounts. Some of the contents are statutory, i.e. required by law, some are professional and some are Stock Exchange requirements, while others are voluntary, i.e. companies can decide for themselves what to put in.

The annual report and accounts of a large international company can be extremely long and highly technical. In order to make your studies a little easier we are going to cover the subject in two chapters. This chapter deals largely with the non-statutory information normally found in an annual report. The next chapter, Chapter 11, covers the annual accounts. These include main the statutory items, especially those relating to financial matters.

This chapter is divided into nine main sections. After listing the learning objectives, the first section explains why the chapter is an important one for non-accountants. The following seven sections cover the contents of a typical annual report, viz. introductory material, a chairman's statement, an operating and financial review statement, a directors' report, a corporate governance statement, a remuneration report, and finally some general information for shareholders. The last main section in the chapter lists some questions that non-accountants should ask about the contents of the chapter.

The outline of the chapter is shown in Figure 10.1. The Figure should make it easier for you to see how the chapter fits together.

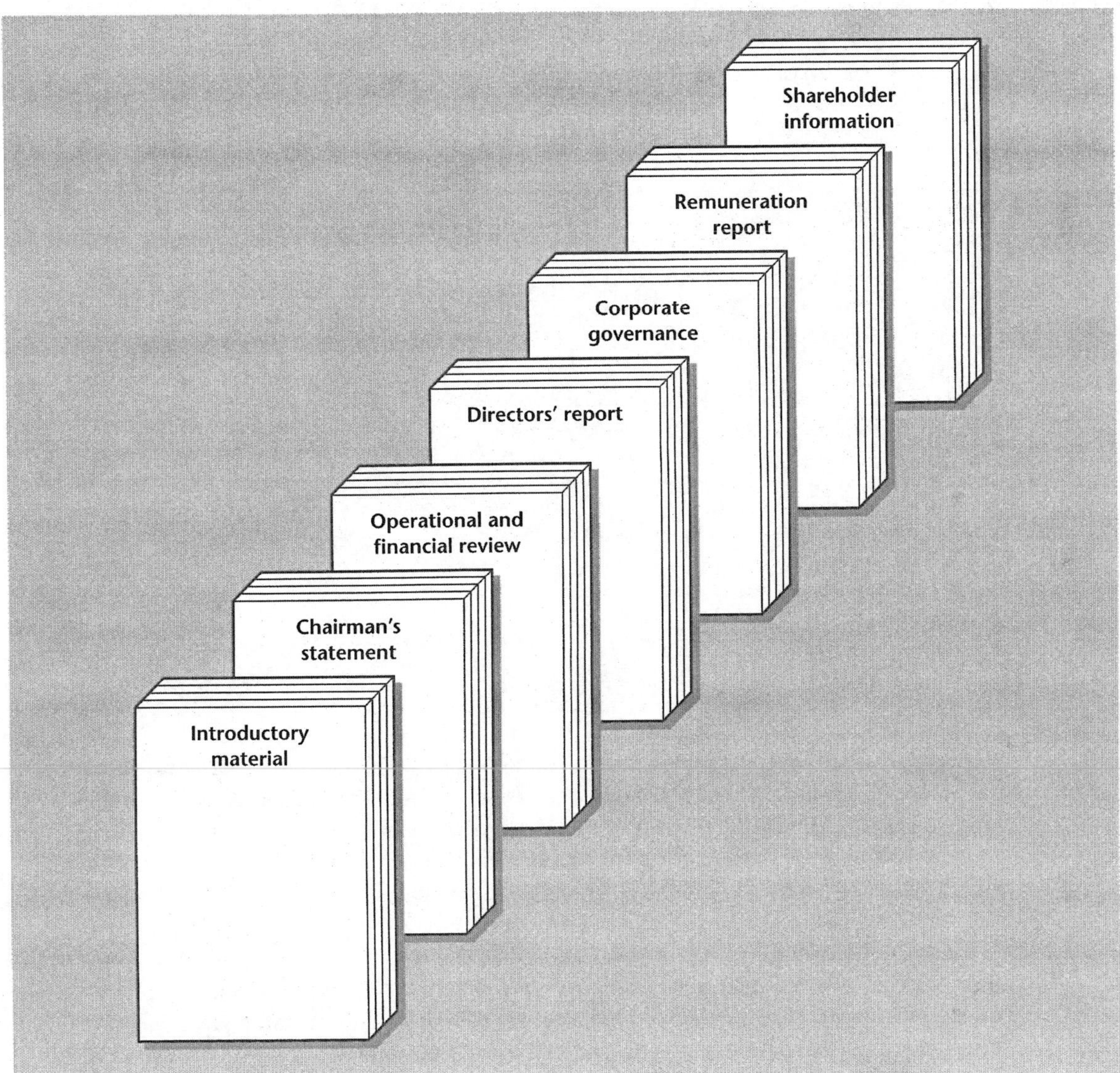

Figure 10.1 Main contents of an annual report

Learning objectives

By the end of this chapter you should be able to:

- **identify the main sections of an annual report;**
- **outline the main contents of a chairman's statement;**
- **list a number of other non-statutory reports and summarize their contents.**

Why this chapter is important for non-accountants

This chapter is important for non-accountants for the following reasons:

1. You will become aware of what an annual report may contain.
2. You will find out where to look for certain types of information.
3. You will learn to distinguish between statutory and non-statutory information.
4. You will be able to use the information contained in the annual report to help assess the company's performance and future prospects.

Activity 10.1

Get hold of an annual report and accounts for three companies.

Guidance: If some of your friends or relatives have shares in a company they should automatically receive a copy of that company's report and accounts. See if they will let you have them. Otherwise select three companies and write to the company secretary. Most companies will let you have a set without any questions being asked. Your library may also hold copies but it is best if you have your copies. Choose commercial or industrial companies and avoid banking and insurance companies as they have their own requirements.

Note: It is important that you do this activity and have some annual report and accounts available otherwise you will find it more difficult to work your way through this chapter.

Introductory material

A company's annual report and accounts can be a formidable document even for those users who have some accounting knowledge. It can easily be over 50 pages long. It is full of jargon and technical detail, and it contains a great deal of numerical analyses. The document can be very off-putting for those users who are frightened of figures. This should not apply to readers of this book because we have gradually been preparing you for what otherwise might have been an alarming experience.

We are going to confine our study of an annual report (we cover the accounts in the next chapter) to seven main types of information that will be found in most companies' annual report. However, the content order, as well as the format, style, print and terminology, can vary. So you might have to refer to the 'contents' of a particular annual report if you want to read a particular report (although not all reports contain a contents list).

Nevertheless, it is likely that the first few pages include what we have called 'introductory material'. Such material probably tells you something about the company along with a brief summary of the financial results for the year. For example, Devro plc makes the following statement on the inside cover of the front page (in a large font):

> Devro is one of the world's leading producers of manufactured casings for the food industry, supplying a wide range of products and technical support to manufacturers of sausages, salami, hams and other cooked meats. The group's main focus is edible collagen-based products, which are a key component of our customers' product offerings to the end consumer, and have been steadily replacing gut casings in markets around the world.

Unless you had heard about Devro, you might be mystified by this statement. 'Collagen' appears to be a technical term (it is explained later) and you might be put off by some of the jargon, e.g. 'key component', 'product offerings', and 'end consumer'. Nevertheless, the statement is very eye-catching.

The bottom of that page also includes a list of the contents of the report. Opposite (on page 1) is a summary of the key financial statistics. This is a very clear, simple summary of the results for the year, so we have reproduced it for you (see Figure 10.2).

Some of the information shown in Figure 10.2 will not mean anything to you yet, so you can appreciate how difficult it must be for those users who have not had any training

Key financials

	2001*	2000*
Earnings per share	**5.1p**	9.0p
Dividends per ordinary share	**2.0p**	5.0p
Turnover	**£208.3m**	£229.5m
Gross profit	**£62.2m**	£70.9m
–margin	**29.9%**	30.9%
Operating profit	**£18.6m**	£24.0m
–margin	**8.9%**	10.5%
Profit before taxation	**£15.2m**	£21.3m
Net cash from operating activities	**£31.1m**	£29.7m
Capital expenditure	**£7.9m**	£13.2m
Net debt	**£24.7m**	£29.0m
Net gearing	**30.2%**	30.9%
Net interest cover	**5.4**	8.8

*Before exceptional charges of £52.1 million (2000: £1.5 million)

Figure 10.2 An example of introductory material

Source: Devro plc, *Annual Report and Accounts 2001*.

in accounting. Pages 2 and 3 of Devro's report provide a summary of the company (headed '*Group at a glance*') and entitled '*A focused business*'. The information presented is in several colours and it is accompanied by various types of pictures. On pages 4 and 5 we are then presented with a '*Market report*' on '*The collagen market*'. A collagen, by the way, is 'the main structural protein found in animal connective tissue'. Such tissue is now being used as a new type of sausage casing.

Devro's introductory material ends after page 5 and we move on to the chairman's statement. In many other companies, especially those that are consumer orientated, you will also find pages of publicity material promoting the company's products.

Activity 10.2

Consult your copies of the three sets of annual report and accounts that you obtained when you completed Activity 10.1. Read through the introductory material and summarize the contents in your notebook.

Chairman's statement

Most company chairmen like to include a report or statement of their own in the annual report. There are no statutory, professional or Stock Exchange specifications requiring chairmen to publish a report, so the format and content will vary from company to company.

You will probably find the chairman's statement in the first few pages of the annual report. You can expect it to be anything from one page to four pages in length. It will be largely narrative in style although it will not be entirely devoid of some quantitative information. Research evidence suggests that chairmen's statements are the most widely read section of an annual report, perhaps because they are usually fairly easy to read.

Chairmen tend to adopt an up-beat approach about the recent performance and are extremely optimistic about the future. You must, therefore, read their reports with a great deal of scepticism, and you should check their comments against the detailed results contained elsewhere within the overall annual report and accounts. Nevertheless, chairmen have to be careful that they do not become too optimistic. Their remarks can have a significant impact on the company's share price and they might have to answer to the Stock Exchange authorities if they publish misleading statements.

The contents of a typical chairman's statement include the following:

- *Results.* A summary of the company's results for the year covering such items as turnover, pre- and post-tax profits, earnings per share, and cash flow.
- *Dividend.* Details about any interim dividend paid for the year and any proposed final dividend.
- *Prospects.* A summary of how the chairman sees the general economic and political outlook and the future prospects for his own company.
- *Employees.* A comment about the company's employees including any notable successes, concluding with the Board's thanks to all employees for their efforts.
- *Directors.* A similar note may be included about the Board of Directors including tributes to retiring directors.

A relatively brief chairman's statement is reproduced in Figure 10.3.

J. Smart & Co. (Contractors) PLC

CHAIRMAN'S REVIEW

ACCOUNTS

As forecast in the interim report, profits for the second half of the year exceeded first half profits resulting in a Group profit for the full year of £4,613,000.

The Board is recommending a Final Dividend of 8.50p nett making a total for the year of 11.40p nett, which compares with 11.00p nett for the previous year. After waivers by members holding approximately 50% of the shares the Dividends will cost the Company £574,000.

Unappropriated profits for the year amounted to £2,879,000 which, when added to the retained profits brought forward and the surplus on the revaluation reserve, bring the consolidated capital and reserves of the Group to £60,964,000.

TRADING ACTIVITIES

Group turnover decreased by 6%, own work capitalised increased by 193% and other operating income increased by 8%. Improvements across all sectors of your Company's activities fuelled an increase in Group profit by 27%.

The amount of contracting work carried out decreased compared with the previous year although margins improved slightly. Sales in precast concrete manufacture improved and losses were substantially reduced. A healthy increase in private house sales boosted profitability.

Commercial and industrial activity increased considerably compared with the previous year. Office developments completed at Carnegie Campus, Dunfermline and Glenbervie Business Park, Larbert and shortly due to complete at East London Street, Edinburgh are attracting varying degrees of interest. Industrial units completed at Arran Road, Perth and Swanfield, Edinburgh were pre-let.

Following on the letting of the second phase of the joint venture development with EDI (Industrial) Ltd at A1 Industrial Estate, Edinburgh the third phase of 31,000 square feet was commenced during the year under review.

FUTURE PROSPECTS

While there is a certain amount of interest expressed in our industrial and commercial floorspace available for let, the sector could not be described as buoyant and development activity in the current year will be substantially less than last year.

The value of the work in hand in contracting is more than at this time last year. Approximately two thirds of this work is on a design and construct basis, the balance having been obtained by traditional competitive tender. Private housing developments are continuing in Edinburgh and Dunfermline and sales are still brisk.

It is not possible at this stage to forecast whether or not the profit for the current year will match the profit for last year.

J. M. SMART
Chairman

19th November 2002

Figure 10.3 A Chairman's Statement

Activity 10.3

Referring to your three sets of annual reports and accounts, find the chairmen's statement and read through each of them carefully. Are there any items not included in the summary shown above?

List the main contents of each chairman's statement in your notebook.

Operating and financial review

An operating and financial review (OFR) may be defined as follows:

> *An OFR is an exposition of a company's performance and prospects supported by both narrative and quantitative information.*

The Cadbury Committee was set up in 1991 by the accountancy profession and the financial community to examine what has come to be called 'corporate governance' (we will be returning to this topic later in the chapter). One of its suggestions was that companies should issue an OFR. The idea was taken up by the business and financial community and in 1993 the ASB issued a statement supporting the suggestion.

An OFR is not covered by any statute or by any accounting standard. The recommendation to publish one is persuasive and not mandatory. The ASB's recommendation is of relevance mainly to listed companies although other entities are encouraged to publish one.

The form and content will vary from company to company but it will normally contain an operating section and a financial section. An OFR can easily be up to ten pages in length so it is not possible to reproduce one here. However, in order to give you an idea of what might be included we summarize below some of the possible contents.

The operating review

- *Review.* A review of the business environment in which the company operates, any developments in the business, and the impact they have had on the company's results.
- *Prospects.* The main factors affecting the company's future prospects.
- *Expansion.* Details of investments aimed at increasing future income and profits.
- *Returns.* The dividends paid to shareholders and the changes in shareholders' funds.

The financial review

- *Capital.* Details of the capital funding of the company and of its capital structure.
- *Taxation.* Additional information about the tax items included in the accounts.
- *Cash.* Details of cash inflows and outflows.
- *Liquidity.* An assessment of the company's liquidity at the end of the period.
- *Going concern.* A statement of the company's ability to remain a going concern.

Activity 10.4

Consult your three annual reports and accounts. Find the pages containing the operating and financial review. Read through them carefully, taking your time over the exercise. Then summarize the contents of each OFR in your notebook.

Directors' report

The directors of the company are required to publish a report of their activities and responsibilities. This is a statutory requirement of the 1985 Companies Act [s234(1)]:

> *The directors of a company shall for each financial year prepare a report –*
>
> *(a) containing a fair review of the development of the business and its subsidiary undertakings during the financial year and of their position at the end of it, and*
>
> *(b) stating the amount (if any) which they recommend should be paid as dividend and the amount (if any) which they propose to carry to reserves.*

The Act also requires some other matters to be disclosed. For example:

- *Business review*: A fair review of the development of the business, the principal activities of the company, important events, future developments, research and development activities, dividend payments, and transfers to reserves.
- *Fixed assets.* Changes to fixed assets and details of differences between book values and market values.
- *Directors.* The names of the directors and their holdings in the company's shares and debentures.
- *Political and charitable donations.* Details of amounts given for (a) political; and (b) charitable purposes.
- *Shares.* Details concerning the purchase of the company's owns shares.
- *Disabled persons.* Information about the employment of disabled persons.
- *Employee involvement.* Details about keeping employees informed and involved in the company's activities.
- *Employees' health, safety and welfare.* This includes what steps the company has taken to protect the employees while they are at work.

In accordance with 'corporate governance' principles (as issued by the London Stock Exchange in a document called the *Combined Code on Corporate Governance*), you may also find other items in a directors' report. The following are examples of items that you might find:

- A statement about the application of the principles in the Combined Code.
- A statement of directors' responsibilities.
- Details of internal financial control procedures.
- A short section explaining how the company deals with its shareholders.
- A statement confirming that the company is a going concern.

• Results and dividends	• Close company status
• Statement of directors' responsibilities	• Corporate governance
• Review of the business and principal activities	• The Board
• Fixed assets	• Directors' remuneration
• Future developments	• Relation with shareholders
• Employee involvement	• Going concern
• Disabled employees	• Accountability and audit
• Political and charitable donations	• Internal control
• Creditor statement policy	• Internal audit
• Directors and their interests	• Audit committee and auditors
• Substantial shareholders	• Auditors

Figure 10.4 Contents of J. Smart & Co. (Contractors) PLC 2002 directors' report

The statutory and corporate governance items required in a directors' report is quite formidable. This part of the annual report can take up many pages, perhaps between six and twelve. The directors' report for even a relatively small company like J. Smart & Co. (Contractors) PLC stretches over five pages and contains 22 separate items (see Figure 10.4).

Activity 10.5

Referring to your three companies' annual reports and accounts, read through each directors' report. Then, in your notebook, list in three adjacent columns the headings used in each report. Try to list them so that similar headings are opposite each other. Are there any items that are only included by one company? Do the other two companies include such items elsewhere within the annual report? If so, make a note of the differences.

Corporate governance

We have already referred to the Cadbury Committee. The idea of 'corporate governance' was taken up by both the business and the financial communities, and the London Stock Exchange has issued some guidance on the subject in its *Combined Code on Corporate Governance.* You will find, therefore, that many annual reports and accounts (especially those of large companies) contain frequent references to corporate governance. These may be scattered through the report and accounts and they may be in the OFR, the directors' report or in separate statement.

Cairn Energy plc (2001)	Devro plc (2001)
• The Board	• The Board and its committees
• Board committees	• Chairman and chief executive
• Relations with shareholders	• Board balance
• Annual General Meeting	• Supply of information
• Directors' responsibility statement	• Appointments to the Board
• Going concern	• Re-election of directors
• Internal control	• Directors' remuneration
• Compliance with combined code	• Dialogue with shareholders
	• The Annual General Meeting
	• Financial reporting
	• Internal control
	• Audit committee and auditors
	• Compliance
	• Going concern

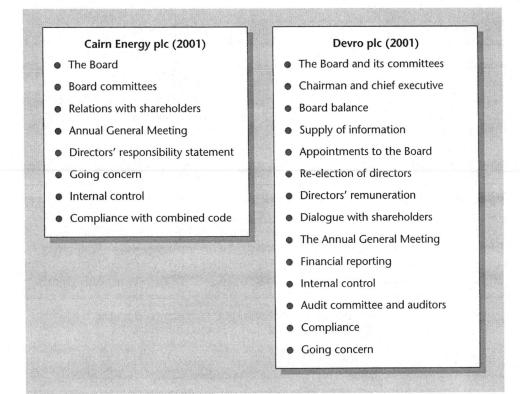

Figure 10.5 Contents of corporate governance statements

In order to give you some idea of what a separate corporate governance statement may include, in Figure 10.5 we have listed the headings used in two such statements, one for Cairn Energy plc and one for Devro plc.

As you can see from Figure 10.5 the contents of both Cairn's and Devro's corporate governance statements include some items that some companies might have included in the directors' report. There may be little disagreement about what should be disclosed but there is obviously an argument about where it should go. This is a good illustration of the difficulties that users of financial statements face when there is some inconsistency about the presentation of annual reports and accounts. Indeed, there is a strong case for the professional bodies to make the requirements prescriptive.

Activity 10.6

Once again turn to your collection of annual reports and accounts. Check whether they include a corporate governance statement. Read through them. Then copy the headings into adjacent columns, listing similar items on the same line opposite each other.

Remuneration report

As part of the corporate governance requirements, companies are expected to set up a remuneration committee. The purpose of this committee is to determine the remuneration (i.e. what they are paid) of the company's directors. The committee members should only include non-executive directors and they should not have a personal or financial interest in the outcome of the committee's deliberations.

The remuneration committee is then expected to submit an annual report to the shareholders, either attached to or included within the annual report and accounts. Their report should set out the remuneration policies and criteria for determining the pay of directors. It should also include the pay of each director by name along with any information about pension entitlements and share options. This information has to be audited.

Remuneration policies are expected to be such that directors are paid a fair rate for the job, the notice attached to service contracts should be for no longer than one year, and compensation schemes should not appear to reward failure. The remuneration report has to state that recognition has been given to these principles. Any departure from them has to be explained.

The contents of Cairn and Devro's remuneration reports are shown in Figure 10.6. Cairn's remuneration report is five pages long, and Devro's three.

Cairn Energy plc (2001)

- Remuneration policy and procedure
- Share option schemes
- Executive share option scheme ('the 1988 scheme')
- 1996 second share option scheme ('the 1996 scheme')
- Directors' interests in share options
- Long-term incentive plan
- Tier one [a share scheme]
- Tier two [another share scheme]
- Save as you earn scheme
- Annual cash bonus scheme
- Pension scheme
- Service contract
- Directors' remuneration

Devro plc (2001)

- Composition of the executive directors' remuneration committee
- Compliance
- Policy on remuneration of executive directors
- Other incentive schemes
- Company policy on contracts of service
- Company pensions policy regarding executive directors
- Pension benefits earned by the directors
- Directors' emoluments
- Directors' interests

Figure 10.6 **Contents of remuneration reports**

As you can see from Figure 10.6 a remuneration report contains a great deal of information about the directors' pay (in all sorts of forms) and the arrangements that they may have to buy shares in the company. Some of it is highly technical and probably most users of accounts are only interested in the directors' basic pay. The range of pay for Cairn's executive directors was from £253,467 to £431,288, and for Devro's executive directors, from £165,000 to £288,000.

Activity 10.7

Consult your set of three annual reports and accounts. Check whether a remuneration report is included. Work your way through each one and then list the headings in columnar form as in Figure 10.6. Try to put similar items on the same line. Note the ones that are specific to one company. List in your notebook the reasons you think the company has decided to disclose them.

Shareholder information

The order and type of the various reports and statements in an annual report and accounts will vary. However, when you are about halfway through you should come across the financial accounts sections. We will deal with these in the next chapter. Following the 'notes to the accounts' you will probably come cross some miscellaneous information. For convenience we have called this 'shareholder information'.

This part of the annual report contains mainly administrative matters. Its likely content includes the following:

- Notice of Annual General Meeting (AGM).
- Company information (names of senior staff and advisers and company addresses).
- Proxy form (to be used if a shareholder cannot attend the AGM).
- Shareholder information (the financial calendar, details about dividend payments and shareholder enquiries).
- List of principal companies of the group.

Activity 10.8

List in your notebook the shareholder information contained in each of your three sets of annual reports and accounts.

Note: Such additional information may not necessarily be towards the end of the annual report and accounts.

Questions non-accountants should ask

In previous chapters we have stressed that the detailed accounting information presented to you will have been prepared by your accountants and that you are unlikely to be involved in that process. This chapter is different. The matters with which we have been dealing will be the responsibility of a large team of non-accountants with the assistance of the accountants. So what do you need to ask if you are involved in preparing your company's annual report? We suggest the following.

- What information is legally required and where should it be shown?
- What information is a professional requirement and where should that go?
- What corporate governance information and other matters are we duty-bound to disclose and where is the best place to put it?
- Are we sure that any statements made are in line with the financial data presented in the annual accounts?
- Do we have some evidence to justify any predictions we make about our future prospects?
- Are we presenting too much information to our shareholders and, if so, can we cut it back?
- Is the design, format and general content of the material likely to encourage recipients to read it?
- Do the various reports contain any jargon and, if so, can we either cut it out or reduce it?
- Are the publicity pages likely to annoy our shareholders?

Conclusion

A company usually publishes an annual report and accounts, supplies a copy to each shareholder, and files one with the Registrar of Companies for public inspection. In this chapter we have examined the contents of the annual *report*. The next chapter examines the contents of the annual *accounts*.

In order to make our study of an annual report a little easier, we have suggested that it can be broken down into seven main sections. The first few pages usually contain some introductory material about the company, such as its objectives and a summary of the financial results for the year. In consumer orientated companies there may also be many pages advertising the company's products. Thereafter contents and order will vary from company to company.

Most companies include a short chairman's report summarizing the company's progress during the year and its prospects for the future. This will probably be followed by a fairly lengthy and detailed operating and financial review (OFR). This is a non-mandatory section recommended by the ASB. It is likely that the directors then present their report. A directors' report is a statutory requirement and the 1985 Companies Act lays down what must be included. These days it may also include a number of 'corporate governance' items. Thus a modern directors' report probably includes much more than the information required by statute.

The annual report and accounts will almost certainly include a separate 'corporate governance' statement even if some such matters are covered elsewhere in the document. In effect, a corporate governance statement informs readers how the company is operated and how it is managed. Again, as part of corporate governance proposals, there will also be a separate report about the remuneration paid and the terms and conditions of employment of the directors.

The annual reports are usually followed by the annual accounts (discussed in the next chapter), and the annual accounts by various items of 'shareholder information' such as company names and addresses and details of the AGM.

Key points

1. An annual report and accounts contains a great many reports and statements. The annual accounts are covered mainly by legislative and professional requirements. These are dealt with in the next chapter. The various annual reports are mainly voluntary.
2. It is possible to identify seven main sections of an annual report. The detailed content and structure varies from company to company. The size of such reports also varies depending partly upon the size of the company and partly on its type, e.g. consumer orientated companies usually include a great deal of publicity material.
3. The introductory section contains some details about the company, a summary of its financial results for the year and possibly some publicity material.
4. The specific reports that follow include a chairman's statement (not mandatory), an operating and financial review statement (recommended by the ASB), a directors' report (statutory), and a corporate governance statement and a remuneration report (both required by listed companies).
5. The annual accounts will normally then be presented followed by the last few pages of the overall document containing some administrative information for shareholders.

Check your learning

The answers to these questions may be found within the text.

1. List three items that may be included in the introductory section of a company's annual report.
2. What mandatory requirement covers the contents of a chairman's statement?
3. Name three items that will normally be included in a chairman's statement.

4 What is an operating and financial review?

5 What statutory and mandatory professional pronouncements require a review to be published?

6 List two items that may be found in the operating section and two items that may be found in the financial review section of an OFR.

7 What statutory and mandatory professional requirements require directors to submit a report to shareholders?

8 Name four items that should be included in a directors' report.

9 What is 'corporate governance'?

10 What is a remuneration report?

11 How has it come about?

12 List four items that it should include.

13 What type of information will normally be included in the last few pages of an annual report?

News story quiz

Remember the news story at the beginning of this chapter? Go back to that story and re-read it before answering the following questions.

Annual reports, especially those for large companies, have become extremely lengthy and complicated in recent years. And yet there are constant demands by various external parties for more and more information to be put in them. This article argues that the changing nature of business calls for more narrative reporting in annual reports.

Questions

1 Does more information supplied to shareholders necessarily make them better informed?

2 Do you think that narrative reports would be more useful to non-accountant users of annual reports than quantitative ones?

3 In terms of format and structure what type of annual report does a small shareholder need?

Tutorial questions

10.1 'A limited liability company's annual report should be made easier to understand for the average shareholder'. Discuss.

10.2 Examine the argument that annual reports are a costly irrelevance because hardly anyone refers to them.

10.3 Should companies be banned from including non-financial data in their annual reports?

Further practice questions, study material and links to relevant sites on the World Wide Web can be found on the website that accompanies this book. The site can be found at ***www.booksites.net/dyson***

7

Assessing financial performance

Objectives

This chapter is really the heart and essence of this book. You should now be reasonably familiar with the terminology, the principal accounting statements and the concepts on which they are based.

When you have completed this chapter you should be able to look at financial statements, i.e. profit and loss accounts and the balance sheets, and be able to do the following:

- ☐ Calculate the ratios illustrated.
- ☐ Appreciate who is interested in them.
- ☐ Understand what they are trying to measure.
- ☐ Know what is meant by value added, and how a value added statement is laid out.
- ☐ Identify the requirements for effective ratio analysis/interfirm comparison.
- ☐ Prepare a ratio analysis using the working notes system.
- ☐ Appreciate the limitations of ratio analysis.

Accounting ratios

Why use ratios?

Ratio analysis is the tool by which we attempt to measure and compare financial performance. However, you must appreciate from the outset that the accounting ratios on their own are pretty meaningless. They should be looked at in conjunction with other data and not in isolation. Three of the principal reasons for using ratio analysis are:

- ☐ To identify areas in which the company needs to carry out further investigations/studies.
- ☐ To pinpoint the areas in which the company may need to improve its performance or would appear to have a differential advantage over its competitors.
- ☐ To provoke questions.

However, you must remember that when it comes to intercompany (interfirm) comparisons the ratios will be meaningless unless you compare like with like. The source data must have been arrived at using similar accounting policies and the ratios must be computed in the same way.

Which ratios?

Ratio analysis is a minefield. There are numerous ratios, conflicting opinions, and a vast amount of terminology and calculation variations.

The ratios which we advocate here are just a small selection of the ratios which can be used. However, they should provide you with a good foundation/framework with which to interpret and assess the financial performance of a company or companies. Ratios may be classified in a number of ways; we will group them as follows:

☐ *Profitability*
This helps you to answer questions such as:
- Am I getting a satisfactory return on my investment?
- Are we getting a good return on all of the capital which has been invested in the business?

☐ *Liquidity*
This is all about the company's ability to pay its debts and the management of its working capital.

☐ *Efficiency*
This looks at the way in which the company uses its assets.

☐ *Capital structure*
This is about the composition and relationship which exist between the equity (i.e. the ordinary share capital or the ordinary share capital plus reserves) and the other long-term sources of finance, such as preference shares, debentures, long-term loans, etc.

☐ *Employee*
This is used to assess the efficiency with which the labour force is being used.

☐ *Investment*
This takes a look at the financial performance of the company's shares.

We will now take a more in-depth view of each group. We will provide you with an indication as to why the ratios are used, who uses them and how they are calculated. To illustrate the calculations in a practical way we will use the data provided in Figure 7.1 relating to Linboo plc. Note that, throughout, all of the calculations are in £000s. Figure 7.1 shows an abridged version of the accounts of Linboo plc.

Profitability ratios

Gross profit to sales

This is of great interest to the management of the company and also the tax authorities. It indicates the average mark-up on the products or services which have been sold during the period. When you are dealing in thousands of pounds, a small percentage increase or decrease in the gross margin (mark-up) can have a significant impact upon the profits.

Linboo plc

Profit and loss account year ended 31 October

(£000s)		20X4		20X5
Sales		2,500		3,200
Less Cost of sales		1,500		2,080
Gross profit		**1,000**		**1,120**
Less Expenses (including debenture interest and depreciation)		750		720
Net profit before tax		**250**		**400**
Corporation tax		50		92
Net profit after tax		**200**		**308**
Less Dividend (paid and proposed)		30		48
		170		260
Balance b/f	(20X3)	430	(20X4)	600
		£600		£860

Balance sheet as at 31 October

			20X4		20X5
Ordinary share capital (in £1 shares)			300		500
Share premium account			—		140
Retained earnings (P&L account balance)			600		860
			900		1,500
Long-term debt:					
12% debenture			300		150
Capital employed			**£1,200**		**£1,650**
Fixed assets:					
Cost			750		1,540
Depreciation			170		340
Net book value		(A)	£580		£1,200
Current assets:	20X3				
Stock	240		300		290
Debtors	320		250		420
Bank			230		40
		(B)	780		750
Less Current liabilities:	20X3				
Trade creditors	145	135		265	
Proposed dividend		25	160 (C)	35	300 (C)
Net worth (A) + (B) – (C)			**£1,200**		**£1,650**
Other information					
Market price per share			£1.50		£1.80
			£000		£000
Interest paid (included in the calculation of the net profit before tax)			36		18
Purchases			1,560		2,070

Figure 7.1 Financial data of Linboo plc

Figure 7.2 gives a worked example of gross profit to sales which is calculated as follows:

$$\frac{\text{Gross profit}}{\text{Sales}} \times 100$$

Possible reasons for the fall of 5% shown in Figure 7.2 could be the following:

- ☐ A reduction in selling prices.
- ☐ An increase in the cost of raw materials.
- ☐ An increase in carriage inwards, i.e. the carriage paid on materials purchased.
- ☐ Stock losses due to pilferage, poor storage or obsolescence.
- ☐ Stocktaking errors, e.g. pricing errors.

Net profit to sales (net margin)

In addition to the factors which affect the gross profit, the net profit/sales percentage is affected by what is happening to the overhead expenses and depreciation.

Figure 7.3 gives a worked example of the net profit to sales ratio, which is calculated as follows:

$$\frac{\text{Net profit before tax}}{\text{Sales}} \times 100$$

Again, this will be useful for management because it helps them to keep a watchful eye on their overhead expenses.

The increase in the net profit/sales percentage seen in Figure 7.3 could be caused by a variety of factors, which may have reduced the overhead expenditure, such as the following:

20X4	20X5
$\frac{£1,000}{£2,500} \times 100 = 40\%$	$\frac{£1,120}{£3,200} \times 100 = 35\%$

Figure 7.2 Gross profits to sales ratio

20X4	20X5
$\frac{£250}{£2,500} \times 100 = 10\%$ i.e. £10 for every £100 of sales	$\frac{£400}{£3,200} \times 100 = 12.5\%$ i.e. £12.50 for every £100 of sales

Figure 7.3 Net profits to sales ratio

- ☐ Moving premises to an area where rents are lower.
- ☐ Changes in the company's policy of financing fixed assets, e.g. renting or leasing fixed assets.
- ☐ Changes in the company's depreciation policy.
- ☐ A reduction in bad debts and/or the provision for bad debts.
- ☐ Less interest to pay on debentures. In Linboo plc debenture interest went down to half its 20X4 level in 20X5.
- ☐ The shedding of personnel, i.e. a reduction in the labour force and/or working less overtime.
- ☐ Creative accounting, e.g. prepaid advertising carried forward to the next accounting period.

Return on investment

Return on investment (ROI) can also be called return on capital employed (ROCE) and the return on assets.

Financial management is particularly concerned with the productivity of all the capital employed. Thus, companies like to have an overall indication of the productivity of all their capital. The following ratio should satisfy this need:

$$\frac{\text{Net profit before tax + loan and debenture interest}}{\text{Capital employed (less intangibles, if any)}} \times 100$$

or in other words:

$$\frac{\text{Net profit before interest and tax (NPBIT)}}{\text{Capital employed (less intangibles, if any)}} \times 100$$

This ratio is demonstrated in Figure 7.4. The debenture interest was added back so that the ratio could show the return on all capital, irrespective of where it came from. Business is about investing money, putting that money to work, and then being able to generate a satisfactory return for those who have provided it.

Other authors may use net profit before tax or net profit after tax over capital employed. Also, note that capital employed equals ordinary share capital plus reserves, plus preference share capital (if any), plus long-term loans and debentures. Capital employed can also equal total assets less intangibles, less current liabilities, i.e. the net tangible assets (net worth less intangibles).

20X4	20X5
$\frac{£250 + £36}{£1,200} \times 100 = 23.84\%$	$\frac{£400 + £18}{£1,650} \times 100 = 25.34\%$

Figure 7.4 Return on investment (ROI) ratio

The reasons for an improvement (or deterioration) in this ratio are those factors which explain the gross profit/sales percentage and net profit/sales percentage plus movements in share capital, reserves and long-term debt.

Liquidity ratios

Liquidity ratios are important to the management, shareholders, lenders and creditors because liquidity ratios provide a measure of the company's ability to pay its debts. A company can be quite profitable but still have liquidity problems. Profitability and liquidity do not go hand in hand. The ratios should provide an indication of whether or not the company has liquidity problems or excess liquidity.

The current ratio

The current ratio (or ratio of current assets to current liabilities) is given as follows:

$$\frac{\text{Current assets}}{\text{Current liabilities}}$$

A worked example of the current ratio is shown in Figure 7.5.

It is difficult to comment on Figure 7.5 without a yardstick. So, assuming that the industry average is 2:1, it would appear that last year 20X4 Linboo plc had excess liquidity. However, it is quite likely that this was used to redeem debentures and/or invest in new fixed assets in 20X5.

The acid test

The acid test (or quick) ratio is expressed as follows:

$$\frac{\text{Liquid assets (i.e. current assets less stocks)}}{\text{Current liabilities}}$$

As a rule of thumb, this ratio should be around 1.00 (i.e. one to one). However, many industries work on less than one to one. If, in the example shown in Figure 7.6, the industry averages for the two years were 0.90 for 20X4, and 0.85 for 20X5, then clearly the picture portrayed by the ratios of 3.00 and 1.54, respectively, signifies excess liquidity.

20X4	20X5
$\frac{£780}{£160} = 4.88$ i.e. for every £1 owing to current liabilities they have £4.88 cover	$\frac{£750}{£300} = 2.50$ i.e. for every £1 owing to current liabilities they have £2.50 cover

Figure 7.5 The current ratio

20X4	20X5
$\frac{£780 - £300}{£160} = 3.00$ i.e. for every £1 owing to current liabilities the company has £3 cover	$\frac{£750 - £290}{£300} = 1.54$ i.e. for every £1 owing to current liabilities the company has £1.54 cover

Figure 7.6 The acid test ratio

Efficiency ratios

The ratios which are grouped under this heading can also be referred to as activity ratios or asset utilization ratios. They are of particular interest to management/analysts because they provide a measure of how efficiently the company is managing its assets and working capital.

The average collection period

This credit control ratio provides an indication of how long it is taking the company to collect its debts. It is, therefore, of particular importance to those who are involved in the company's financial management. The ratio is expressed as follows:

$$\frac{\text{Average debtors}}{\text{Sales}} \times 365 = \text{Average collection period in days}$$

Average debtors is last year's balance sheet debtors plus this year's balance sheet debtors, divided by two.

From the example shown in Figure 7.7 it can be seen that Linboo plc's credit control has improved: the money owing from debtors is coming in that little bit quicker in 20X5 than in 20X4. If the industry average is 60 days, which is not untypical, then the company's credit control function would appear to be doing a reasonable job.

The credit period taken

Creditors, from whom goods and services have been purchased on credit, are a source of short-term finance. Financial managers will be interested in this ratio to see if they are

20X4	20X5
(£000) Average debtors = $\frac{320 + 250}{2}$ = 285 $\frac{285}{2,500} \times 365 = 42$ days (rounded up)	(£000) Average debtors = $\frac{250 + 420}{2}$ = 335 $\frac{335}{3,200} \times 365 = 39$ days (rounded up)

Figure 7.7 Debt collection (average collection period) ratio

paying off their debts too slowly or too quickly when compared with industry figures. The creditors will be interested in the figure so that they can compare it with the time it is taking the company to pay their amounts owing. Two example calculations follow:

- ☐ $\frac{\text{Average creditors}}{\text{Sales}} \times 365 = \text{Credit period taken in days}$
- ☐ $\frac{\text{Average creditors}}{\text{Purchases}} \times 365 = \text{Credit period taken in days}$

Average creditors is last year's balance sheet creditors plus this year's balance sheet creditors divided by two.

The second of the two calculations is the more realistic of the two. However, if the purchases figure is not available, then you have no choice but to use the sales figure. The purchases of Linboo plc were £1,560 for 20X4 and £2,070 for 20X5 (both £000), from the data provided in Figure 7.1.

If the industry average is 45 days, it would appear from the data in Figure 7.8 that the company is paying off its debts too quickly. However, if this is to secure generous cash discounts for prompt payment it may not be such a bad idea. After all, as a small percentage discount allowed does have a high annual percentage rate (APR).

Stock turnover

Stock turnover is also known as 'stock turn', and it shows the number of times which the average stock held is sold in a given period. Stock does represent capital tied up, so it is preferable to have a rapid rate of stock turnover to ensure that it is tied up for a minimum amount of time. The average stock is computed by dividing the opening stock plus the closing stock of the period by two. Two example calculations follow:

- ☐ $\frac{\text{Sales}}{\text{Average stocks}} = \text{The rate of stock turnover}$
- ☐ $\frac{\text{Cost of sales}}{\text{Average stocks}} = \text{The rate of stock turnover}$

20X4	20X5
(£000)	(£000)
Average creditors $= \frac{145 + 135}{2}$	Average creditors $= \frac{135 + 265}{2}$
$= \underline{140}$	$= \underline{200}$
(a) $\frac{140}{2{,}500} \times 365 = 21$ days	(a) $\frac{200}{3{,}200} \times 365 = 23$ days
Using the purchases figure:	Using the purchases figure:
(b) $\frac{140}{1{,}560} \times 365 = 33$ days	(b) $\frac{200}{2{,}070} \times 365 = 36$ days

Figure 7.8 Finance from creditors (credit period taken) ratio

The second of the two calculations is the more realistic of the two because stocks tend to be valued at their cost price or lower. However, because the cost of sales information is not always available the first calculation is used quite extensively.

If we divide the rate of stock turnover by 365, it tells us the average time for which the stock is held before being sold. Using the figures from calculation (a) in Figure 7.9 the position is as follows:

- ☐ For 20X4: $\frac{365}{9.26}$ = 40 days (rounded up)
- ☐ For 20X5: $\frac{365}{10.85}$ = 34 days (rounded up)

The higher the rate of turnover, the smaller the period of time for which stock is being carried. Thus, the above figures illustrate that the position has improved, i.e. stock is being tied up for a shorter period of time.

This means that there is also likely to be lower wastage caused by deterioration and obsolescence. A rapid rate of turnover equals fast-moving stock and less capital tied up.

Sales to fixed assets

This ratio provides a measure of asset utilization. It should be treated with caution when attempting to carry out an interfirm comparison. This is because companies may rent or lease a lot of their fixed assets. Fixed assets which are rented or leased (other than leasehold property) do not appear in the balance sheet, and are described as 'off-balance-sheet' financing.

A decision also has to be taken as to which fixed assets should be included in the ratio. Should we include all of the fixed assets or just the manufacturing fixed assets?

Thus, we can calculate it in a number of ways, two of which are as follows:

- ☐ $\frac{\text{Sales}}{\text{Fixed assets}}$
- ☐ $\frac{\text{Sales}}{\text{Manufacturing fixed assets}}$

Note that there is insufficient information provided in Figure 7.1 for Linboo plc from which to calculate the second of these ratios.

20X4	20X5
(£000)	(£000)
Average stock = $\frac{240 + 300}{2}$ = 270	Average stock = $\frac{300 + 290}{2}$ = 295
(a) $\frac{2{,}500}{270}$ = 9.26 times	(a) $\frac{3{,}200}{295}$ = 10.85 times
(b) $\frac{1{,}500}{270}$ = 5.56 times	(b) $\frac{2{,}080}{295}$ = 7.05 times

Figure 7.9 The rate of turnover (stock turn) ratio

According to the figures shown in Figure 7.10 the company became less efficient in 20X5, generating a lower sales figure per £1 invested in fixed assets. However, the dramatic increase in fixed assets may not have taken place until towards the end of 20X5 and, therefore, the benefit of the new investment should have a more dramatic impact on next year's performance. On the other hand, the company could have been caught out by a downturn in the economy.

Capital structure (gearing) ratios

Gearing (or leverage) is all about the relationship between the equity, i.e. ordinary share capital plus reserves, and *the other forms of long-term financing* which may be described as debt, including preference shares, long-term loans, debentures, and, if circumstances warrant it, the bank overdraft.

A company which has a high proportion of debt financing is referred to as being **high-geared**. A company with a low proportion of debt financing is said to be **low-geared**. In the event of adverse trading conditions it is the more highly geared companies which suffer, because of their obligations to make interest payments/repayments of capital on long-term loans and debentures. It is of particular importance to the company's financial management and the external providers of capital.

Gearing (leverage)

Examples of gearing ratios are as follows:

1. $$\frac{\text{Debt, i.e. other forms of long-term financing (excluding the bank overdraft)}}{\text{Debt (excluding the bank overdraft)} + \text{Ordinary share capital} + \text{reserves}} \times 100$$
2. As above, but including the bank overdraft if it is being used as a long term source of finance.
3. $$\frac{\text{Debt}}{\text{Equity (i.e. issued ordinary shares + reserves)}}$$

   This is also called the debt/equity ratio or borrowings/ordinary shareholders' funds.

From the example shown in Figure 7.11, it can be seen that the gearing for Linboo plc has gone down significantly during 20X5 because some of the debentures have been

20X4	20X5
(a) $\frac{2,500}{580} = 4.31$ i.e. generating £4.31 of sales for every £1 invested in fixed assets	(a) $\frac{3,200}{1,200} = 2.67$ i.e. generating £2.67 of sales for every £1 invested in fixed assets

Figure 7.10 Sales to fixed assets ratio

20X4	20X5
(£000)	(£000)
(a) $\frac{300}{1,200} \times 100 = 25\%$	(a) $\frac{150}{1,650} \times 100 = 9.09\%$

Figure 7.11 Gearing ratio (using the example 1 calculation)

redeemed and new ordinary share capital and share premium have been introduced. To make a more informed comment you need to look at industry figures. What is high- or low-geared will depend upon the industry in which the company operates, e.g. below the industry average could be classed as low, above could be classed as high.

Why include the bank overdraft? If the company is using its bank overdraft as a long-term source of funds, then it should, quite rightly, be included in the gearing calculation.

If, and when, your see other gearing ratios, remember the following:

- ☐ Equity = issued ordinary share capital plus reserves, i.e. ordinary shareholders' funds.
- ☐ Net worth = capital employed.
- ☐ Net worth = total assets less current liabilities, i.e. the net assets.
- ☐ Net worth = ordinary shareholders' funds plus the other forms of long-term financing.

Be warned that there are many more gearing ratios. However, they are all trying to say something similar, about the relationship which exists between the equity and the debt financing.

Some analysts/writers include preference shares with the long-term debt, others add them on to the equity. The reason for this conflict of opinion is that preference shares do not carry as high a risk to the company as do long-term loans and debentures, i.e. the obligation to make interest payments/repayments by stated dates. It is possible to defer paying a preference dividend should the company so decide. However, a company cannot defer a payment of interest to debenture holders.

Interest cover

This is an income-based measure of gearing. It is of interest to the company's financial management and long-term lenders, such as debenture holders, bankers, etc. It shows how well the company can cover their interest payments, and is calculated as follows:

$$\frac{\text{Net profit before interest and tax (NPBIT)}}{\text{Loan and debenture interest}}$$

It can be observed from a review of Figure 7.12 that the reduction in the gearing, coupled with the increase in profits, has made a dramatic improvement in the interest cover. Because of their low gearing and increased investment in fixed assets (i.e. additional security), Linboo plc are in a very good position to raise further debt capital, i.e. long-term loans and debentures, should they need more finance.

20X4		20X5	
	(£000)		(£000)
Net profit before tax	250	Net profit before tax	400
Add back Debenture interest	36	*Add back* Debenture interest	18
NPBIT	286	NPBIT	418
$\frac{286}{36}$ = 7.95 times		$\frac{418}{18}$ = 23.23 times	

Figure 7.12 Interest cover ratio

If we include the preference dividend in the calculation, the ratio then becomes known as **the fixed charge cover,** the calculation being as follows:

$$\frac{\text{Net profit before interest and tax}}{\text{Loan interest plus debenture interest plus preference dividend}}$$

Employee ratios

Employee ratios tend to be used in an attempt to assess the productivity and efficiency of the labour force. Again, care has to be exercised when carrying out interfirm comparisons to take account of the degree of mechanization, the use of robotics, and the location, for instance, wage rates for the same type of work could be higher or lower in other parts of the United Kingdom and in Europe.

Four types of employee ratios are detailed as follows:

1. Average remuneration per employee:
$$\frac{\text{Total wages/salaries paid to employees for the year}}{\text{Average number of employees on the payroll}}$$
2. Net profit per employee:
$$\frac{\text{Net profit before tax}}{\text{Average number of employees on the payroll}}$$
3. Sales per employee:
$$\frac{\text{Sales}}{\text{Average number of employees on the payroll}}$$
4. Directors' efficiency:
$$\frac{\text{Directors' remuneration (salaries, fees, etc.)}}{\text{Net profit before tax + directors' remuneration}} \times 100$$

The fourth of these ratios shows the directors' earnings as a percentage of the profits generated after adding back their earnings, which is useful for interfirm comparisons and trade unions. Why a directors' efficiency ratio? Directors are responsible for the success of their company, especially when it comes to the bottom line, i.e. the profit or loss.

Investment ratios

This group of ratios looks at financial performance of the company relating to the ordinary shares. The financial management, existing ordinary shareholders, would-be investors, analysts and competitors will all be very interested in these ratios.

Earnings/shareholders' equity (return on equity)

The earnings/shareholders' equity (or return on equity) ratio is a measure of the return on investment applicable to the ordinary shareholders. It is computed as follows:

$$\frac{\text{Net profit after tax less preference dividend (if any)}}{\text{Equity, i.e. issued ordinary share capital plus reserves}} \times 100$$

This ratio helps answer the question asked by ordinary shareholders of, what is in it for me? The ratio looks at what is left for the ordinary shareholders after paying/providing for the business expenses, including debenture and loan interest, directors' remuneration, taxation and preference dividends. Thus, it is in fact a ratio which reflects the self-interest of the ordinary shareholders, i.e. the equity shareholders.

The decrease in the figures shown in Figure 7.13 is probably due to the new and significant investment in fixed assets, which should benefit future accounting periods.

Dividend yield (on ordinary shares)

The dividend yield ratio simply relates the dividend to the market price of an ordinary share. However, it does give some idea to a potential investor of the expected rate of return on investment in terms of cash paid out. The ratio is expressed as follows:

$$\frac{\text{Dividend per share}}{\text{Market price per ordinary share}} \times 100$$

A worked example for Linboo plc is shown in Figure 7.14.

However, the question of which share price to use is debatable. Should it be the share price at the start or end of the period, or an average covering the whole of the period? Because share prices fluctuate a lot it is perhaps fairer that an average be used. Thus the return calculated gives the return on the average value of the shares for the period.

Earnings per ordinary share

The earnings per ordinary share ratio is also called the earnings per share (EPS) ratio and is expressed as follows:

20X4	20X5
$\frac{200}{900} \times 100 = 22.23\%$	$\frac{308}{1,500} \times 100 = 20.54\%$

Figure 7.13 Earnings/shareholders' ratio

20X4	20X5
£000 £000 Dividend per share = 30 ÷ 300 = 0.10 $\frac{£0.10}{£1.50} \times 100 = 6.67\%$ i.e. generating £6.67 for every £100 invested at the share price concerned	£000 £000 Dividend per share = 48 ÷ 500 = 0.096 $\frac{£0.096}{£1.80} \times 100 = 5.34\%$ i.e. generating £5.34 for every £100 invested at the share price concerned

Figure 7.14 The dividend yield ratio

$$\frac{\text{Net profit after tax less preference dividend (if any)}}{\text{Number of ordinary shares issued}}$$

The EPS is a measure of the earning power of each share and is closely linked to the share's market value. Thus, it shows the amount generated per share for the period (see Figure 7.15). Usually, a portion will be paid out as dividends and the balance ploughed back.

Dividend cover

The dividend cover ratio shows the number of times that the current earnings cover the ordinary dividend which has been paid and/or proposed. It can be calculated as follows:

$$\frac{\text{Earnings per share}}{\text{Dividend per share}}$$

or using the totals:

$$\frac{\text{Net profit after tax less preference dividend}}{\text{Total ordinary share dividend}}$$

Thus, it could be said that this ratio provides an indication of the likelihood that the company will be able to maintain its dividends while being able to enjoy a healthy plough-back of profits. A worked example of this ratio for Linboo plc is shown in Figure 7.16.

The price earnings ratio

A high price earnings (PE) ratio means a high price in relation to earnings. This possibly reflects market expectations of great things to come, i.e. a bright future is forecast.

20X4	20X5
$\frac{£200}{300}$ = £0.67 per share	$\frac{£308}{500}$ = £0.62 per share

Figure 7.15 Earnings per ordinary share ratio

20X4	20X5
$\frac{£0.67}{0.10}$ = 6.7 times i.e. for every £1 needed to pay the dividend £6.70 has been generated	$\frac{£0.62}{0.096}$ = 6.46 times i.e. for every £1 needed to pay the dividend £6.46 has been generated

Figure 7.16 Dividend cover ratio

A low PE implies a low price in relation to earnings. The reason for this could be low expectations on the part of the market. However, entrepreneurs have been known to take over companies with low PEs and over a period of two to five years perform a turnaround and then sell them, making millions of pounds in the process. The price earnings ratio is calculated as follows:

$$\frac{\text{Market price per ordinary share}}{\text{Earnings per ordinary share}}$$

This is the most commonly accepted relationship between a company's ability to generate profits and the market price of its ordinary shares.

The higher PE in 20X5 shown in Figure 7.17 could be attributable to an increase in market expectations of anticipated good results in the future, possibly as the new investment in fixed assets begins to bear fruit.

The inversion of this ratio provides a ratio known as the **capitalization rate** (or earnings yield), the rate at which the market is capitalizing the value of current earnings, and is expressed as follows:

$$\frac{\text{Earnings per ordinary share}}{\text{Market price per ordinary share}} \times 100$$

As with the dividend yield, this ratio also gives an indication of the return on investment (ROI), i.e. return on capital – an indication of the cost of the equity share capital. A worked example of this for Linboo plc is shown in Figure 7.18. These ratios can be compared to those of other similar-sized companies within the same industrial sector.

20X4	20X5
$\frac{£1.50}{£0.67}$ = 2.24 times	$\frac{£1.80}{£0.62}$ = 2.91 times

Figure 7.17 The price earnings (PE) ratio

20X4	20X5
$\frac{£0.67}{1.50} \times 100 = 44.67\%$	$\frac{£0.62}{1.80} \times 100 = 34.45\%$

Figure 7.18 The capitalization rate (or earnings yield) ratio

Value added statements

The value added approach is an alternative way of looking at the information provided in the profit and loss account. Value added is the difference between the amount we receive from sales and the materials and services which we buy from external suppliers. Thus, value added represents the additional wealth created by the company's own efforts through the application of its labour force, and its resources such as plant, machinery and equipment.

The value added statement (see Figure 7.19) shows how the value added has been arrived at and how it is shared out between the stakeholders. The stakeholders of a company are the following:

- ☐ The employees (including directors) for their remuneration.
- ☐ The providers of capital, for example, interest payments on loans and debentures, and dividends to preference and ordinary shareholders.

Value added statement

	£000
Sales	
Less Materials and services bought from outside suppliers	———
= **Value added**	
Add Other income, e.g. investment income	———
Value added available	═══
Shared out between the stakeholders as follows:	
Employees' remuneration	
Debenture and loan interest	
Preference shares	
Ordinary shares	
Taxation	
Depreciation	
Retained earnings	
	═══

Note that 'other income' would also have to be accounted for in the statement.

Figure 7.19 The value added statement

- ☐ The government for taxation.
- ☐ The company, by means of depreciation of fixed assets and retained earnings which are reinvested in the business.

There are a number of ratios that can be used that look at relationships with value added, for example:

- ☐ Value added per employee:

$$\frac{\text{Value added}}{\text{Number of employees}}$$

A measure of the productivity of labour.

- ☐ Value added/input:

$$\frac{\text{Value added}}{\text{Materials and services from external sources}} = \textbf{Value added per £ of input}$$

The extent to which the original input has grown.

- ☐ Value added/manufacturing fixed assets

$$\frac{\text{Value added}}{\text{Manufacturing fixed assets}} = \textbf{Value added generated per £ of manufacturing fixed assets}$$

Provides a measure of plant utilization.

- ☐ Value added/capital employed

$$\frac{\text{Value added}}{\text{Capital employed}} = \textbf{Value added per £ of capital employed}$$

Gives an indication of the productivity of capital.

Using the information

The information which is generated can be presented using a comparative statement which could be drawn up on the lines of Figure 7.20. The statement illustrated in Figure 7.20 includes a working notes column at the right-hand side reserved for explanations of reasons for variances and comments, e.g. strengths and weaknesses and inter-relationships between variances.

The comparative statement could also include other ratios covering liquidity, profitability, gearing, etc.

The format used in Figure 7.20 could also be used to compare two different companies, e.g. company A compared with company B, instead of this year with last year, as shown.

Having made the working notes during the course of the analysis, the principal findings could then be summarized in a conclusions section together with any recommendations. Look at Figure 7.21 and see if you can spot the year in which Zimte plc experienced difficulties, i.e. a year which looks out of line when compared to other years.

Ratio	This year	Last year	Reasons for variances/comments
Turnover	£531 m	£452 m	
Profit before tax	£38 m	£24 m	
Earnings per share	24.4p	11.75p	
Dividend cover	3.0 times	1.4 times	

Figure 7.20 Suggested layout for the comparative statement

	20X1	20X2	20X3	20X4	20X5	20X6
Zimte plc						
Liquidity						
Current ratio	1.34	1.65	0.89	1.13	1.32	1.40
Acid test	0.69	0.91	0.45	0.55	0.65	0.85
Debtors' average collection period (months)	2.30	1.90	1.70	1.60	1.50	1.50

Figure 7.21 Suggested layout for company financial analysis

From your review of Figure 7.21 you should have observed that the year 20X3 was out of line and, yes, the company did encounter problems in that year. What were the problems? On the current ratio the company only had £89 of current assets to cover every £100 of current liabilities which it owed. The acid test position had also deteriorated significantly. For every £100 owing to its current liabilities, the company only had £45 worth of cover in terms of its liquid assets. However, its average collection period, i.e. the speed at which it collects its debts in from debtors, improved. This could be due to the adverse liquidity position in which it found itself. If you are short of cash you are encouraged to collect your outstanding debts more quickly. This trend has continued, and currently in year 20X6 the company is, on average, taking around 45 days to collect its debts. Also, you can see from the figures that since 20X3, the problem year, the company has improved its liquidity position.

The important message of Figure 7.21 concerning financial analysis is that you need at least five or six years' worth of figures to be in a position to make a more realistic appraisal, e.g. the identification of trends. It is difficult to make sound judgements simply on the basis of a two-year analysis.

A comparison of ratios, one year with another for the same company, does not indicate whether the performance was good, bad or indifferent. Hence, the quest for a yardstick, i.e. a standard against which performance can be measured. The yardsticks which can be used are industry figures, either by comparing with other companies in the same area which are of a similar nature or by looking at industry averages. A wealth of this type of information is available on computer databases, on the World Wide Web and in numerous publications. However, it is not always an easy task to carry out; for example, company T in Figure 7.22 has a different year end from the other companies. Thus, the comparison does not cover the same trading period.

	Motor Component Industry		
Company	S	T	U
Year end	Dec 20X6	July 20X6	Dec 20X6
Ratio:			
Return on capital employed	17.0%	17.5%	19.1%
Profit margin	6.3%	8.5%	8.3%
Average collection period (months)	4.4	5.0	4.6
Gearing	47.7%	32.8%	39.1%
Interest cover (times)	6.1	7.1	6.4
Current ratio (times)	1.8	1.8	1.7
Acid test (times)	0.9	1.0	0.8

Figure 7.22 Industry figures – motor components

Self-assessments

This chapter has provided you with the ratios, i.e. the tools, with which you can analyse and assess company performance. There now follow two separate self-assessments for you to use to check your understanding of the ratios. They are as follows:

- ☐ Woodcroft plc.
- ☐ Nether Ltd and Thong Ltd.

Self-assessment

Woodcroft plc

You have been supplied with the following data relating to Woodcroft plc for the years 20X7 and 20X8:

		20X7		20X8
		£000		£000
Sales		1,200		1,600
Net profit before tax		120		180
Net profit after tax		80		130
Ordinary dividends (paid and proposed)		60		70
Balance sheet				
Employment of capital:				
Fixed assets		100		120
Current assets (20X6)				
Stock (160)	200		180	
Debtors (260)	300		340	
	500		520	

Less **Current liabilities** (20X6)				
Creditors (120)	160		180	
Proposed dividend	40		60	
Bank overdraft	200		140	
	400	100	380	140
		200		260
		20X7		20X8
Capital employed:	£000	£000	£000	£000
Ordinary shares (£1 each)		100		100
Reserves		100		160
		200		260

Calculate the following ratios for both 20X7 and 20X8, making brief comments about each of your answers:

Liquidity:
- Current ratio
- Acid test (quick ratio)

Profitability:
- Net profit to sales
- Return on investment (return on assets)

Efficiency:
- Average collection period
- Credit period taken
- Stock turnover

Investment:
- Earnings/shareholders' equity
- Dividend cover
- Earnings per ordinary share (EPS)

When you have completed this exercise, please check your answers with the suggested answers on pages 119–21.

Self-assessment

Nether Ltd and Thong Ltd

You are provided with the following accounting information for Nether Ltd and Thong Ltd for the year 20X8:

	Nether Ltd	*Thong Ltd*
	£000	£000
Sales	125	250
Net profit before tax	25	40
Net profit after tax	20	32

		Nether Ltd		*Thong Ltd*
Balance sheet details:		£000		£000
Fixed assets		100		120
Current assets:				
Stock	25		60	
Debtors	20		30	
Cash	15		—	
	60		90	
Current liabilities:				
Creditors	40		35	
Bank overdraft	—		25	
	40	20	60	30
Net assets		£120		£150
Share capital (£1 shares)		100		100
Reserves		20		50
		£120		£150

Calculate the following ratios for 20X8 for both Nether Ltd and Thong Ltd in order to compare the performances of both companies. The industry average for each ratio is given below:

Liquidity:
- Current ratio (2.00)
- Acid test (quick ratio) (0.90)

Profitability:
- Net profit before tax to sales (20%)
- Return on investment (return on assets) (24%)

Efficiency:
- Average collection period (60 days)
- Credit period taken (70 days)
- Stock turnover (7 times)

Investment:
- Earnings/shareholders' equity (20%)
- Earnings per ordinary share (£0.30)

Having made your calculations and comparisons, prepare a brief draft of your conclusions and recommendations.

When you have completed this self-assessment, please check your answers with the suggested answers on pages 122–4.

The limitations of ratio analysis

One of the principal limitations of ratio analysis is the inadequacy of the source data (i.e. profit and loss accounts and balance sheets) which may be affected by the following:

- ☐ The way in which the accounting concepts are applied, for instance the use of subjective judgement, and the inconsistency with which certain figures are calculated.

- ☐ Preparing accounts with the tax authorities in mind, e.g. the distinction between repairs and renewals and fixed assets is open to differing interpretations. Should we charge the expenditure (i.e. **write it off**) in the profit and loss account or carry it forward into the future as an asset in the balance sheet?
- ☐ A change in the accounting policies.
- ☐ Off-balance-sheet financing, e.g. the renting or leasing of machinery and plant, equipment and motor vehicles.
- ☐ **Window dressing (creative accounting)**, i.e. making the accounts look better or worse than they really are, e.g. having a special effort to collect cash in from debtors in the last few months of the accounting period. This means that the debtors' figure at the year end could be totally unrepresentative of the position that existed throughout the period.

Interfirm comparisons can therefore be extremely difficult because the firms concerned could be using different accounting policies, applying the concepts in different ways and could be affected by off-balance-sheet financing, etc. This is why the most accurate and realistic comparisons are those which are done for internal reporting purposes which look at the company over a number of years. Even then, adjustments may have to be made, to allow for changes in accounting policies, inflation, etc.

Another major limitation arises from the way in which some of the ratios are computed, for example the following:

- ☐ The treatment of the bank overdraft. Is it really a current liability? Nowadays, many companies use it as a long-term source of funds. The way in which it is treated affects the liquidity ratios and gearing ratios.
- ☐ Certain ratios use the sales figures when the cost of sales or the purchases figure is more appropriate.
- ☐ Which profit figure should be used? Should it be:
  - net profit before tax?
  - net profit after tax?
  - net profit before interest and tax (NPBIT)?
- ☐ The average creditors, debtors and stocks are calculated using opening and closing balances. What happens throughout the period would thus appear to be irrelevant. For an external analysis the information is simply not available, but for internal analysis purposes it should be.

Finally, the terminology used also acts as a limitation in that it does tend to confuse the user, for example capital employed, net assets and net worth can mean the same thing. Most gearing ratios exclude the bank overdraft, others include it. Return on investment can be called return on assets or return on capital employed, and so on.

Self-assessment

The problems of interfirm comparison

Study the data given in Figure 7.23 for some companies in the textile industry. Listed below are two possible reasons why a comparison of the financial performance of the textile companies is difficult:

- Some of them may be highly diversified and others may not be.
- Their product ranges could be significantly different.

See if you can think of four more reasons why it is difficult to make comparisons.

When you have completed this self-assessment, please check your answers with the suggested answers on pages 124–5.

The balanced scorecard

Ratios which review past performance such as the return on capital employed are used in the balanced scorecard method. This approach, which aims to ensure that businesses succeed and prosper, is, however, much more than a financial analysis. It also takes an in-depth look at customers, internal business processes, learning and growth, and is concerned with organizational goals, strategy and future performance.

Industry		**Performance**			
Textiles	Year end	Turnover £m	Return on capital %	Net profit/sales %	Stock turnover
Company					
A	Sept X2	30.7	24.5	9.7	3.7
B	Dec X2	24.1	20.7	11.3	2.7
C	Mar X3	82.6	41.3	18.8	3.6
D	Mar X3	15.6	13.8	8.0	3.1
E	Jun X3	23.9	32.2	13.1	10.3
F	Mar X3	10.7	14.4	7.2	2.6
G	Mar X3	119.7	15.1	6.1	3.2
H	Dec X2	7.5	15.8	7.4	4.1
I	Sept X2	7.6	31.1	13.3	16.0
J	Feb X3	29.2	22.4	9.4	3.5
K	Mar X3	76.4	22.2	10.7	3.6
L	Apr X3	10.2	30.1	13.3	3.1

Figure 7.23 Industry figures – textiles

Summary: assessing financial performance

Ratio analysis

Ratio analysis is a tool which is used in order to compare and evaluate financial performance. The source data from which the ratios are calculated may be internal, e.g. the company's own profit and loss account, appropriation account, balance sheet and data relating to debtors, creditors and stocks, etc.; or external in the form of the published accounts of other companies and industry figures which are available from a variety of sources.

Ratios can help to:

- ☐ Indicate areas in which further investigation is needed.
- ☐ Highlight strengths and weaknesses.
- ☐ Provoke questions.

Ratios are of little value if they are used in isolation. To be useful, they need to be viewed in conjunction with other data, such as the following:

- ☐ Information about the management.
- ☐ Industry figures, which provide a yardstick with which more realistic comparisons can be made.
- ☐ The value of fixed assets and investments.
- ☐ Opportunity costs, e.g. the returns available from alternative investments.
- ☐ Government regulations/legislation already passed or pending.
- ☐ Security, i.e. the degree to which the company has used its assets as security for loans and debentures.

The ratios

The following ratios should help you to make a reasonable assessment of the financial performance of a company.

Profitability

The gross profit to sales ratio is expressed as follows:

$$\frac{\text{Gross profit}}{\text{Sales}} \times 100$$

It indicates the average gross margin (mark-up) which is being made on the products/services which are being sold.

The net profit to sales (net margin) ratio is expressed as follows:

$$\frac{\text{Net profit before tax}}{\text{Sales}} \times 100$$

This shows how much profit is being generated by sales and provides an indication as to what is happening to the overheads.

The return on investment (ROI) ratio (also called return on capital employed (ROCE) return on assets) is expressed as follows:

$$\frac{\text{Net profit before interest and tax (NPBIT)}}{\text{Capital employed (less intangibles, if any)}} \times 100$$

This gives the overall return on all of the capital which has been invested in the business, i.e. it is a measure of the productivity of all the capital invested in the business irrespective of its source.

Liquidity ratios

The current ratio (or the ratio of current assets to current liabilities) is expressed as follows:

$$\frac{\text{Current assets}}{\text{Current liabilities}}$$

This provides an indication of whether the company has excess liquidity, satisfactory liquidity or liquidity problems. It provides an indication of the company's ability to pay its short-term debts.

The acid test (or quick) ratio is expressed as follows:

$$\frac{\text{Liquid assets (i.e. current assets less stocks)}}{\text{Current liabilities}}$$

This is a key ratio used in the management of working capital, which looks at the ability to pay short-term debts with the liquid assets. As a general rule, this ratio is expected to be around one to one, i.e. £1 of liquid assets to every £1 owing to current liabilities. However, in practice the liquid assets tend to be less than £1 for every £1 owing to current liabilities.

Efficiency ratios

These ratios look at asset utilization and provide an insight into the efficiency of inventory (stock) control and credit control.

The average collection period ratio is expressed as follows:

$$\frac{\text{Average debtors}}{\text{Sales}} \times 365$$

This provides us with an indication of how long it is taking us to collect the amounts owing from our credit customers, i.e. our debtors.

The credit period taken ratio is expressed as follows:

$$\frac{\text{Average creditors}}{\text{Purchases (or sales if the purchases figure is not available)}} \times 365$$

This tells us the average time it takes us to pay our suppliers of goods on credit. Note that creditors do represent a source of short-term financing to the company.

The stock turnover ratio is expressed as follows:

$$\frac{\text{Cost of sales (or sales)}}{\text{Average stock (i.e. opening plus closing stock divided by two)}} = \text{The rate of turnover}$$

This shows the number of times which the average stock held is sold in a given period of time.

The sales to fixed assets ratio is expressed as follows:

$$\frac{\text{Sales}}{\text{Fixed assets}} = \text{The overall efficiency with which the fixed assets are used}$$

or

$$\frac{\text{Sales}}{\text{Manufacturing fixed assets}} = \text{A measure of the utilization of manufacturing fixed assets}$$

Capital structure ratios

The gearing (or leverage) ratio is expressed as follows:

$$\frac{\text{Debt, e.g. long-term loans and debentures (with or without the bank overdraft, as appropriate)}}{\text{Debt (with or without the bank overdraft) + ordinary share capital + reserves}} \times 100$$

This looks at the proportion of debt financing in relation to the total long-term financing and is of particular significance to financial management and the providers of finance.

The debt/equity ratio is expressed as follows:

$$\frac{\text{Debt}}{\text{Equity}}$$

Those companies with a high proportion of debt to equity, i.e. those which are highly geared, tend to be at greater risk in periods where trading conditions are poor. This is because they have to pay interest or repay capital and interest on debentures/loans irrespective of whether they are performing well or badly.

Many companies nowadays do use their bank overdraft as a long-term source of funds. Note that there are many more gearing ratios and that some authorities include the preference shares with the equity, whilst others include it with the debt!

The interest cover ratio is expressed as follows:

$$\frac{\text{Net profit before interest and tax}}{\text{Loan and debenture interest}}$$

This ratio shows how well the company can cover the interest that it has to pay out. It is expressed as the number of times that it can cover the interest payments. If the preference dividend is added to the loan and debenture interest the ratio then becomes the fixed charge cover.

Employee ratios

Employee ratios assess the productivity of labour in terms of sales and net profit. The ones which were covered earlier in this chapter were:

- ☐ Average remuneration per employee.
- ☐ Net profit per employee.
- ☐ Sales per employee.
- ☐ Directors' efficiency.

Investment ratios

Investment ratios are of particular significance to directors, shareholders, analysts, would-be investors and competitors.

The earnings/shareholders' equity (return on equity) ratio is expressed as follows:

$$\frac{\text{Net profit after tax, less preference dividends (if any)}}{\text{Equity (i.e. issued ordinary share capital + reserves)}} \times 100$$

This ratio provides the ordinary shareholders with an idea of what their return on investment is. The profit figure which is used in the calculation represents what is left for them after paying everything else including interest, tax, and dividends on preference shares.

The dividend yield ratio can be expressed as follows:

$$\frac{\text{Dividend per ordinary share}}{\text{Market price per ordinary share}} \times 100$$

This ratio relates the profit distributed as dividend to the share price. It does not measure the return on investment for a shareholder because there are also the capital gains on their shares to consider. However, it does provide a potential investor with an indication of the expected rate of return on investment in terms of cash paid out.

The earnings per ordinary share or earnings per share (EPS) ratio is expressed as follows:

$$\frac{\text{Net profit after tax less preference dividend}}{\text{Number of ordinary shares issued}}$$

This represents the earning power per share.

The dividend cover (on ordinary shares) ratio is expressed as follows:

$$\frac{\text{Earnings per share}}{\text{Dividend per share}}$$

This ratio shows how many times the company can cover its ordinary share dividends from its current earnings. It can also be calculated in the following way:

$$\frac{\text{Net profit after tax less preference dividend}}{\text{Total ordinary share dividend}}$$

The price earnings (PE) ratio is expressed as follows:

$$\frac{\text{Market price per ordinary share}}{\text{Earnings per ordinary share}}$$

This ratio expresses the relationship between the company's ability to generate profits and the market price of its ordinary shares.

The capitalization rate (or earnings yield) ratio is the PE ratio turned upside down, and is expressed as follows:

$$\frac{\text{Earnings per ordinary share}}{\text{Market price per ordinary share}} \times 100$$

It provides shareholders and investors with an indication of the current performance of the ordinary shares, i.e. it provides a measure of the cost of the equity share capital.

Value added statements and ratios

Value added statements show how the value added (the wealth created), i.e. sales less materials and services bought from outside suppliers, is distributed between the stakeholders. The stakeholders of a company are the employees, the providers of capital, the government, and the company itself by means of depreciation and retained earnings.

Ratios can be computed using value added to measure the productivity of labour, capital and fixed assets and also the growth of the original inputs.

Using the information

Information can be used in the following ways:

- ☐ When you look at comparative figures. For example, this year compared to last year, or company A compared to company B. It is useful to make working notes on each ratio/group of ratios to explain the variances and to highlight strengths and weaknesses, etc.
- ☐ If a ratio analysis is to be useful, it needs to be based on several years' figures so that trends can be identified and emerging problems detected.
- ☐ The quest for a 'yardstick', i.e. something against which performance can be measured, can be partly solved by using industry figures.

Limitations

Ratio analysis does have limitations, the principal ones being:

- ☐ The inadequacy of the source data, i.e. the final accounts, for example concerning the application of concepts and accounting policies, '**off-balance-sheet financing**' and '**window dressing**' (creative accounting) etc.
- ☐ The way in which the ratios are computed, for example the treatment of the bank overdraft as a long- or short-term source of finance; using the sales figure when purchases or cost of sales figures would be more appropriate; the profit figure could be one of many, for example, net profit before tax, net profit after tax, etc.; the way in which the average debtors, creditors and stock are arrived at, i.e. taking no account of what happens during the intervening period.
- ☐ The terminology can be very confusing.

Interfirm comparison

If you have to carry out an interfirm comparison, beware! You cannot just compare with another firm in the same industrial sector. You also need to try to select companies which are in the same industrial sector and which also have some of the following characteristics:

- ☐ Have a similar product range.
- ☐ Are of a similar size.
- ☐ Have the same year end.
- ☐ Use similar accounting policies.
- ☐ Finance their assets in a similar manner, i.e. the extent to which they use 'off-balance-sheet financing'.
- ☐ Have revalued their buildings and/or other fixed assets around the same date.
- ☐ Employ the same kind of production methods.
- ☐ Are located in an area where overhead costs are similar.
- ☐ Arrive at the year-end stock valuations using similar methods/practices.

The balanced scorecard approach

This reviews financial, customer, internal business processes, learning and growth. In addition to reviewing past performance via selected ratios it also uses forecasts to enable it to focus on future performance.

Further reading

Glautier, M. W. E. and Underdown, B., *Accounting Theory and Practice*, Pitman Publishing, 1997.
Holmes, G. and Sugden, A., *Interpreting Company Reports and Accounts*, Financial Times Prentice Hall, 1999.
Parker, R. H., *Understanding Company Financial Statements*, Penguin Business, 1999.
Pendlebury, M. and Groves, R., *Company Accounts, Analysis, Interpretation and Understanding*, International Thomson Business Press, 1999.

Sources of industry data

- *U.K. Industrial Performance Analysis* (published annually, ICC Business Publications Ltd).
- Extel Cards.
- The Company Reports Section of a library, e.g. covering *The Times* 1,000 companies.
- On the computer *Micro View* by Extel and *Micro Extat* as used by leading business schools.
- Internet sources.

1

Introduction to management accounting

Objectives

The principal aim of this chapter is to introduce you to the purpose and scope of management accounting. When you have completed this chapter you should be able to do the following:

- ☐ Appreciate why predetermined cost and management accounting systems are needed.
- ☐ Understand what is meant by elements of cost.
- ☐ Distinguish between direct and indirect costs, and fixed and variable costs.
- ☐ Appreciate the way in which management accounting can meet the needs of management.

Cost and management accounting systems

Cost and management accounting systems can be divided into two, as shown in Figure 1.1. Historic costing looks back at past performance. However, it must be remembered that simply comparing current performance with past performance is not such a satisfactory way of controlling business activities.

Why not? Because it is hard to say whether or not past performance has been good, bad or indifferent.

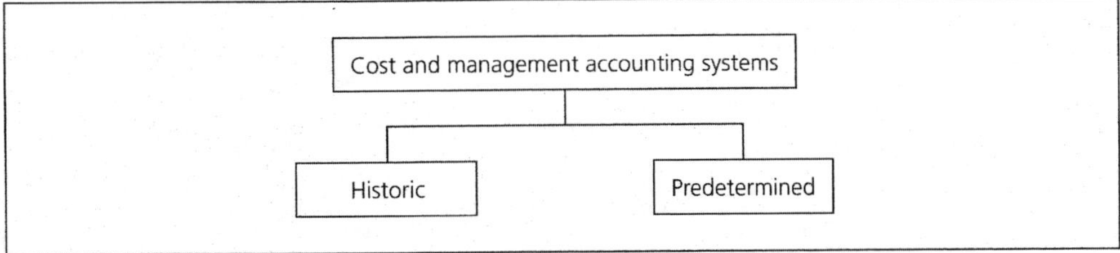

Figure 1.1 Cost and management accounting

However, management accounting tends to make extensive use of predetermined systems such as budgetary control and standard costing.

Why? The principal reasons are as follows:

- ☐ A lot of the management accounting information produced is about the future. Management needs to be able to assess what its decisions/proposed decisions will mean in terms of future costs and revenues, etc.
- ☐ The quest for a 'yardstick', i.e. a way of assessing and measuring performance, e.g. a sales target, budgeted expenditure on advertising, etc.

The budgets and standards used should provide targets at which to aim; they should *not* merely reflect what is expected to happen. Thus, control can be exercised by comparing the planned (budgets or standards) figures with the actual results at regular intervals.

The elements of cost

The cost of a product, job or service is made up of the elements of cost, i.e. materials, labour and overheads (see Figure 1.2). The last of the three (overheads) is the most difficult to deal with. In later chapters we will look at how overheads are dealt with in total absorption costing, activity based costing and marginal costing.

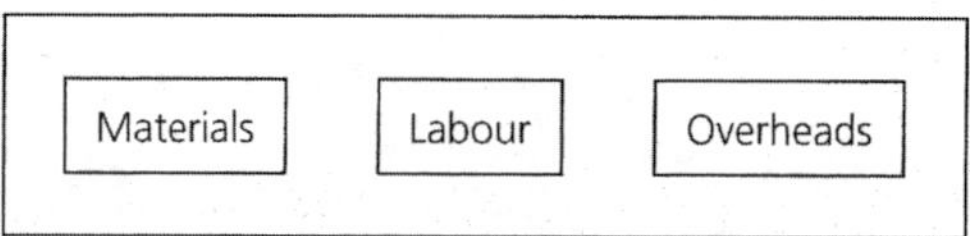

Figure 1.2 The elements of cost

The classification of costs

Costs can be classified in a number of ways (see Figure 1.3):

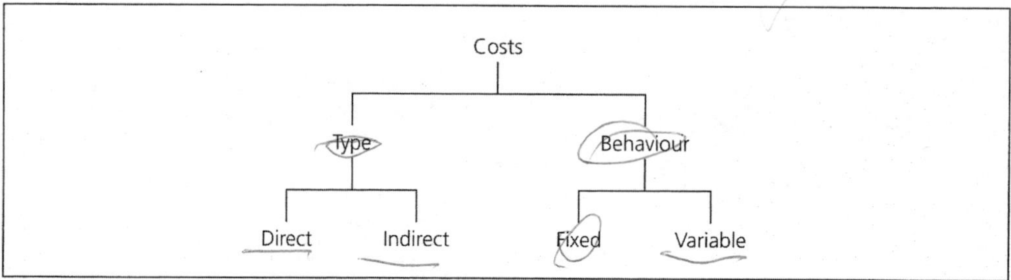

Figure 1.3 The classification of costs

- **Direct costs** can be identified as forming part of the product or service, e.g. manufacturing wages and raw materials which are used in the production process.
- **Indirect costs** are usually referred to as **overheads**; they are expenses which do not form part of the product or service, e.g. the wages of cleaners and canteen staff, materials used for cleaning, and maintenance.
- **Fixed costs** have to be paid out irrespective of the level of activity, but within a relevant range. Examples are insurance of buildings, rent of premises and maintenance contracts.
- **Variable (marginal) costs** comprise the direct costs referred to above plus variable overheads. They may be described as those costs which vary with the level of activity within a relevant range. Examples of variable costs are direct materials plus those expenses which vary with the level of output, e.g. power for machines.

A combination of fixed and variable costs may be referred to as a **semi-variable** cost, e.g. a fixed rental for some equipment plus a variable element charged according to usage.

Costs may be further divided up between products, services, departments, sections and functions. These may be referred to as **cost centres.** A cost centre is simply a location, person or function, etc., to which costs are allocated and apportioned. The aim is to collect and accumulate the costs applicable to each specific cost centre.

What is management accounting?

Management accounting is very closely linked to cost accounting; so closely, in fact, that it is difficult to say where cost accounting ends and where management accounting begins. **Cost accounting** simply aims to measure the performance of departments, goods and services. However, **management accounting** is much, much more, and involves the following.

- *The provision of information for management*
  Indeed, the role of the management accountant could well be described as that of an 'information manager'. The information generated should be designed to assist management, to control business operations, and to help management with decision making. In fulfilling this role the management accounting department/section must consult with the users of the information, i.e. management, to assess their needs in terms of precisely what information is required and when, etc. The aim is to provide management with a flow of relevant information, e.g. reports, statements, spreadsheets, etc., as and when required. A frequent flow of information (weekly or monthly) should enable management to respond to emerging problems/situations as soon as possible. The early detection of problems means earlier solutions and early action.

- *Advising management*
  A key part of management accounting is to advise management about the economic consequences and implications of its (proposed) decisions and alternative courses of action. In particular, this advice should answer a frequently overlooked question: **what**

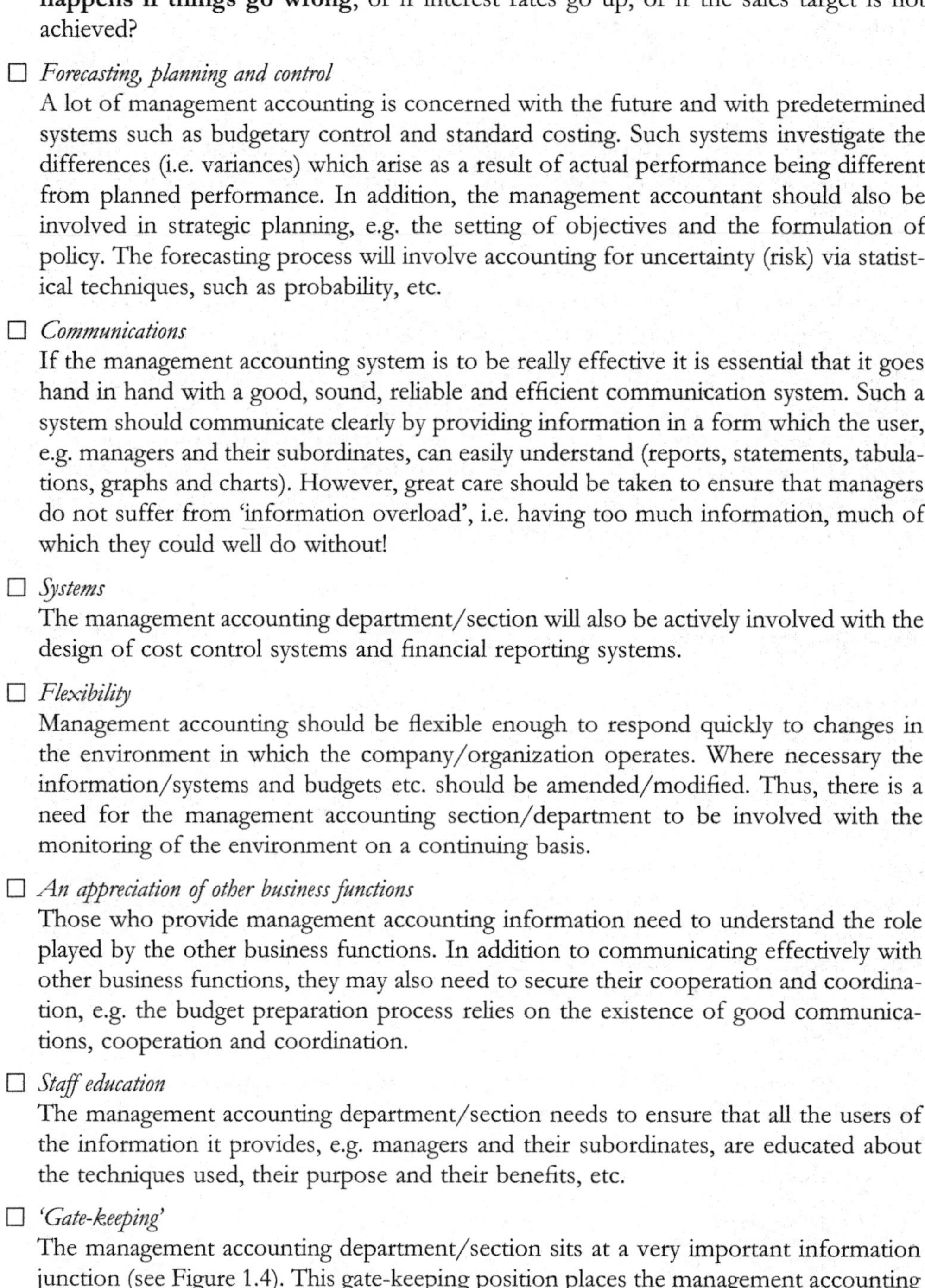

happens if things go wrong, or if interest rates go up, or if the sales target is not achieved?

- ☐ *Forecasting, planning and control*
  A lot of management accounting is concerned with the future and with predetermined systems such as budgetary control and standard costing. Such systems investigate the differences (i.e. variances) which arise as a result of actual performance being different from planned performance. In addition, the management accountant should also be involved in strategic planning, e.g. the setting of objectives and the formulation of policy. The forecasting process will involve accounting for uncertainty (risk) via statistical techniques, such as probability, etc.

- ☐ *Communications*
  If the management accounting system is to be really effective it is essential that it goes hand in hand with a good, sound, reliable and efficient communication system. Such a system should communicate clearly by providing information in a form which the user, e.g. managers and their subordinates, can easily understand (reports, statements, tabulations, graphs and charts). However, great care should be taken to ensure that managers do not suffer from 'information overload', i.e. having too much information, much of which they could well do without!

- ☐ *Systems*
  The management accounting department/section will also be actively involved with the design of cost control systems and financial reporting systems.

- ☐ *Flexibility*
  Management accounting should be flexible enough to respond quickly to changes in the environment in which the company/organization operates. Where necessary the information/systems and budgets etc. should be amended/modified. Thus, there is a need for the management accounting section/department to be involved with the monitoring of the environment on a continuing basis.

- ☐ *An appreciation of other business functions*
  Those who provide management accounting information need to understand the role played by the other business functions. In addition to communicating effectively with other business functions, they may also need to secure their cooperation and coordination, e.g. the budget preparation process relies on the existence of good communications, cooperation and coordination.

- ☐ *Staff education*
  The management accounting department/section needs to ensure that all the users of the information it provides, e.g. managers and their subordinates, are educated about the techniques used, their purpose and their benefits, etc.

- ☐ *'Gate-keeping'*
  The management accounting department/section sits at a very important information junction (see Figure 1.4). This gate-keeping position places the management accounting section in a position of power; it has access to (can send information to and from)

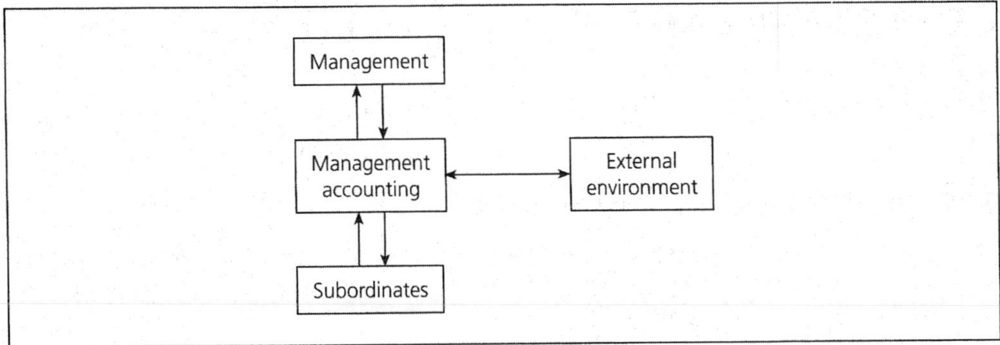

Figure 1.4 Management accounting: the gate-keeper

management and subordinates, and communicates with and receives a certain amount of information from the external environment. Its power arises because it can control the flow of information upwards to management or downwards to subordinates.

- ☐ *Limitations*
  Although management accounting can, and does, provide a lot of useful information, it must be stressed that this is *not* an exact science. A vast amount of the information generated depends upon subjective judgement, e.g. the assessment of qualitative factors or assumptions about the business environment. Management accounting is not the be-all-and-end-all of decision making – it is just one of the tools which can help management to make more informed decisions.

- ☐ *Being the servant*
  Finally, having established that management accounting is a tool, it must be emphasized that it is there to serve the needs of management.

Summary: an introduction to management accounting

Cost and management accounting systems

- ☐ **Historic** looks backwards at past events.
- ☐ **Predetermined** looks forward to the future.

Management accounting makes extensive use of predetermined systems such as budgetary control and standard costing.

The elements of cost

- ☐ Materials.
- ☐ Labour.
- ☐ Overheads.

The classification of costs

- ☐ Direct or indirect.
- ☐ Fixed or variable.

The role of management accounting

Management accounting attempts to provide managers and executives with a regular supply of relevant information which will enable them to manage more effectively, efficiently and economically. It also involves:

- ☐ Advising management about the possible consequences of its actions.
- ☐ Forecasting, planning and control.
- ☐ Communications.
- ☐ Systems.
- ☐ Flexibility.
- ☐ An appreciation of other business functions.
- ☐ Staff education.
- ☐ 'Gate keeping'.
- ☐ Limitations.
- ☐ Being the servant and 'information manager' of the management.

Management accounting should thus assist management with decision making and problem solving. It should help managers and executives to make the best use of their valuable time and talents in fulfilling their responsibilities and enable them to take advantage of emerging opportunities.

Further reading

Drury, C., *Costing: An Introduction*, International Thomson Business Press, 1998.
Dyson, J., *Accounting for Non-accounting Students*, Financial Times Pitman, 2000.
Weetman, P., *Management Accounting*, Financial Times Prentice Hall, 1999.

4

Total absorption costing

Objectives

By the time you have finished studying this chapter, you should be able to do the following:

- ☐ Understand how overheads are incorporated into the cost of a job, product or service.
- ☐ Prepare an overhead distribution summary and calculate:
  - a machine hour rate;
  - a direct labour hour rate;
  - the cost of a job, product or service.
- ☐ Appreciate the limitations of total absorption costing.

The aim of total absorption costing

The principal aim of total absorption costing (also called **absorption costing** or **total costing** or the **full cost method**) is to attempt to ensure that all overhead costs are covered by the revenues received. It should be mentioned here that this is *not an attempt to produce accurate costs*. It is, however, an attempt to answer the question of how much should be included for overheads in costing jobs, products or services.

Overheads

Overheads comprise the indirect expenditure of a business, i.e. that expenditure which does not form part of the product, job or service and includes such costs as:

- ☐ **Indirect labour**: cleaners, canteen staff, security staff, supervisory staff, etc.
- ☐ **Indirect materials**: e.g. cleaning materials, maintenance materials, etc.
- ☐ **Indirect expenses**: rent, insurance of buildings, heating, lighting, etc.

The overheads can also be subdivided into fixed overheads and variable overheads.

Cost centres

Cost centre is the name given to a unit/section to which costs are allocated and apportioned. It could be a department, a process, a function, a service, a group of machines or a person. The aim is to arrive at a total overhead cost for each cost centre. All organizations/companies, including those which provide a service, e.g. the BBC, banking, insurance, education, may have numerous cost centres.

You may also come across the term **profit centre**. This is much the same as a cost centre, but is also revenue-earning. Thus, a profit or loss for the centre can be computed.

Overhead absorption

Overhead absorption (also called **overhead recovery**) is the process of sharing out the overheads between jobs, products or services by means of **absorption rates/recovery rates**, e.g. a rate per direct labour hour or a rate per machine hour.

Absorption costing differs from marginal costing (which we will look at in Chapter 6) in that it attempts to include most of the overheads in product, job or service costs. Marginal costing, on the other hand, includes only the variable overheads in product costs.

We will now describe how a typical absorption costing system in a manufacturing environment works by reference to the absorption of overheads diagram (see Figure 4.1). Because the overheads have to be charged to jobs/products/services throughout the period/year, the recovery rates must be calculated before the period/year begins, i.e. they have to be predetermined.

Stage 1
The production overheads, i.e. the indirect materials, labour and expenses have to be estimated for the forthcoming period/year.

Stage 2
Those overheads which can be identified with and traced to a department/cost centre are charged to the department/cost centre concerned, i.e. they are *allocated* to the cost centre.

Stage 3
Overheads which cannot be allocated to cost centres, i.e. those which cannot be identified and traced to departments/cost centres will have to be *apportioned* to departments/cost centres using some arbitrary basis. A number of overheads tend to *vary more with time than output* and will have to be shared out between the cost centres using some method of apportionment (see Table 4.1).

Stage 4
Having collected all the overheads applicable to the service departments, the total overhead cost of each service department can be shared out between the user departments/

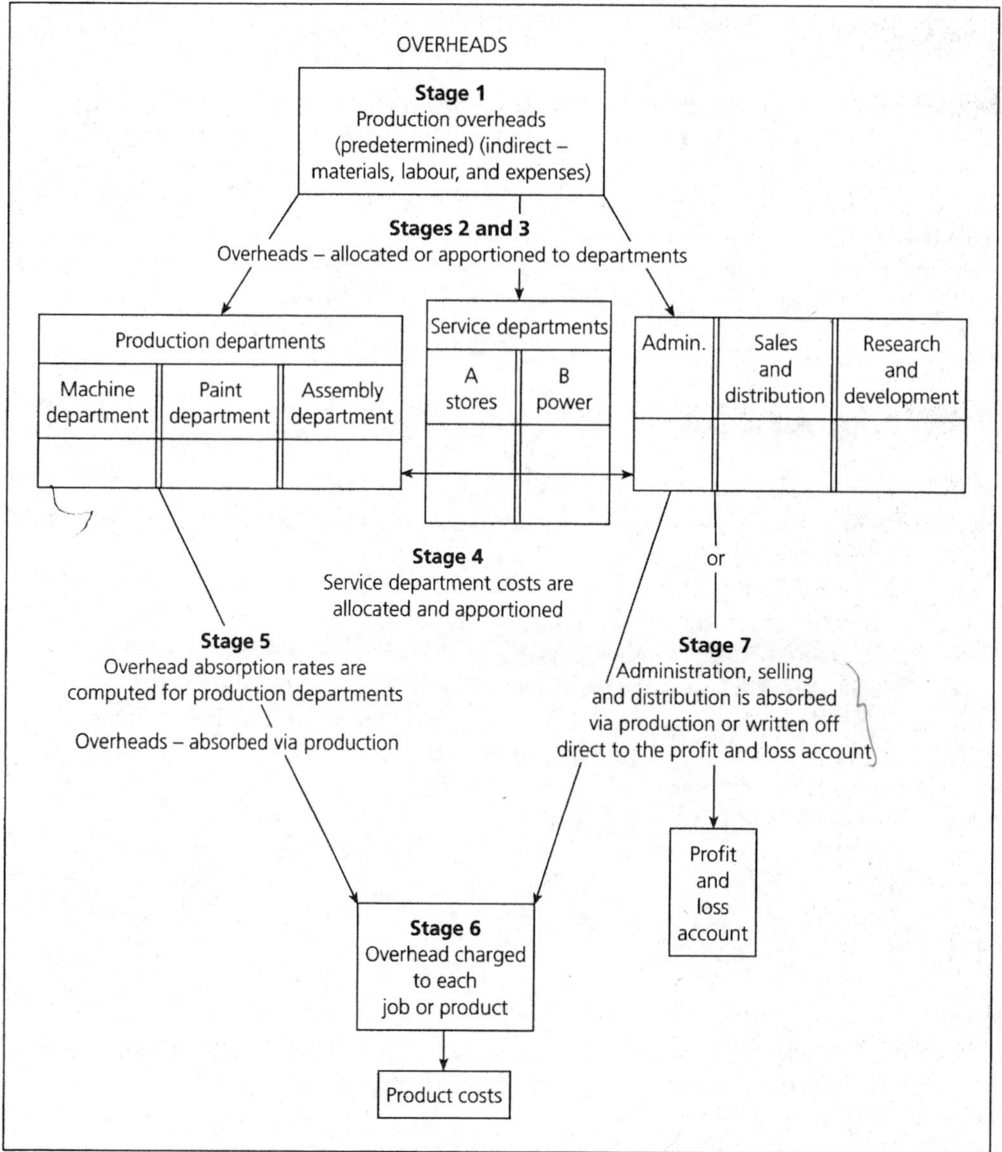

Figure 4.1 Absorption costing in a manufacturing environment

Table 4.1 The apportionment of overheads

Item of overhead expenditure	Basis of apportionment
Rent/heating	Floor area or cubic capacity
Supervision/canteen	Number of employees

costs centres according to technical estimates or by using some arbitrary basis of apportionment, e.g. in proportion to the number of issue notes for the stores department.

Stage 5

The overhead absorption (overhead recovery) rates are calculated. The total overhead for each production department, inclusive of its share of service department costs, is divided by the estimated machine hours or direct labour hours, as appropriate:

$$\frac{\text{machine department overheads}}{\text{estimated no. of machine hours}} = \text{the rate per machine hour}$$

$$\frac{\text{paint department overheads}}{\text{estimated no. of direct labour hours}} = \text{the rate per direct labour hour}$$

There are quite a number of other overhead absorption (overhead recovery) rates which could have been used. A study of them is outside the scope of this book.

Stage 6

The overheads are then charged to products in one of two ways:

- if a job/product spends 8 machine hours in the machine department, it will be charged with 8 machine hours of overheads at the rate per machine hour;
- if a job/product spends 1½ direct labour hours in the paint department, it will be charged with 1½ direct labour hours' worth of overheads at the rate per direct labour hour.

As products move from department to department they *accumulate* a portion of each department's overheads. The overheads are being recovered hour by hour.

Stage 7

The administration, selling and distribution expenses are charged either to the profit and loss account or to jobs/products. The way in which they are treated is at the discretion of the management.

The following simplified, but comprehensive, example should help you to understand the process more fully.

Example 4.1 Van Chiu Ltd

We have been provided with the information shown in Tables 4.2 and 4.3 relating to Van Chiu Ltd, for their forthcoming period. The estimated number of direct labour hours in department F was 15,500 and the estimated number of machine hours in department G was 22,500.

1. Prepare a departmental overhead summary and calculate a direct labour hour rate for department F and a machine hour rate for department G.

Table 4.2 Van Chiu Ltd: estimated overhead expenditure

Estimated overhead expenses	£	Allocation or apportionment
Indirect materials and labour:		
Production department F	9,925	Allocation
Production department G	7,900	Allocation
Service department H	15,875	Allocation
Service department I	7,300	Allocation
Rent of buildings	24,000	Floor area
Insurance of buildings	3,000	Floor area
Supervision	28,000	Number of employees
Repairs and renewals	18,000	Technical estimate: F 30%, G 50%, H 10%, I 10%
Depreciation of machinery:		
Production department F	4,000	Allocation
Production department G	9,000	Allocation
Service department H	5,000	Allocation
Service department I	2,000	Allocation
	134,000	

Table 4.3 Van Chiu Ltd: apportionment data

	F	G	H	I
Area (in square metres)	250	600	100	50
Number of employees	17	10	3	2
Technical estimates for service departments				
The use of service H	60%	30%	–	10%
The use of service I	25%	75%	–	–

2. Prepare a quotation for a job, number WW658, to which the following data are applicable:
   (a) direct material: £394;
   (b) direct labour:
      department F: 6 hours at £8 per hour;
      department G: 2 hours at £9 per hour;
      machine hours in department G were 5.

   The company uses a mark-up of 30% on cost.

Answer

Having been provided with the predetermined overheads, we can prepare the departmental overhead summary in which we allocate and apportion the overheads to departments/cost centres. When this has been completed, we then share out the service department costs between user departments according to the technical estimates supplied. This will take us up to the point of having total overhead figures for departments F and G. See Table 4.4 for the overhead distribution summary.

We now know the total overhead which has been allocated and apportioned to production departments F and G, and the overhead absorption (recovery) rates for the two departments can now be calculated. The rate for production department F is:

Table 4.4 Van Chiu Ltd: overhead distribution summary

Overhead	Allocation or apportionment	Total	Production departments F		Service departments H	I
				G		
		£	£	£	£	£
Indirect materials and labour	Allocated	41,000	9,925	7,900	15,875	7,300
Rent and insurance	Floor area	27,000	6,750 (25%)	16,200 (60%)	2,700 (10%)	1,350 (5%)
Supervision	No. of employees	28,000 (17/32)	14,875 (10/32)	8,750 (3/32)	2,625 (2/32)	1,750
Repairs and renewals	Technical estimates	18,000	5,400 (30%)	9,000 (50%)	1,800 (10%)	1,800 (10%)
Depreciation	Allocated	20,000	4,000	9,000	5,000	2,000
		£134,000	40,950	50,850	28,000	14,200
Service H	Technical estimates		16,800 (60%)	8,400 (30%)	−28,000	2,800 (10%)
						17,000
Service I	Technical estimates		4,250 (25%)	12,750 (75%)	–	−17,000
		£134,000	£62,000	£72,000		

Table 4.5 Quotation for job WW658

		£
Direct materials		394
Direct labour	£	
(6 × £8) Department F	48	
(2 × £9) Department G	18	66
Overheads		
Department F 6 hrs @ £4	24	
Department G 5 hrs @ £3.20	16	40
Cost		500
add mark up @ 30% (profit)		150
		650

$$\frac{\text{overheads}}{\text{direct labour hours}} = \frac{£62{,}000}{15{,}500} = £4 \text{ per direct labour hour}$$

For production department G it is:

$$\frac{\text{overheads}}{\text{machine hours}} = \frac{£72{,}000}{22{,}500} = £3.20 \text{ per machine hour}$$

The quotation for the job WW658 can now be prepared, and is as shown in Table 4.5.

Comments

You should note that the quotation for the job WW658 is made up of four elements:

- Direct materials.
- Direct labour.
- Overheads.
- Mark-up/profit.

The direct materials and direct labour were given, but you should remember that they also will also have to be predetermined/estimated in practice.

Finally, note that for department G the hours used to arrive at the overhead cost of £16 were the 5 machine hours, *not* the direct labour hours. Why? Because the overheads for that department are being recovered using a machine hour rate.

Now see if you can solve a similar problem in order to firmly fix the overhead absorption process in your mind, before we take a look at the limitations of absorption costing.

Self-assessment Question 4.1

Throngfirth Manufacturing

Throngfirth Manufacturing operates three production departments: the machine department, paint department and assembly department, and two service departments:

stores and power. The budgeted overheads for the forthcoming period are as shown in Table 4.6.

They have also supplied you with the information given in Table 4.7, which should help you to apportion those overheads which cannot be allocated to departments.

From the data provided in Tables 4.6 and 4.7 you are required to:

1. Prepare a departmental overhead summary and calculate a machine hour rate for the machine department and direct labour hour rates for the other two production departments.

Table 4.6 Throngfirth Manufacturing: budgeted overheads

	£
Indirect materials and labour:	
Machine department	36,730
Paint department	11,270
Assembly department	11,900
Stores	16,680
Power	15,120
Other overheads:	
Fuel for power department	74,000
Building insurance	5,800
Lighting	3,800
Supervision	19,000
Machinery insurance	4,800
Canteen	24,200
Depreciation:	
Machine department	12,400
Paint department	6,300
Assembly department	2,100
Stores	1,400
Power	3,500
	249,000

Table 4.7 Throngfirth Manufacturing: apportionment data

	Machine department	Paint department	Assembly department	Stores	Power
Floor area (m^2)	8,000	2,000	4,000	1,000	1,000
Number of employees	6	2	8	2	2
Value of machinery (£000)	75	25	–	–	25
Direct labour hours	6,400	5,000	8,000		
Machine hours	20,000	–	–		
Stores usage (technical estimate)	25%	25%	40%	–	10%
Power usage (technical estimate)	60%	25%	15%	–	–

2. Calculate how much product PQ will cost if it takes £1,277 of raw materials and 15 hours of machine time in the machine department, and the following direct labour costs:
   (a) machine department: 4 hours @ £9 per hour;
   (b) paint department: 3 hours @ £8 per hour;
   (c) assembly: 16 hours @ £7 per hour.
3. Calculate the proposed selling price if a mark-up of 40% on cost is used.

The answers are to be found on pages 113–15.

The limitations of total absorption costing

The first limitation of absorption costing is the *accuracy of the predetermined overheads*. You should not lose sight of the fact that the overheads which are used are only estimates.

The selection of the bases of apportionment, e.g. floor area, number of employees, etc., depends upon the judgement of whoever has to make the selection. Different people could adopt differing bases of apportionment for the same type of expense, e.g. the rent of premises could be shared out according to floor area or cubic capacity.

There are many different methods which can be used for dealing with the distribution of service department costs to user departments. For example, the stores cost could be shared between user departments/cost centres according to the number of issue notes (material requisitions). However, although this may seem a reasonable and appropriate method, you should note that it does not take account of the value, weight or size of the materials.

Another problem arises because the *machine hours and/or the direct labour hours for the period also have to be estimated.*

Thus, when the actual figures become available the overheads may be more or less than those which were estimated for the period. This means that there will be either an *over- or under-absorption of overheads* charged to products. However, we cannot go back and rework the costs of the jobs/products; they are now history. The over- or under-absorption will have to be adjusted for in the profit and loss account.

You should also note that the treatment of administration, selling and distribution overheads, and research and development expenditure varies; they can be included in the job/product/service costs or charged direct to the profit and loss account as an expense.

It has been found that certain companies that did charge some of their research and development expenditure to products, tended to understate the profits earned by existing products and overstate the profits earned by newly introduced products. As a result they discontinued some of the existing products – products which were really more profitable than the new products!

An introduction to ABC (activity-based costing), an extension of the absorption costing method, will be covered in Chapter 5.

Summary: total absorption costing

Figure 4.1 sums up the essence of absorption costing. The overheads, i.e. indirect expenditure, both fixed and variable, have to be estimated, i.e. *predetermined* before the period to which they relate commences. Total absorption costing is also called **absorption costing, full costing** or **total costing**. It is just an attempt to ensure that all costs are covered. It does not profess to produce accurate job, product or service costs.

Overheads

Overhead/indirect cost is defined by CIMA (The Chartered Institute of Management Accountants) in the UK as 'Expenditure, labour, materials or services which cannot be economically identified with a specific saleable cost unit'. A cost unit could be a job, product or service.

Those overheads which can be identified and traced to a department or cost centre can be charged direct to the department or cost centre concerned, i.e. allocated. Those which cannot be identified or traced to a department or cost centre will have to be apportioned according to some arbitrary basis, e.g. floor area, number of employees, etc.

The costs of running the various service departments, such as stores and power, have to be accumulated to arrive at a cost for running each service. The service department cost is then shared out between user departments via technical estimates or some other arbitrary basis.

Overheads can be analysed into groups, e.g. production, administration, selling and distribution, research and development. They can also be subdivided into fixed overheads and variable overheads.

However, whatever the analysis or subdivision used, you should note that we are still dealing with *the same estimated overhead/indirect costs.*

Overhead absorption

In deciding which basis of apportionment (arbitrary basis) to use, the selector has to choose the method which is considered to be the most appropriate for the type of expense which has to be shared out between departments/cost centres.

Before the absorption rate can be calculated the machine hours and the direct labour hours have to be estimated for the forthcoming period. The absorption rates which we have used were selected because they reflect time, as a lot of overheads vary more with time than output. These rates were as follows:

$$\text{machine hour rate} = \frac{\text{machine department overheads}}{\text{number of machine hours for the department concerned}}$$

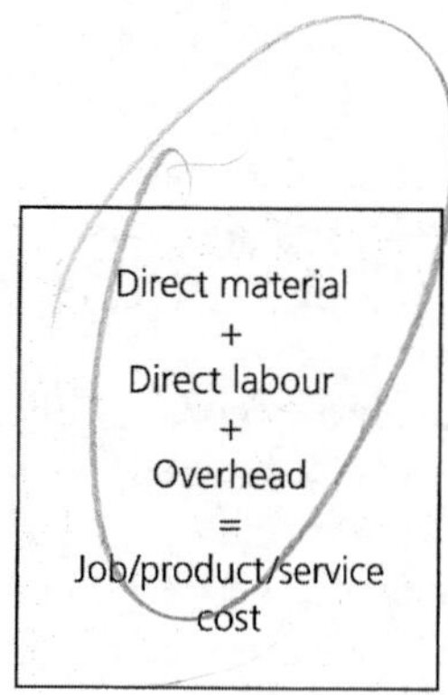

Figure 4.2 Job/product/service cost

$$\text{direct labour hour rate} = \frac{\text{overheads for the department}}{\text{number of direct labour hours for the department concerned}}$$

Decisions have to be made about the treatment of administration, research and development, and selling and distribution overheads.

As jobs/products/services pass through a department/cost centre, they in effect 'clock up' a share of that particular department's/cost centre's overheads, e.g. at so much per machine hour or so much per direct labour hour. Thus, as a job/product/service goes from department to department it *accumulates a share of the firm's overheads.*

Note that a job/product/service cost is made up of the elements shown in Figure 4.2. Some businesses use this figure plus a mark-up to fix their selling price or their quotation for a job/product/service.

Services

Although the illustrations in this chapter relate to a manufacturing type of environment and internal services, those organizations which provide services, e.g. health, auditing, education, radio and television, etc. do face similar problems. They also have to cost their services and account for overheads, as illustrated in Figure 4.2.

Limitations

Finally, remember that absorption costing does have limitations, e.g. the accuracy of the forecast overheads, the accuracy of the estimated machine hours and direct labour hours, the selection of methods of apportionment, etc.

Further reading

Drury, C., *Costing: An Introduction*, International Thomson Business Press, 1998.
Hussey, J. and Hussey, R., *Cost and Management Accounting*, Macmillan, 1998.

6

Marginal costing and breakeven analysis

Objectives

When you have completed your study of this chapter you should:

- ☐ Know how marginal costing differs from absorption costing.
- ☐ Understand the relationship between selling price, variable cost and the contribution.
- ☐ Be able to calculate the contribution and profit volume ratio and use them to calculate the breakeven point.
- ☐ Be able to solve problems involving profit targets and limiting factors.
- ☐ Understand and be able to prepare an elementary breakeven chart.
- ☐ Appreciate the limitations and drawbacks of marginal costing and breakeven analysis.

Marginal costing

Marginal costing (which is also known as **variable costing** or **direct costing** or **differential costing**) is concerned with the treatment of fixed costs and the relationship which exists between three figures: sales, variable cost and the contribution.

What is the contribution? The **contribution** is the name given to the difference between sales and variable cost in the marginal cost equation.

Example 6.1 Contribution and profit

A product sells at £50 and has a variable cost of £30, and during the period ended 30 June 20X0 2,000 units were sold. Fixed costs for that period amounted to £25,000. The contribution and profit would be calculated as shown in Table 6.1.

It can be observed from Example 6.1 that the *contribution contributes towards the recovery of the fixed costs and profit.* Marginal costing is a technique which can be used as part of the decision-making process to show the effect of changes/possible changes in demand and/or selling prices and/or variable costs. It can, for example, be used: to identify the most

Table 6.1 Marginal costing relationships

	per unit (£)	2,000 units (£)	% of sales
Selling price	50	100,000	100
less Variable costs	30	60,000	60
Contribution	20	40,000	40
less Fixed costs (overheads)		25,000	
Profit		15,000	

Table 6.2 A multi-product environment

£000	Products A	B	C	D	Total £
Contribution	20	34	36	20	110
less Fixed costs					78
Profit					32

profitable projects, in make-or-buy decisions, or in deciding whether or not to enter into a special contract. Variable costs include only those costs which can be identified with and traced to products (or services), e.g. direct labour, direct materials, direct expenses and variable overheads. The fixed costs (overheads) are those which cannot be identified with and traced to the products (or services). They tend to vary more with time than output, and are treated as **period costs**. This means that the fixed costs are not included in product (service) costs. They are simply written off, in total, against the total contribution(s) generated from the sale of all the firm's products (services), for the period in which they were incurred: see Table 6.2. This treatment of fixed costs also means that because they are not included in product costs they are *not carried forward into the future as part of the valuation of the stocks of work in progress and finished goods.*

The profit volume ratio (PV ratio)

The profit volume ratio explains the relationship between the contribution and sales and is calculated as follows:

$$\frac{\text{contribution}}{\text{sales}} \times 100 \quad \text{or} \quad \frac{\text{contribution per unit}}{\text{selling price per unit}} \times 100$$

Using the figures in Table 6.1 this works out as:

$$\frac{£40{,}000}{£100{,}000} \times 100 = 40\%$$

You may have observed that this has already been shown in Table 6.1. It is simply the contribution expressed as a percentage of sales. We now have enough information to

C = FC

calculate the **breakeven point**, *the point at which sales revenue and costs are equal*, or the point at which the contribution generated is equal to the fixed costs:

$$\frac{\text{fixed costs}}{\text{contribution per unit}} = \text{breakeven point in units}$$

$$\frac{£25{,}000}{£20} = 1{,}250 \text{ units}$$

To convert this to the breakeven point in terms of value, we just multiply the 1,250 units by the unit selling price of £50:

1,250 units × £50 = £62,500

Or we could calculate the breakeven point using the profit volume ratio, as follows:

$$\text{Fixed cost} \div \text{PV ratio} = £25{,}000 \times \frac{100}{40} = £62{,}500$$

The contribution table

A good way of dealing with problems involving changes in selling prices and/or variable costs is to construct a contribution table (see Table 6.4). The table shows the effect of the change or changes on the contribution.

Example 6.2 The effect of a change on the contribution

Using the figures from Table 6.3 as our starting point, we can work out the effects of different strategies for the forthcoming period (see Table 6.4).

It can be seen that Strategy 2 will generate the highest profit in the forthcoming period, provided the forecast demand materializes.

Table 6.3 Strategic alternatives

	Selling price per unit £	Variable cost per unit £	Demand (units)	Fixed costs £
Current period	50	30	2,000	25,000
Strategy 1	Increase by £5	No change	1,800	28,000
Strategy 2	No change	Reduce by £3	2,500	35,000
Strategy 3	No change	Increase by £2	2,200	28,000

Table 6.4 Contribution table

		Current period	1	2	3
		£	£	£	£
	Selling price (per unit)	50	55	50	50
less	Variable cost (per unit)	30	30	27	32
	Contribution (per unit)	20	25	23	18
	Units sold (demand)	2,000	1,800	2,500	2,200
	Total contribution	40,000	45,000	57,500	39,600
less	Fixed costs	25,000	28,000	35,000	28,000
	Profit	15,000	17,000	22,500	11,600

It should be apparent, from a study of Example 6.2, that a movement in either the selling price or variable cost will be reflected by a movement in the contribution, as follows:

- ☐ An increase in the selling price or a decrease in the variable cost will result in an increase in the contribution.
- ☐ Vice versa, a decrease in the selling price or an increase in the variable cost will bring about a decrease in the contribution.

Note also that the fixed costs may vary, e.g. if the decision is taken to purchase a new machine, the fixed machine cost will increase.

Profit targets

If management sets a profit target, all you have to do is remember that the contribution is equal to the *fixed costs plus the profit target* (see Figure 6.1). Adding the fixed costs which have to be covered to the profit target will give you the total contribution which needs to be generated. The total contribution required must then be divided by the contribution per unit. This tells you how many units will have to be sold in order to generate the required contribution:

$$\frac{\text{contribution required}}{\text{contribution per unit}} = \text{the number of units which must be sold in order to generate the contribution required}$$

Fixed costs
plus Profits or *less* Loss
=
Contribution required

Figure 6.1 The contribution required

Example 6.3 Generating the required contribution

Using the current period information in Table 6.4, and assuming management has set a target profit of £24,000, we can work out how many units we would have to sell to achieve this (see Table 6.5).

Table 6.5 Dealing with profit targets

		£
	Fixed costs	25,000
add	profit target	24,000
	Contribution required	49,000

$\therefore$ must sell $\frac{£49{,}000}{£20} = 2{,}450$ units

In terms of value, this would be
2,450 units @ £50 unit selling price = £122,500

Self-assessment Question 6.1

Now attempt the following self-assessment question. When you have completed it, compare your answer with the suggested solution on pages 116–18.

Heaton Postex plc

Heaton Postex plc manufactures CD players and has provided you with the following information on variable costs per unit for the current year, 20X8.

Direct labour:	£20
Direct materials:	£64
Variable overheads:	£12
Total variable costs:	£96

Fixed costs: £164,000.
Selling price per unit: £120.
Expected sales: 40,000 units.

The sales target for next year, 20X9, has been set at 50,000 units, and fixed costs are expected to rise to £186,000. The selling price would rise to £125 per unit and the total variable costs would increase by £4 per unit.

Calculate the following:

1. The total contribution and net profit for 20X8 and 20X9.
2. The breakeven point for 20X8 and 20X9.
3. The sales level which would have to be attained in 20X9 in order to generate a profit equal to that which was earned in 20X8.
4. The maximum amount which could be spent on additional fixed costs at a sales level of 56,000 units to produce a profit of £1,200,000.

Table 6.6 Limiting factors: material supply

	Product P	Product Q
Selling price (per unit)	800	500
Variable cost (per unit)	500	300
Material required to produce one unit	4 litres	2 litres

Limiting factors

The limiting factor (also called the **key factor** or **principal budget factor**) is the factor which constrains/limits the activities of a business. Thus, when budgets are being prepared, the limiting factor is the starting point of the budgeting process and has to be taken into account first. For example, if sales demand were the limiting factor, i.e. if the company could only sell a limited number of products during a period, this would limit the production needed, the amount of labour, the material requirements, and so on. It is not a sound business policy to produce more than you can sell!

Other examples of limiting factors are as follows:

- ☐ The supply of materials, e.g. Table 6.6.
- ☐ The availability of labour.
- ☐ Production capacity.
- ☐ Finance.
- ☐ Legislation.

However, limiting factors are not static. Management can, by its actions, eliminate them altogether or reduce their effect.

What can management do where the supply of certain materials is limited?
Answer: lots. Management can search for new supplies; investigate the use of a substitute; have the product redesigned to use none or less of the material concerned; improve production and inspection techniques to reduce waste and the number of defectives.

What can be done if there is a shortage of labour?
Answer: quite a lot. Where labour is the limiting factor management can bring workers in from other areas; attract labour from other countries; introduce overtime and shift work; undertake to train or organize the training of new operatives; lease or buy labour-saving machines/robots; use subcontractors.

What can management do if there is insufficient production capacity?
Answer: again, quite a lot. Managers can introduce more overtime and shift work; lease or buy more machinery/robots; use subcontractors; reorganize the production flow to reduce idle/non-productive time; review the design of the product, e.g. the degree of precision needed, etc., so as to reduce the time spent making the product.

Can management do anything if finance is in short supply?
Answer: yes, finance is always available from a multitude of sources, but usually at a cost which reflects the risk to the lender! In addition to loans from various sources there are also government schemes/grants; EU schemes/grants; sale and lease back; the sale of the company's own surplus fixed assets, e.g. buildings, machines, equipment and current assets such as stocks of raw materials, fuels and finished goods; the issue of share capital, etc.

What can be done if the limiting factor is legislation?
Answer: not a lot. However, management can approach local council representatives, MPs, trade associations, chambers of trade and pressure groups.

When a business's activities are constrained because of a limiting factor, it has to attempt to maximize its contribution. This can be done by means of a simple technique. The technique calculates *the contribution per unit of the limiting factor.* The course of action which gives the highest contribution per unit of the limiting factor, e.g. per hour or per kilo, is the one which will maximize the contribution.

Example 6.4 Maximizing the contribution

The supply of a particular material is limited to 5,000 litres per period. It can be used to produce either product P or product Q, details of which are given in Table 6.6.

The contribution per unit of the limiting factor, i.e. the contribution per litre, would be calculated as shown in Table 6.7.

The maximum contribution possible is therefore:

quantity of material available × contribution per litre

Product P 5,000 litres × £75 = £375,000
Product Q 5,000 litres × £100 = £500,000

Product Q is therefore the one which should be produced. By producing it, a contribution of £500,000 is generated, £125,000 greater than the contribution which could be generated by producing product P.

Table 6.7 Contribution per litre

	Product P £	product Q £
Selling price (per unit)	800	500
less Variable cost (per unit)	500	300
Contribution	300	200
$\frac{\text{contribution}}{\text{quantity needed}}$	$\frac{£300}{4}$ = **£75/litre**	$\frac{£200}{2}$ = **£100/litre**

Table 6.8 Scoubado Manufacturing: product information

	Product J £	K £	L £
Selling price (per unit)	75	108	59
Cost per unit			
Direct material	30	64	20
Direct labour	6	9	4
Variable overhead	14	11	15
	50	84	39
Time taken to produce one unit	30 min	45 min	20 min

Self-assessment Question 6.2

Now see if you can solve the following limiting factor problem; the figures do change and are more complex, but the principles/techniques remain unchanged.

Scoubado Manufacturing

Scoubado Manufacturing make three products – J, K and L. Details are given in Table 6.8.

The constraint under which the company is currently working is that, until management can take appropriate action, its *productive hours are limited to 42 hours per day.* However, all sales of J in excess of 30 units will have to be sold at £72 per unit; all sales of K in excess of 24 units will have to be sold at £105 per unit; and all sales of L in excess of 60 units will have to be sold at £49 per unit.

Work out the maximum contribution which could be earned per day. (For the suggested answer please turn to pages 118–19 *but only* after you have attempted to solve the problem yourself.)

The limitations and drawbacks of marginal costing

It will always be difficult to assess how both fixed costs and variable costs will be affected by changes in output. Direct labour, direct materials and variable expenses can be affected in a multitude of ways. It must be pointed out here that one of the drawbacks, which is frequently not appreciated, is that it is not always such an easy task to segregate costs into their fixed and variable elements. Some items of expenditure which are very similar can be treated differently, e.g. the rent of machinery paid on a fixed rental would be treated as a fixed cost, but if the rental paid was based on output it would be treated as a variable cost! Direct labour paid at a fixed amount irrespective of the level of output would be a fixed cost!

Oversimplified marginal costing can lead to the underpricing of products and a loss-making situation. The incorrect assumption made by certain users that fixed costs tend to remain constant, irrespective of the level of activity, may account for the underpricing of certain products and loss-making situations.

Breakeven analysis

In Chapter 1 you were introduced to cost behaviour. However, a quick recap may prove helpful.

- *Fixed costs*
  Those costs which, in the short term, remain unchanged within a relevant range of activity (see Figure 6.2).
- *Variable costs*
  Those costs which, in the short term, vary directly with the level of activity (output) within a relevant range (see Figure 6.3).

A combination of the two is known as a semi-variable or a semi-fixed cost, e.g. a cost which is made up of a fixed rental plus an amount which is paid per unit of output produced.

At the outset you should note that breakeven analysis is a short-term planning device and should not be used in isolation but in conjunction with other data/information. Note that in the short term fixed and variable costs will only remain constant within a relevant range of output/level of activity.

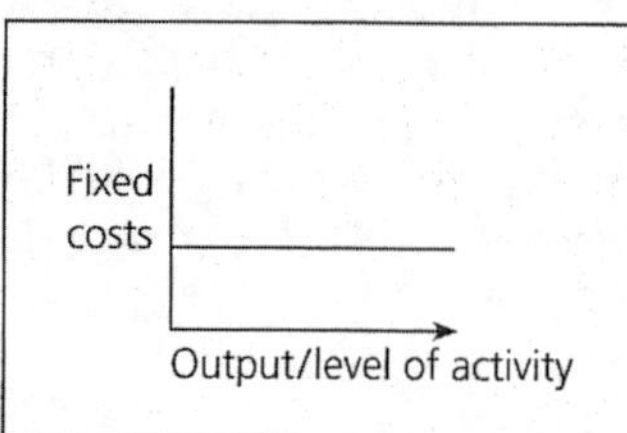

Figure 6.2 Fixed costs

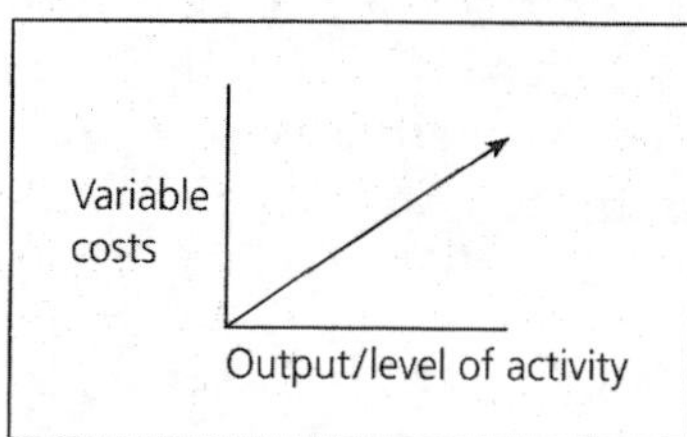

Figure 6.3 Variable costs

The traditional breakeven chart (graph)

Example 6.5 Constructing a breakeven chart

We will now construct a breakeven chart using the following information:

Output:	125,000 units
Sales:	£500,000
Variable cost:	£250,000
Fixed cost:	£100,000

We first draw up our chart and then insert the sales line (see Figure 6.4).

Next we draw the fixed-cost line which runs parallel to the base of the chart (i.e. the output) (see Figure 6.5).

Finally, we include the variable costs by adding them on to the fixed costs. This line is drawn from £100,000 at 0 output to £350,000 at 125,000 output. This line is the total-cost line, i.e. fixed cost £100,000 plus variable cost £250,000 = £350,000 total cost (see Figure 6.6).

Having completed our breakeven chart (Figure 6.6) we can read off the breakeven point at £200,000 sales and costs and 50,000 output, the point at which costs and revenue (sales/income) are equal, i.e. where the sales line crosses the total cost line, or the point at which the contribution generated is equal to the fixed costs.

For proof see Table 6.9.

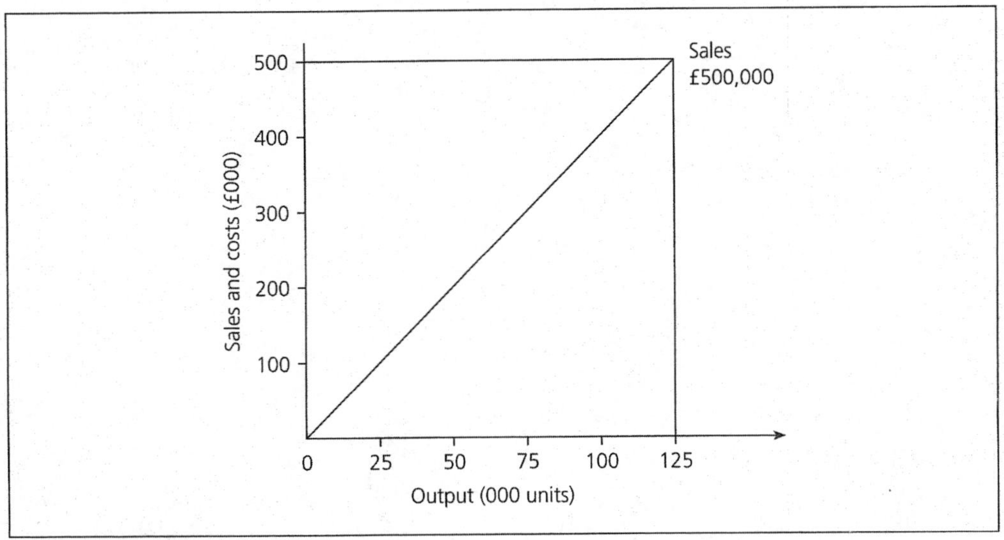

Figure 6.4 Sales

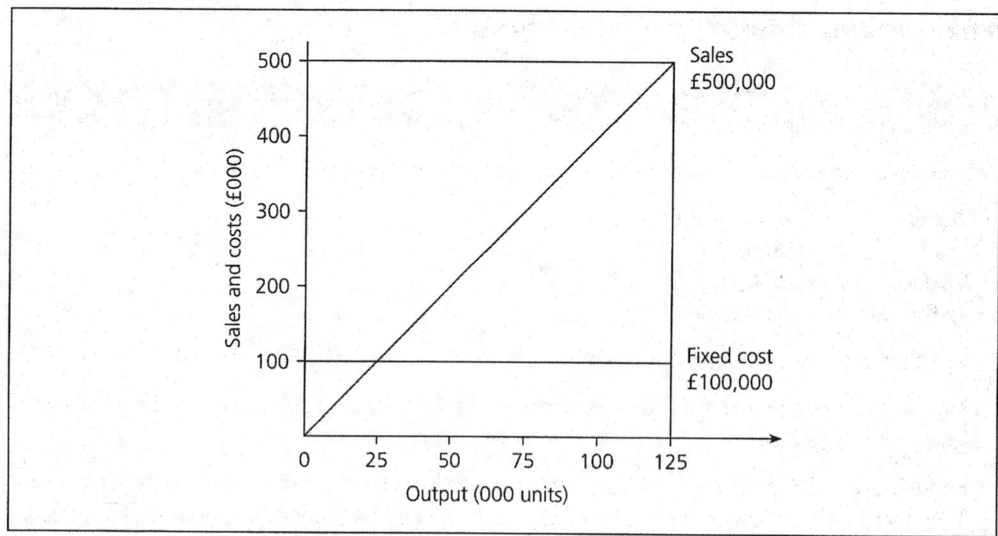

Figure 6.5 Sales and fixed costs

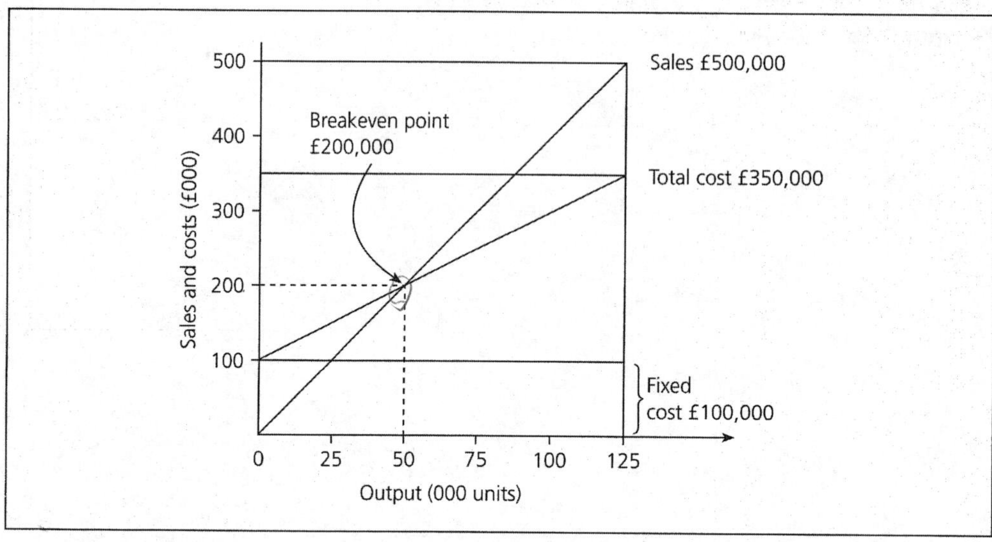

Figure 6.6 Breakeven point

Table 6.9 Calculating the breakeven point

		Per unit £		125,000 units £000	
	Sales	4		500	
less	Variable cost	2		250	
	Contribution	2		250	(50% profit volume ratio)
less	Fixed cost			100	
			Profit	150	

Breakeven point = fixed cost ÷ PV ratio = $£100{,}000 \times \frac{100}{50} = £200{,}000$

or

$= \frac{\text{fixed cost}}{\text{contribution per unit}} = \frac{£100{,}000}{£2} = 50{,}000 \text{ units}$

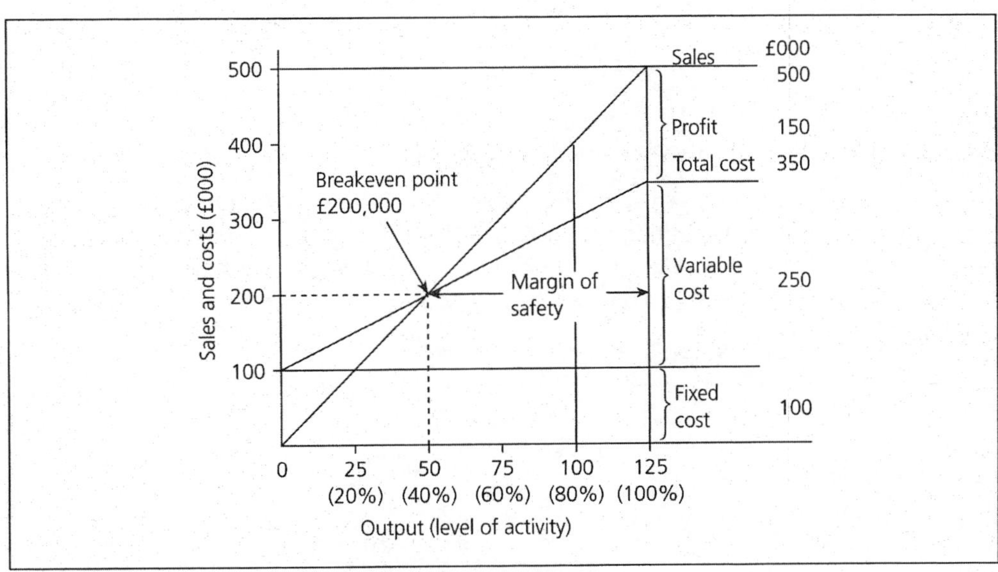

Figure 6.7 Conventional breakeven chart

Now let us take a closer look at the chart which we have just completed, and see what else it can tell us (Figure 6.7).

- ☐ The logic of the calculations involved can be followed as per the right-hand side of the chart, i.e. sales £500,000 less total cost £350,000 = profit £150,000, total cost £350,000 = variable cost £250,000 + fixed cost £100,000.
- ☐ Above the breakeven point we make a profit, below it we make a loss.
- ☐ The margin of safety is the difference between the breakeven point and the selected output/level of activity. This indicates the extent to which the level of activity must fall before a loss-making situation is reached, and vice versa.

Table 6.10 A profit proof: using marginal costing

		£000
	Contribution from 100,000 units @ £2 per unit	200
less	Fixed cost	100
	Profit	100

- ☐ The horizontal base line of the chart can be expressed in terms of either output or level of activity.
- ☐ By projecting a vertical line from the base line, e.g. at 100,000 units output (80% level of activity) we can use the chart to read off the fixed cost, total cost and sales applicable to this particular level of activity. You can see that the vertical line drawn from 100,000 units output (80% level of activity) cuts the fixed-cost line at £100,000, the total-cost line at £300,000 and the sales line at £400,000. The gap between sales and total cost of £100,000 represents the profit which should be achieved at the 80% level of activity: see Table 6.10 for proof.

The contribution breakeven chart (graph)

The contribution breakeven chart is an alternative way of showing the information which we used to construct our traditional breakeven chart. Using the same information as Example 6.5 we will look at its construction in two phases. First, we draw up the chart and then insert the sales line and the variable-cost line, both of which are drawn from the base line point 0 (see Figure 6.8).

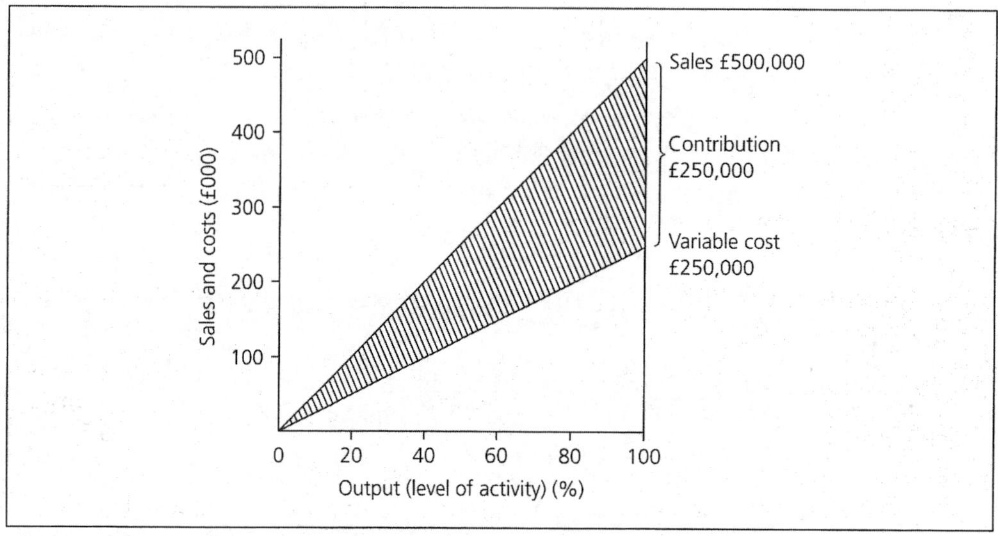

Figure 6.8 Contribution, sales and variable cost

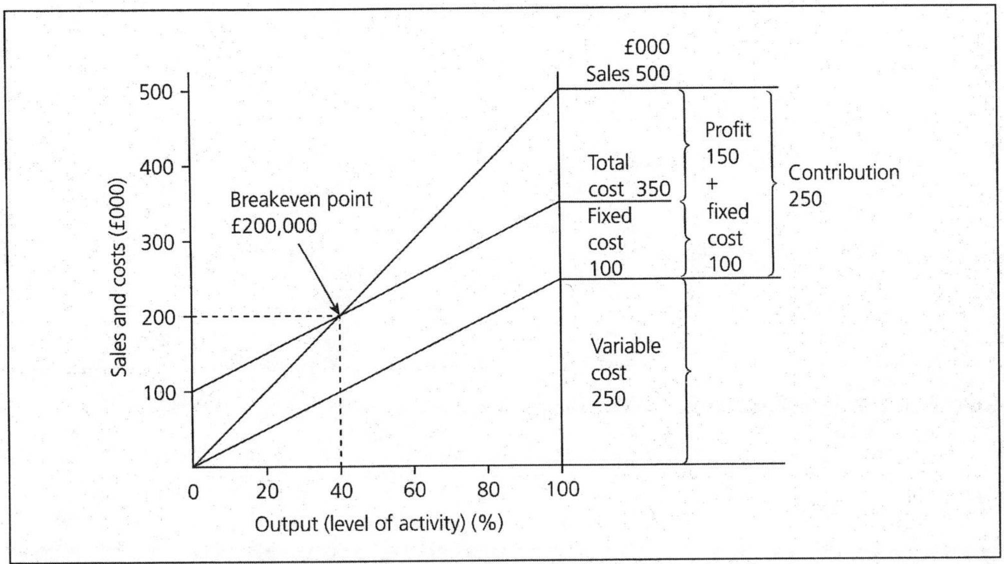

Figure 6.9 Contribution breakeven chart

This incomplete breakeven chart (Figure 6.8) illustrates that sales of £500,000 less variable cost £250,000 = contribution £250,000. The principal advantage of this chart is that it shows, very clearly, the contribution which is being generated at different levels of activity.

The fixed costs of £100,000 are then added to the variable costs and the total-cost line drawn from £100,000 at 0% level of activity to £350,000 at 100% level of activity; the fixed costs are plotted parallel to the variable costs (see Figure 6.9).

- ☐ Figure 6.9 shows that below the breakeven point the fixed costs are not being covered. When the contribution generated has covered fixed costs, the remainder is profit.
- ☐ The final contribution breakeven chart (Figure 6.9) illustrates that the contribution £250,000 less fixed cost £100,000 = profit £150,000.

The profit graph/profit volume diagram

This is an alternative type of breakeven chart and should help you to understand the profit volume ratio more clearly. To draw it you need to know any two of the three figures: fixed cost, profit and breakeven point. Again, using the same figures as in Example 6.5, the graph would be as shown in Figure 6.10.

- ☐ The line which joins the fixed costs to the profit is, in fact, the contribution line, i.e. it represents fixed costs £100,000 + profit £150,000 = £250,000 contribution.
- ☐ The breakeven point is again £200,000.

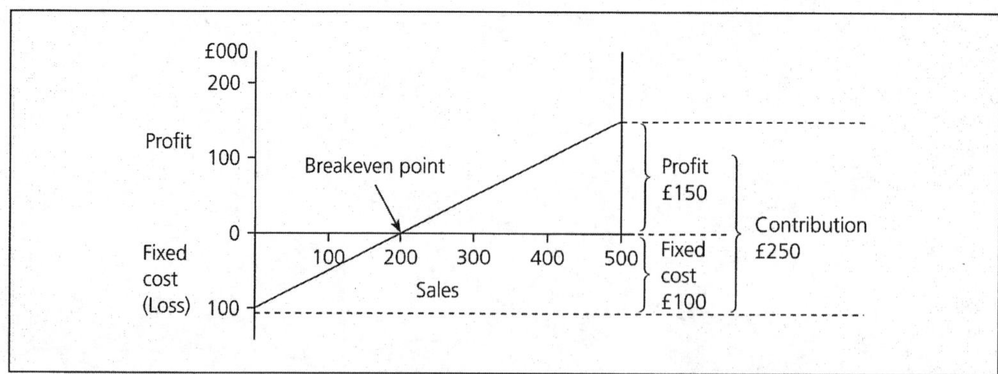

Figure 6.10 Profit graph/profit volume diagram

Self-assessment Question 6.3

Now it's your turn. May I suggest that you find some graph paper and then attempt the following problem. When you have completed your answer, compare it with the suggested answer on pages 119–20.

Holme Honley Products plc

The firm's forecast figures for the forthcoming period are as shown in Table 6.11.

1. Prepare a breakeven chart and show the breakeven point and margin of safety.
2. Show what the position would be if the output achieved was only 15,000 units (i.e. a 60 per cent level of activity).

Table 6.11 Holme Honley Products plc forecast figures

Output (units)	25,000
	per unit
Sales	£100
Variable cost	£40
Fixed costs	£1,200,000

The limitations and drawbacks of breakeven analysis

The assumptions upon which breakeven analysis is based, e.g. how costs behave, a constant product mix, constant selling prices, etc., do not always hold true in the real world, even in the short term.

- ☐ Fixed and variable costs will not always behave as expected.
- ☐ Sales of a product may have to be made to different customers/market segments at different prices.

- ☐ The decisions made by management can affect variable and fixed costs.
- ☐ Efficiency levels within a manufacturing concern are not always constant.
- ☐ The product mix will have to respond to changes in demand and cannot therefore be forecast with accuracy.

Remember also that the breakeven chart is most useful if used in the short term and in conjunction with other data.

Summary: marginal costing and breakeven analysis

Marginal costing

Marginal costing differs from absorption costing because of the way in which it deals with fixed costs (overheads):

- ☐ Fixed costs, in marginal costing, are treated as **period costs**, i.e. they are written off in the period in which they are incurred.
- ☐ Fixed costs are not included in stock valuations and are not therefore carried forward to future accounting periods.

The marginal cost equation expresses what marginal costing is all about (see Figure 6.11). It is about the relationship between sales, variable cost and the contribution. Movements in the selling price and/or variable cost will be reflected by a corresponding movement in the contribution. If the selling price goes up or the variable cost goes down, the contribution will go up by the same amount and vice versa. The contribution generated contributes towards the recovery of fixed costs, the remainder being the profit. The contribution per unit can be very useful when it comes to solving problems such as the following:

How many units must be sold in order to break even?

$$\frac{\text{fixed costs}}{\text{contribution per unit}} = \text{breakeven point in units}$$

How many units must be sold to produce a specified profit target?

$$\frac{\text{fixed cost} + \text{profit target}}{\text{contribution per unit}} = \text{no. of units which must be sold to achieve the profit target}$$

Sales
less
Variable cost
=
Contribution

Figure 6.11 Marginal cost equation

Note that, when dealing with profit target problems, the key is to calculate the total contribution which must be generated:

total contribution required = fixed cost + profit target.

The **profit volume ratio** explains the relationship between the contribution and sales:

$$\text{PV ratio} = \frac{\text{contribution}}{\text{sales}} \times 100 \quad \text{or} \quad \frac{\text{contribution per unit}}{\text{selling price per unit}} \times 100$$

This can also be used to help solve problems, e.g. to compute the breakeven point in terms of value:

breakeven point = fixed costs ÷ PV ratio

If a constraint, e.g. the supply of materials, productive hours available, etc., limits the activities of a business, there is a **limiting factor** (**key factor** or **principal budget factor**) at work and a simple technique can be applied in order to solve the problems which emerge. The technique expresses the *contribution per unit of the limiting factor*, e.g. contribution per kilo, contribution per litre, contribution per hour, etc. Where a choice has to be made between alternative products, the products which give the highest contribution per unit of the limiting factor should be produced, as this will maximize the contribution.

The impact of a limiting factor can be eliminated/reduced by the actions of management.

Marginal costing, which is also called 'direct costing' or 'variable costing' or 'differential costing', is certainly a very useful decision-making technique. However, it must be appreciated that its use can lead to underpricing and that it is not always as easy as might be imagined to separate the fixed from variable costs.

Breakeven analysis

The construction of a breakeven chart is a relatively straightforward activity. The breakeven point can be computed mathematically, so why produce a chart? The answer lies in the fact that with the chart you can read off the position at various levels of output/activity and highlight the margin of safety. The limitations of breakeven analysis stem from the fact that in practice costs do not always behave as might be expected: sales of a product may have to be made using a variety of prices and the product mix is difficult to forecast.

Further reading

Atrill, P. and McLaney, E., *Management Accounting for Non-specialists*, Prentice Hall Europe, 1998.
Drury, C., *Management Accounting for Business Decisions*, International Thomson Business Press, 1997.
Upchurch, A., *Management Accounting*, Prentice Hall Europe, 1998.

7

Budgeting and budgetary control

Objectives

When you have reached the end of this chapter, you should:

- ☐ Know the principles of effective budgeting.
- ☐ Be able to explain the following terms:
  - a budget;
  - budgetary control;
  - the principal budget factor;
  - control by responsibility;
  - management by exception.
- ☐ Know why it is important to prepare a cash budget (cash flow forecast).
- ☐ Be able to prepare a cash budget, budgeted profit and loss account and a budgeted balance sheet.
- ☐ Be able to identify the differences between a cash budget and a budgeted profit and loss account, and also to appreciate why the increase/decrease in the cash balance is different from the profit (loss) for a period.
- ☐ Appreciate that budgets are interrelated.
- ☐ Understand how flexible budgets are constructed and why it is important to use them.
- ☐ Be familiar with the behavioural aspects of budgeting.
- ☐ Know how zero base budgeting (ZBB) works.

We will now take a look at the household budget and see how the principles followed there apply (even more so) to both public- and private-sector organizations.

Introduction: the household budget

The family depicted in our diagram (Figure 7.1) will have to do as follows:

- ☐ Work in harmony.
- ☐ Adopt a common-sense approach.
- ☐ Set targets which are realistic and attainable.
- ☐ Decide upon the allocation of their scarce resources.

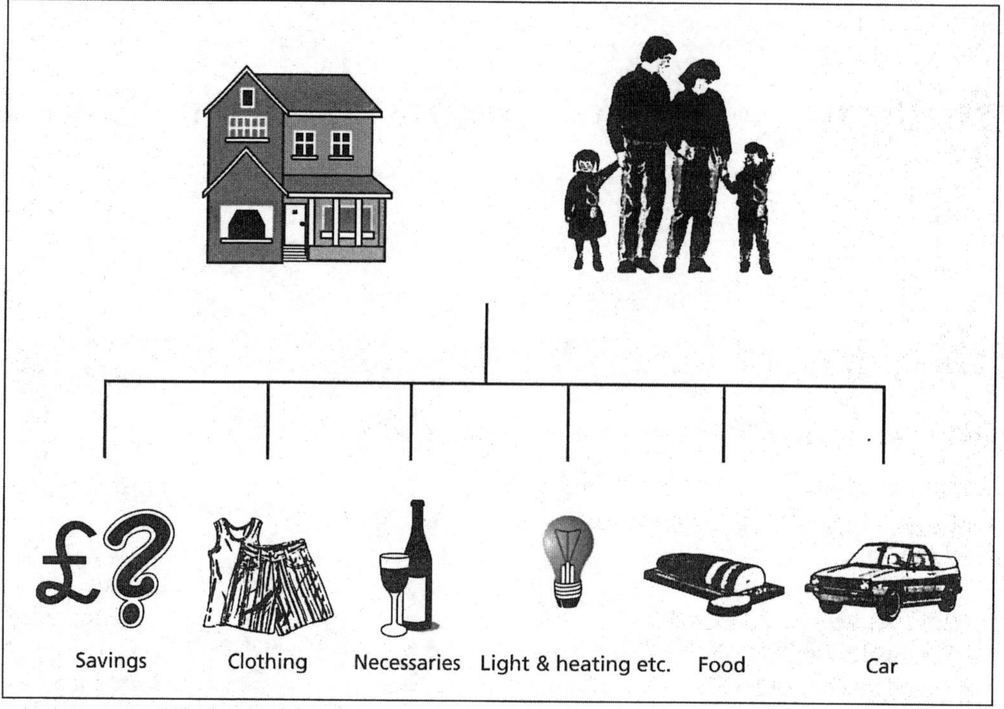

Figure 7.1 The household budget

- ☐ Consider trade-offs, i.e. all of the various alternatives.
- ☐ Appreciate the interrelationships between the various budgets.
- ☐ Hold meetings to discuss targets etc.
- ☐ Set objectives.
- ☐ Formulate policy.
- ☐ Participate in setting budgets.
- ☐ Cooperate, coordinate and communicate effectively.
- ☐ Prepare in advance of the budget period.
- ☐ Work to a budget preparation timetable.
- ☐ Identify the principal budget factor (i.e. limiting factor or key factor).
- ☐ Prepare flexible budgets.
- ☐ Delegate responsibility.
- ☐ Monitor progress.
- ☐ Take corrective action.
- ☐ Ensure that behavioural factors are taken into account.
- ☐ Make assumptions about the future.
- ☐ Revise the budgets to take account of changes in the assumptions which were made, e.g. changes in the business environment.

Quite a list; but also a good indication of exactly what effective budgeting and budgetary control entails.

Principles

Having listed the principles we will now look at them in a little more depth. Managers/ executives responsible for the budgeting process will need to:

- ☐ Work together in *harmony* and *adopt a common-sense approach* throughout the budgeting process. This will involve the realistic appraisal of income and expenditure and the employment of capital.
- ☐ *Set attainable targets.* A budget which includes unattainable targets is most likely to be rejected by the people involved. From a management point of view, it is most important that budgets are accepted as being fair and reasonable.
- ☐ Decide upon how they are going to *share out the scarce resources* which they have at their disposal between the competing factions, e.g. alternative projects, production needs v. research and development needs v. marketing needs, and so on. This will involve discussions, negotiations, inter-personal skills and trade-offs.
- ☐ Appreciate the fact that *budgets are interrelated*, e.g. there is a link between the income budget and the expenditure budget. If income is to be used for one particular type of expenditure then it is not available to finance other expenditure. (See budget relationships and Figure 7.3 later in this chapter.)
- ☐ Attend meetings to discuss the setting of **objectives**, and the formulation of the **policy**, which they must follow in order to achieve the objectives. Many organizations do in fact have a budget committee which consists of representatives from all of the functional areas, e.g. production, marketing, finance, research and development, administration, selling and distribution, etc., and *a budget controller*, i.e. a person who oversees and coordinates their activities. The budget controller will seek to ensure that relevant information/data are collected, analysed, collated and distributed, to assist those who need it for their budget preparation. He/she must also attempt to secure the cooperation of others and to see that committee decisions are communicated clearly and effectively.
- ☐ Ensure that all those who should be involved get a chance to *participate in the budget preparation process.* Participation/involvement by, e.g., certain worker-representatives and/ or supervisors can result in the setting of more realistic budgets and improved morale/ motivation. The people involved may even bring to the attention of management, information which is vital to the success of the budgeting process.
- ☐ Hold their meetings well before the new budget period commences. They will have to devote time to the discussion of plans, the review of data and the revision of plans, etc. Hence the need for a *timetable for the budget preparation period*, so that by the time the new budget period commences, the budget is ready to be implemented. This preparation of budgets in advance is a prerequisite for effective budgeting.

Simple Budget and Actual Comparative Statement (Details of purpose, etc.) Date				
Item	Actual £000	Budget £000	Variance £000	Reasons for variance

Figure 7.2 Simple budget and actual comparative statement (*details for the previous year could also be included for comparison*).

- ☐ From the outset, *identify their principal budget factor* (*limiting factor, key factor*), e.g. demand, as this will constrain their activities (see also limiting factors in marginal costing in Chapter 6). They will also have to decide whether or not to take action designed to eliminate or reduce the effects of the principal budget factor.
- ☐ *Plan for changes* in the basic assumptions upon which the budgets were based. This is why budgets should, where possible, be flexible, i.e. designed to change as levels of activity (output) change, and be revised to take account of environmental change.
- ☐ *Delegate the authority/responsibility* for a specific part of the budget to a particular person. This is known as '*control by responsibility*'. The person concerned will have to attempt, for example, to keep their spending in line with the targets set and provide explanations for periods in which targets are exceeded.
- ☐ *Monitor progress* at frequent intervals, e.g. monthly, by looking at budget and actual comparative statements, drafted along the lines of Figure 7.2.

  Just like the householder, company/organization managers/executives will be particularly interested in significant adverse variances. These would be highlighted on the above type of statement/report (Figure 7.2), together with the reasons why they occurred. Managers can then devote their time and energy into putting right whatever is going wrong.

  To focus on these reported significant adverse variances is known as *management by exception*. This should ensure the early detection of items which are not going according to plan. *Early detection means early action!*
- ☐ Appreciate that *budgets do affect people's behaviour* and that behavioural factors cannot and should not be ignored.

The variance is the difference between the actual and the budget. For example, if the actual expenditure exceeds the budgeted expenditure, it is adverse, i.e. an overspend. If the actual expenditure falls short, it is a favourable variance.

Self-assessment Question 7.1

Budgetary control self-check

From what you have read in this chapter so far, see if you can define, in your own words, the following key terms:

- A budget.
- Budgetary control.
- The principal budget factor.
- Control by responsibility.
- Management by exception.

When you have attempted to answer this self-assessment question, please turn to pages 121–2 and compare your answer with that suggested.

Practical considerations

Having established the principles of budgeting and budgetary control, we will conclude this section of the chapter by pointing out a number of practical considerations.

First, there needs to be an acceptance throughout the company/organization that budgeting is *a management planning technique* and that its use can greatly improve efficiency. Yes, budgeting/budgetary control should help the company/organization to compete in the market place and promote its long-term survival. Managers should therefore show by their actions that they *accept and approve of the budget.* Their *acceptance/approval* should be very clearly communicated to all those concerned. They should ensure that all of the personnel involved in the budgeting process are *educated* as to its benefits/principles and the way in which it operates within the company/organization.

A minor point, worthy of note, is that the actual and budgeted figures must match as regards content, i.e. they must be computed in the same way.

Finally, control should really be directed towards problem solving, constructive comments and the taking of corrective action by management, rather than recrimination.

Budget relationships

The budgeting process is rather like a large jigsaw, i.e. all the pieces must fit together, in order to form a coherent picture (see Figure 7.3). Budgets are interrelated. Something which affects one budget will tend to have a ripple effect in that it will also affect other budgets. Thus, during the budget preparation period the budget committee has to meet regularly to ensure that the individual functional budgets, e.g. sales, production, plant utilization, etc., all fit together. Examples 7.1 and 7.2 illustrate how the production budget would be arrived at, and the close link with the sales budget.

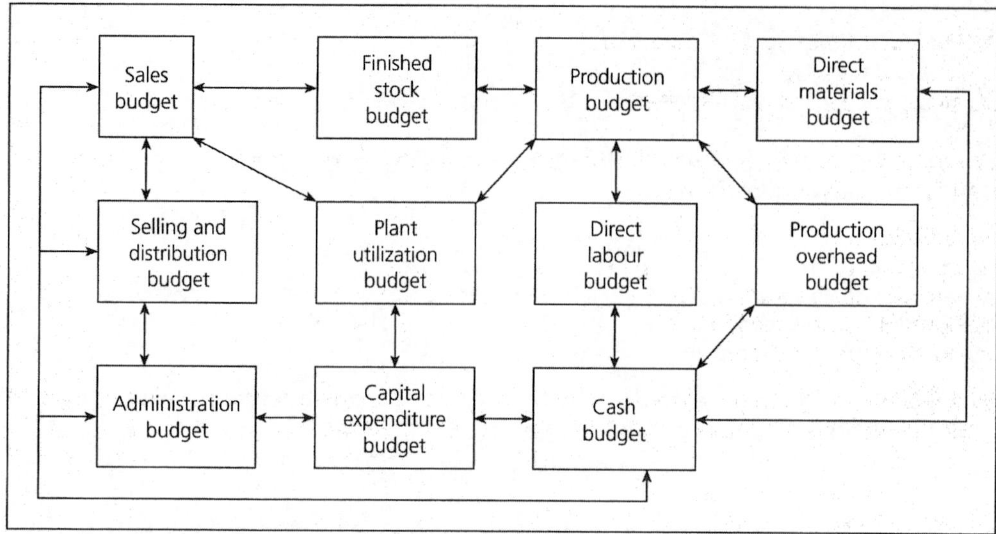

Figure 7.3 Budget interrelationships

Example 7.1 The calculation of budgeted production

Data relating to the forthcoming budget period are shown in Table 7.1.

The production budget would be as in Table 7.2.

The 12,700 units could be produced provided the company/organization had sufficient plant capacity, could organize an adequate supply of direct materials and direct labour, and had enough finance available. Thus, if the sales budget, which in the absence of a principal budget factor is the most usual starting point, is increased, the production budget will also have to be increased, as will the direct material budget and so on.

Table 7.1 Calculation of budgeted production to satisfy the sales budget

	Budget (units)
Opening stock of finished goods	500
Closing stock of finished goods	800
Sales	12,400
To satisfy sales would need:	
Opening stock	500
Production	11,900
	12,400

Table 7.2 The production budget

	Units
Made to resell	11,900
Made to stock	800
Production budget	12,700

The cash budget

The diagram about budget interrelationships, Figure 7.3, which we have just looked at, clearly illustrates that the cash budget (also called a 'cash flow forecast') interacts with numerous other budgets. A common cause of business failure has been identified as poor cash flow management. The cash budget is a very important and integral part of good cash flow management. Cash budgeting aims to do the following:

- ☐ Make sure that cash is available when it is needed.
- ☐ Identify shortages in good time, so that appropriate remedial action can be taken.
- ☐ Identify surpluses of cash, so that where possible they can be transferred/invested where they can earn a satisfactory return. Nowadays, the **treasury function** of a company/organization deals with the investment of surplus cash in the short term, e.g. overnight or for, say, a week or a month.

The cash budget is drawn up using predetermined figures. It records them during the month in which they are expected to come in or go out. In doing this it has to take periods of credit allowed by suppliers or to customers into account. So, for example, it does not really matter about the month in which a sale is made or the period covered by a dividend received. What does matter is when the cash from the sale or the dividend is actually received. Thus, non-cash items, e.g. depreciation, are not included in the cash budget. The cash moves when the asset is paid for, not when it is depreciated.

We will now take you through a step-by-step example, which will show you how the cash budget is prepared.

Example 7.2 A cash budget

Brendug and Co. Ltd

1. First of all we have to estimate the cash flows for the forthcoming period, taking into account past performance, future plans and relevant data. Let us assume that this has now been done for Brendug and Co. Ltd and the information generated is as given in Table 7.3.
2. Insert the opening balance for the period. (Our example is a start-up situation, so this does not apply.)

Table 7.3 Brendug and Co. Ltd: cash budget data

20X3	
January	During this month the company planned to commence trading and receive cash of £100,000 from an issue of £1 ordinary shares.
January	To pay £48,000 for plant and machinery. This will be depreciated at 10% of cost per annum.
January	To pay a half-year's rent in advance of £12,000.

Sales would be £8,000 in January and then £16,000 per month thereafter. Customers (i.e. debtors) would be given *two months' credit.*

Purchases of raw materials would be £6,000 in January and then £12,000 per month thereafter. Suppliers (i.e. creditors) will only allow *one month's credit.*

Wages and general expenses have been estimated to be £3,000 per month, payable during the month in which they are incurred.

The budgeted closing stock of raw materials is £6,000.

Table 7.4 Brendug and Co. Ltd: cash budget (1) (£000)

	Inflows			Outflows				
	Opening balance	Share capital	Sales	Purchases	Rent	Wages & general expenses	Fixed assets	Closing balance
Jan	–	100	–	–	12	3	48	
Feb		–	–	6	–	3	–	
Mar		–	8	12	–	3	–	
Apr		–	16	12	–	3	–	
May		–	16	12	–	3	–	
Jun		–	16	12	–	3	–	

Table 7.5 Brendug and Co. Ltd: calculating the closing balance for January

		£000
	Inflows	100
less	Outflows (12 + 3 + 48)	63
	= Closing balance	37

3. Fill in the above information vertically, column by column, taking into account the periods of credit. The cash budget will then appear as shown in Table 7.4, for the period of six months to 30 June 20X3.
4. Add up the January inflows and subtract the January outflows to calculate the closing balance, as in Table 7.5.

   The closing balance of £37,000 for January is then carried down as the opening balance for February; to this will be added any February inflows and the February outflows will be deducted, as shown in Table 7.6.

Table 7.6 Brendug and Co. Ltd: calculating the closing balance for February

		£
	Opening balance + inflows	37
less	Outflows	9
		28

Table 7.7 Brendug and Co. Ltd: cash budget (2) (£000)

	Inflows			Outflows				
	Opening balance	Share capital	Sales	Purchases	Rent	Wages & general expenses	Fixed assets	Closing balance
Jan	–	100	–	–	12	3	48	37
Feb	37		–	6	–	3	–	28
Mar	28		8	12	–	3	–	21
Apr	21		16	12	–	3	–	22
May	22		16	12	–	3	–	23
Jun	23		16	12	–	3	–	24
	(Step 5)	100	56	54	12	18	48	

This process will be repeated until the closing balance for June has been computed. When it has, the cash budget will then look like Table 7.7.

5. Having worked out the June closing balance of £24,000, we can then add up each column (other than the opening and closing balance columns) as indicated above. Why?

   Although this is not part of the cash budget, we can then use this information together with the outstanding debtors and creditors to produce information for the budgeted profit and loss account and balance sheet. This will help you understand:

   - ☐ The difference between a cash budget and a budgeted profit and loss account, and
   - ☐ The difference between profit and cash.

Notice that we did not use the closing stock of raw materials or deal with any depreciation in the cash budget.

The budgeted profit and loss account and the budgeted balance sheet

We adjust the totals for the cash budget (step 5 in Example 7.1) to provide the figures which we need to produce the budgeted profit and loss account and balance sheet, as shown in Table 7.8.

Table 7.8 Brendug and Co. Ltd: converting cash budget information to provide some of the figures for the budgeted profit and loss account and balance sheet (£000)

Share capital	Sales		Purchases	Rent	Wages & general expenses	Fixed assets
100	56		54	12	18	48
Debtors (2 mth × £16)	32	Creditors (1 mth × £12)	12			
	88		66			

Table 7.9 Brendug and Co. Ltd: budgeted profit and loss account

	(£000)		
	Sales (£56 received in cash + £32 owing from customers)		88
less	Cost of Sales		
	Opening stock	–	
add	Purchases (£54 in cash + £12 owing to suppliers)	66	
		66	
less	Closing stock	6	60
	Gross profit		28
less	Expenses:		
	Rent	12	
	Wages and general expenses	18	
	Depreciation of plant and machinery	2.4	32.4
	Net profit (Loss)		(4.4)

Taking into account the closing stock of £6,000 and depreciation of £2,400 (£48,000 × 10% for half a year) we can now draft the budgeted profit and loss account, as shown in Table 7.9.

Finally, we can list all of the budgeted balances as at 30 June 20X3 to produce the budgeted balance sheet (see Table 7.10).

The master budget

You should note that the cash budget, budgeted profit and loss account, and the budgeted balance sheet are frequently referred to as the **master budget**. If management approves it, it will be implemented. If it is not approved, then it is back to the drawing board to review and revise targets, policies, etc. The master budget, once approved, is the culmination of the budget preparation process.

Table 7.10 Brendug and Co. Ltd: budgeted balance sheet

	£000	£000
EMPLOYMENT OF CAPITAL		
Fixed assets:		
Plants and machinery	48	
less Depreciation	2.4	45.6
Working capital		
Current assets:		
Stock	6	
Debtors (2 months × £16)	32	
Cash and bank (per cash budget)	24	
	62	
less **Current liabilities**		
Creditors (1 month × £12)	12	50
		95.6
CAPITAL EMPLOYED		
Share capital	100	
Reserves		
Retained profits (loss)	(4.4)	95.6

Self-assessment Question 7.2

The difference between profit and cash

Now compare the cash budget in Table 7.7 (Example 7.2) with the budgeted profit and loss account of Brendug and Co. Ltd and explain why the cash balance of £24,000 differs from the loss of £4,400. You will find the answer to this assessment on pages 122–3.

SELF-assessment Question 7.3

Having completed the above self-assessment question now see if you can prepare a cash budget, budgeted profit and loss account and balance sheet for Jeanles Ltd.

Jeanles Ltd

Jeanles Ltd are to commence trading in a few months' time on 1 January 20X4 with cash from issued share capital of £60,000. They have provided you with estimates relating to their first six months (Table 7.11).

Prepare a cash budget for the half-year to 30 June 20X4, a budgeted profit and loss account for the half-year and a budgeted balance sheet as at 30 June 20X4.

You will find the suggested answer on pages 123–4.

Table 7.11 Jeanles Ltd: cash budget data

	£	
Quarterly rent of premises, payment due in January and April	1,400	(per quarter)
Cash outlay on equipment – payable January	59,000	
payable March	16,000	
Monthly planned purchase of stock for resale:		
January	10,000	
February	15,000	
March–June (per month)	21,000	
All stock is bought on two months' credit (i.e. January purchases are paid for in March)		
Monthly planned sales are:		
January	8,000	
February	20,000	
March–June (per month)	28,000	

All sales are on one month's credit. No bad debts or arrears of payments are expected. The budgeted closing stock for 30 June 20X4 should be £4,000.

The monthly cash outlay on general expenses is expected to be £500, and wages and salaries are expected to be £1,000 per month. Depreciation of equipment is to be at 20% of cost per annum. The agreed overdraft limit is £7,500.

Flexible budgets

A company/organization can use either a fixed budget or a flexible budget. A fixed budget is a budget which is designed to remain unchanged irrespective of the level of activity (i.e. level of output) actually attained, whereas a flexible budget is a budget which, by recognizing the differences between fixed, semi-fixed and variable costs, is designed to change in relation to the level of activity attained. An example of a flexible budget is shown in Table 7.12.

Table 7.12 Monthly departmental flexible budget

	£000	£000	£000	£000	£000
Sales	80	90	100	110	120
Direct costs (e.g. finished goods, wages)	24	27	30	33	36
Variable overheads	8	9	10	11	12
Semi-fixed overheads	5	6	7	8	9
Fixed overheads	15	15	15	15	17 (step)
	52	57	62	67	74
Profit	28	33	38	43	46

A fixed budget is not really suitable for comparing performance because you could be comparing two completely different levels of activity. The idea behind flexible budgeting is to overcome that problem so that the actual level of activity attained can be compared with a budget appertaining to the same level of activity.

Example 7.3 Fixflex plc

We have been supplied with the information given in Table 7.13. If we compare these figures we will see that a significant proportion of the variances is a direct result of comparing two different levels of activity, i.e. a budget of 30,000 units with an actual performance of 25,000 units.

Taking cost behaviour into account we can recompute (i.e. *flex*) the budget to the actual level achieved and this will provide us with a more realistic and valid comparison, as given in Table 7.14.

The aim of this section is for you to appreciate how flexible budgets are constructed and understand why a business/organization should use them. It is not the intention that you should become proficient in the 'number crunching' aspect of flexible budgeting.

Table 7.13 Fixflex plc: budget/actual information

	Budget August 20X4	Actual August 20X4
Production (units)	30,000	25,000
	£	£
Labour – variable	36,000	33,000
Variable overheads	4,500	3,625
Fixed overheads	5,400	5,400

Table 7.14 Fixflex plc: budget/actual comparative statement

	Budget August 20X4 Per unit £	25,000 units £	Actual August 20X4 25,000 units £	Variance £
Labour $\frac{(£36,000)}{(30,000)}$	1.20	30,000	33,000	(3,000)
Variable overheads $\frac{(£4,500)}{(30,000)}$	0.15	3,750	3,625	125
Fixed overheads	–	5,400	5,400	–
		39,150	42,025	2,875

Note: The fixed costs are assumed to remain unchanged in this example.

The behavioural aspects of budgeting

Budgeting takes place within a human environment and behavioural factors cannot be pushed aside and ignored. Budgets are in fact designed to affect people's behaviour. However, people do not always respond as expected. Their response could be affected by the way in which the budget was drawn up; their involvement/lack of involvement in the preparation of the budget; the way in which it was communicated; their education and training; the way in which the budget is to be implemented; and so on. Some of the causes of the behavioural problems relating to budgeting which are frequently encountered in a company/organization are as follows:

- *Perceptions*
  Perceptions about the objectives of a company/organization and the interpretation of policy. This is caused by poor communications and a lack of participation.
- *Personal goals*
  Those who have to abide by the budget, and achieve the targets set, also have their own personal objectives. These personal objectives may conflict and run counter to the objectives laid down by management. For example, departmental heads may become too preoccupied with their own advancement and empire-building, at the expense of achieving budget targets.
- *Participation*
  A principle of budgeting that is sometimes overlooked, which results in those who should be involved and consulted deciding to withdraw their full-hearted cooperation and support. They may even fail to point out something to management which could well have saved a lot of money and a great amount of time dealing with unnecessary problems.
- *Aspiration levels*
  The achievement of the budget is perceived or treated as success and non-achievement perceived or treated as failure. This can affect *motivation and morale.*
- *Targets*
  If targets are set too high, employees may opt out of trying to achieve them. However, if they are set too low, e.g. in an incentive scheme, employees may agree between themselves what the level of production should be! This is because they are afraid that targets will be revised if managers realize they have set the targets too low.
- *Obsession*
  Some managers are obsessed by the idea that the budget must be achieved at all costs. This is partly due to their aspirations and an uncalled-for perception of accuracy. Some managers tend to forget that the budgeted figures are only estimates.
- *An excuse*
  If things do go wrong, e.g. where there are organizational problems, it is not uncommon for the budget to get the blame. And if some managers/supervisors wish to justify something which has to be done, they say 'Oh well, we have to do this to keep within our budget'. This then leads their subordinates to treat the budget as a whipping post.

- *Resource allocation*
  This is always an area in which conflict can arise, possibly as a result of departmental goals/empire-building.
- *Imposition*
  If management imposes budgets 'from above', i.e. a 'top down' approach, the personnel who 'work below' may reject them and fail to pledge their support or generally just show a lack of enthusiasm.
- *Sub-optimal decisions*
  If budgets have to be cut, an across-the-board cut will weaken both the strong and the weak! Again, this will undoubtedly result in conflict.

Management therefore needs to tread very carefully when preparing and introducing budgets. To some extent success will depend upon the way in which managers deal with the education and training of other employees, employee participation, good clear communications and the regular review and monitoring of behavioural factors.

The benefits of budgeting

Effective budgeting improves efficiency in that it demands the following:

- Careful planning and the provision of information/data for management.
- The participation of both management and workers.
- Coordination and cooperation.
- A sound accounting system.
- That new trends and inefficiencies are detected at an early stage of the planning/control process.
- The delegation of duties/authority. This will mean that job specifications will have to be clear and unambiguous.
- Control by responsibility.
- Management by exception.
- A sound evaluation system for comparing/reporting on budgeted and actual results.
- The motivation of the work force.
- Good clear communications.
- Corrective action by management to remedy adverse situations.

This can happen only if all those who are involved understand what budgeting is trying to do and are able to express their views during the budget preparation process, and if the budget is flexible enough to take account of changes in circumstances.

Zero base budgeting

Another approach to budgeting is that of zero base budgeting (ZBB). This has been found to be particularly useful in service/support areas, e.g. canteen, welfare, research and development. It forces the managers who are responsible for budgets to justify them and to rank them according to their importance, and also to evaluate more/less costly alternatives. Top management can then screen and discuss the proposals and decide which ones will go ahead. This, it is claimed, promotes a much more efficient allocation of resources. This is because managers have to justify the following:

- ☐ How much they want.
- ☐ Why they want it.
- ☐ How else they could achieve the same result.
- ☐ The degree of importance which they attach to it.

Summary: budgeting and budgetary control

Managerial aspects

Budgeting is a management technique. Management needs to set objectives and formulate policy. The budgets provide targets which reflect the objectives, and the policy is the means by which those targets should be achieved. Management must see that the targets which are set are fair, reasonable and attainable. To produce effective budgets managers must do the following:

- ☐ Secure the cooperation and participation of employees, e.g. supervisors, and certain shop-floor workers.
- ☐ Communicate clearly and indicate acceptance of the budget.
- ☐ Possess negotiation/inter-personal skills and be able to cope with behavioural problems.
- ☐ Delegate the authority and responsibility for budgets to subordinates.
- ☐ Plan the budget preparation process well in advance of the forthcoming budget period, e.g. timetables for meetings, etc. The aim is to ensure that the budget is ready to be implemented before the start of the new budget period.
- ☐ Host/attend the appropriate meetings at which their own budget/certain other budgets will be reviewed/discussed.
- ☐ Appoint a person to act as budget controller.
- ☐ Set up an effective monitoring and reporting system to compare budgeted with actual results at frequent intervals.
- ☐ Be prepared to take action to put right something which is going wrong, as indicated by the feedback from comparative statements/reports.

Budget preparation

It is essential that the budget preparation process commences well before the budget period to which it relates and that the principal budget factor (i.e. a constraint) is identified. The preparation process will be coordinated by the budget controller. The authority and responsibility for a particular budget/section of a budget will be delegated to a named individual. The budget controller will supply that person with appropriate information/data to help with their budget preparation. From the outset all those involved will have to be issued with instructions and a timetable. The timetable will state when schedules and other information will be required and the dates and times of meetings. Meetings are needed to plan, discuss, review and revise the budgets, to ensure that everything fits together. This is because budgets are interrelated. One budget cannot be prepared in isolation and without reference to the other budgets. When the process is complete, managers must ensure that the information on objectives, policy, targets, etc. is communicated to the appropriate personnel, which indicates managers' acceptance of the budget.

Budgetary control

Control in budgeting is exercised by regular comparisons (e.g. monthly) between budgeted and actual results. The statements/reports produced inform management of where in their company/organization things are not going according to plan. Management can then decide on the form of corrective action which needs to be taken (see Figure 7.4).

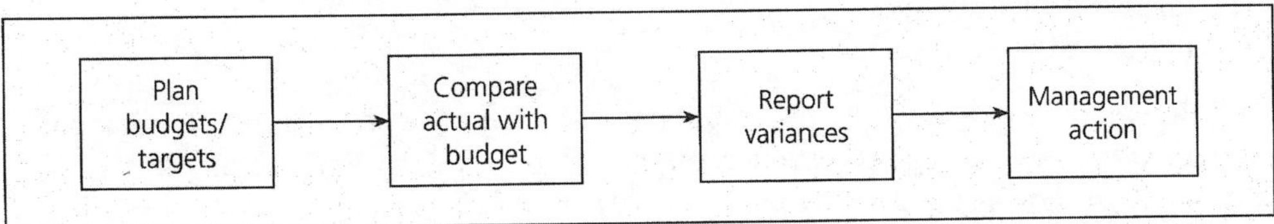

Figure 7.4 Budgetary control

Cost control

Management will be particularly interested in the significant adverse variances which will be highlighted in statements and reports. This system, which singles out those variances which management should look at very carefully, is known as *management by exception.* Managers spend their time and energy putting right things which are going wrong and keeping the company/organization on course to achieve its objectives. Frequent comparisons do provide an early warning system/early detection system of inefficiencies, the emergence of new trends and environmental changes.

Control is also exercised by delegating to an individual the responsibility for a particular budget or subsection of a budget, i.e. *control by responsibility.* That person alone has to justify and explain to management why targets have hot been achieved.

However, if the reported variances are to be any use it is essential that the budgeted and actual figurers have been computed the same way and relate to the same level of activity. This is why, if at all possible, a flexible budget should be used, i.e. a budget which is designed to change as the level of activity changes.

Finally, remember that control should be directed towards problem solving and not the creation of conflict!

More effective budgeting

If budgeting is to become really effective it must be remembered that it is only a forecast. The budget itself, once implemented, must be monitored at frequent intervals, and if necessary amended to take account of changes in the basic assumptions upon which it was based.

Management will also have to monitor *behavioural factors* on a regular basis. People problems, if allowed to fester and multiply, can become the principal reason for the non-attainment of budget targets.

Staff education can be a most worthwhile investment. If staff know more about budgeting and what it is trying to do then, provided that they are able to *participate* and express their opinions, more reasonable, accurate and realistic budgets should be produced.

The master budget

This consists of the following:

- ☐ A cash budget.
- ☐ A budgeted profit and loss account.
- ☐ A budgeted balance sheet.

It is the coming together of all the component parts of the budgeting jigsaw. It communicates in advance of the budget period commencing (e.g. a six- or twelve-month period) the outcome in terms of cash flow, profits, assets and liabilities, etc.

Zero base budgeting

This provides a system of ranking budget packages according to their importance and is suitable for services/non-profit making activities.

Further reading

Drury, J.C., *Management Accounting for Business Decisions*, International Thomson Business Press, 1997.
Horngren, C.T., Foster, G. and Srikant, M.D., *Cost Accounting, A Managerial Emphasis*, Prentice Hall, 2000.
Hussey, J. and Hussey, R., *Cost and Management Accounting*, Macmillan, 1998.

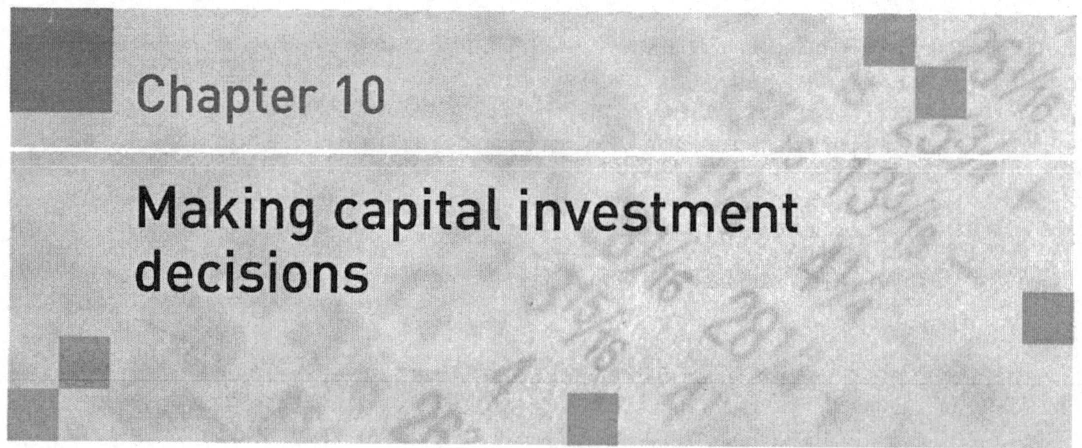

Chapter 10

Making capital investment decisions

Introduction

In this chapter we shall look at how businesses can make decisions involving investments in new plant, machinery, buildings and similar long-term assets. Though we shall be considering this topic in the context of businesses making decisions about the type of assets that were just mentioned, the general principles can equally well be applied to investments in the shares of businesses, irrespective of whether the investment is being considered by a business or by a private individual. This chapter is the first of the three that deal with the area generally known as *business finance* or *financial management*.

Objectives

When you have completed your study of this chapter you should be able to:

- **explain the nature and importance of investment decision making**
- **identify the four main investment appraisal methods used in practice**
- **use each method to reach a decision on a particular practical investment opportunity**
- **discuss the attributes and defects of each of the methods.**

The nature of investment decisions

The essential feature of investment decisions is the time factor. Investment involves making an outlay of something of economic value, usually cash, at one point in time, which is expected to yield economic benefits to the investor at some other point in time. Typically, the outlay precedes the benefits. Also, the outlay is typically one large amount and the benefits arrive in a stream of smaller amounts over a fairly protracted period.

Investment decisions tend to be crucial to the business because:

- *Large amounts of resources are often involved.* Many investments made by a business involve laying out a significant proportion of its total resources (see Exhibit 10.1 below). If mistakes are made with the decision, the effects on the business could be significant, if not catastrophic.
- *It is often difficult and/or expensive to 'bail out' of an investment once it has been undertaken.* It is often the case that investments made by a business are specific to its needs. For example, a hotel business may invest in a new, purposely designed hotel complex. The specialist nature of this complex will probably lead to it having a rather limited second-hand value to another potential user with different needs. If the business found, after having made the investment, that room occupancy rates were not as buoyant as was planned, the only possible course of action might be to close down and sell the complex. This would probably mean that much less could be recouped from the investment than it had originally cost, particularly if the costs of design are included as part of the cost, as they logically should be.

Exhibit 10.1 indicates the level of annual investment for a number of randomly selected, well-known UK businesses. It can be seen that the scale of investment varies from one business to another. (It also tends to vary from one year to the next for a particular business.) In nearly all of these businesses the scale of investment is very significant. The exhibit is limited to considering the fixed asset investment, but most fixed asset investment also requires a level of current asset investment to support it (additional stock-in-trade, for example), meaning that the real scale of investment is even greater than indicated by the exhibit.

Exhibit 10.1

Business	*Expenditure on additional fixed assets as a percentage of:*	
	Annual sales	*Start of year fixed assets*
Associated British Foods plc	10.1	28.6
The Boots Company plc	3.2	7.6
British Airways plc	9.3	7.0
BT plc	19.9	17.0
British Sky Broadcasting Group plc	5.0	5.8
J D Wetherspoon plc	25.1	24.1
Manchester United plc	27.5	20.5
Stagecoach Group plc	6.0	5.4
Tesco plc	8.5	20.1
Vodafone Group plc	79.4	11.8

Source: Annual reports of the businesses concerned for the accounting years ending in 2002

Activity 10.1

When managers are making decisions involving capital investments, what should the decision seek to achieve?

The answer to this question must be that any decision must be made in the context of the objectives of the business concerned. For a private-sector business, this is likely to include increasing the wealth of the shareholders of the business through long-term profitability.

Methods of investment appraisal

Given the importance of investment decisions to the viability of the business, it is essential that proper screening of investment proposals takes place. An important part of this screening process is to ensure that the business uses appropriate methods of evaluation.

Research shows that there are basically four methods used in practice by businesses throughout the world to evaluate investment opportunities.

They are:

- accounting rate of return (ARR);
- payback period (PP);
- net present value (NPV);
- internal rate of return (IRR).

It is possible to find businesses that use variants of these four methods. It is also possible to find businesses, particularly smaller ones, that do not use any formal appraisal method, but rely more on the 'gut feeling' of their managers. Most businesses, however, seem to use one of the four methods listed above that we shall now review.

We are going to assess the effectiveness of each of these methods and we shall see that only one of them (NPV) is not flawed to some extent. We shall also see how popular these four methods seem to be in practice.

To help us to examine each of the methods, it might be useful to consider how each of them would cope with a particular investment opportunity. Let us consider the following example.

Example 10.1

Billingsgate Battery Company has carried out some research that shows that it could manufacture and sell a product that the business has recently developed.

Production would require investment in a machine that would cost £100,000, payable immediately. Production and sales would take place throughout the next five years. At the end of that time, it is estimated that the machine could be sold for £20,000.

Production and sales of the product would be expected to occur as follows:

	Number of units
Next year	5,000
Second year	10,000
Third year	15,000
Fourth year	15,000
Fifth year	5,000

It is estimated that the new product can be sold for £12 a unit, and that the relevant material and labour costs will total £8 a unit.

To simplify matters, we shall assume that the cash from sales and for the costs of production are paid and received, respectively, at the end of each year. (This is clearly unlikely to be true in real life – money will have to be paid to employees on a weekly or a monthly basis, and customers will pay within a month or two of buying the product. On the other hand, it is probably not a serious distortion. It is a simplifying assumption that is often made in real life, and it will make things more straightforward for us now. We should be clear, however, that there is nothing about any of the four approaches that *demands* this assumption being made.)

Bearing in mind that each product sold will give rise to a net cash inflow of £4 (that is £12 – £8), the total net cash flows (receipts less payments) for each year of the life of the product will be as follows:

Time		*£000*
Immediately	Cost of machine	(100)
1 year's time	Net profit before depreciation (£4 × 5,000)	20
2 years' time	Net profit before depreciation (£4 × 10,000)	40
3 years' time	Net profit before depreciation (£4 × 15,000)	60
4 years' time	Net profit before depreciation (£4 × 15,000)	60
5 years' time	Net profit before depreciation (£4 × 5,000)	20
5 years' time	Disposal proceeds from the machine	20

Note that, broadly speaking, the net profit before deducting depreciation (that is, before non-cash items) equals the net amount of cash flowing into the business. Apart from depreciation, all of this business's expenses cause cash to flow out of the business. Sales revenues lead to cash flowing in.

Having set up the example, we shall go on to look at the techniques used to assess investment opportunities and see how they deal with this particular decision.

Accounting rate of return (ARR)

The **accounting rate of return** method takes the average accounting profit that the investment will generate and expresses it as a percentage of the average investment in the project as measured in accounting terms.

Thus:

$$\text{ARR} = \frac{\textbf{Average annual profit}}{\textbf{Average investment to earn that profit}} \times 100\%$$

We can see that to calculate the ARR, we need to deduce two pieces of information:

- the annual average profit;
- the average investment for the particular project.

In our example, the average profit before depreciation over the five years is £40,000 [that is, £(20 + 40 + 60 + 60 + 20)/5]. Assuming straight-line depreciation (that is, equal annual amounts), the annual depreciation charge will be £16,000 [that is, £(100,000 – 20,000)/5]. Thus the average annual profit is £24,000 (that is, £40,000 – £16,000).

The average investment over the five years can be calculated as follows:

$$\text{Average investment} = \frac{\text{Cost of machine + disposal value}}{2}$$

$$= \frac{£100{,}000 + £20{,}000}{2}$$

$$= £60{,}000$$

Thus, the ARR of the investment is:

$$\text{ARR} = \frac{£24{,}000}{£60{,}000} \times 100\%$$

$$= 40\%$$

To decide whether the 40 per cent return is acceptable, we need to compare this percentage with the minimum required by the business.

Activity 10.2

Chaotic Industries is considering an investment in a fleet of ten delivery vans to take its products to customers. The vans will cost £15,000 each to buy, payable immediately. The annual running costs are expected to total £20,000 for each van (including the driver's salary). The vans are expected to operate successfully for six years, at the end of which period they will all have to be sold, with disposal proceeds expected to be about £3,000 per van. At present, the business uses a commercial carrier for all of its deliveries. It is expected that this carrier will charge a total of £230,000 each year for the next five years to undertake the deliveries.

What is the ARR of buying the vans? (Note that cost savings are as relevant a benefit from an investment as are actual net cash inflows.)

The vans will save the business £30,000 a year (that is, £230,000 – (£20,000 × 10)), before depreciation, in total.

Activity 10.2 continued

Thus, the inflows and outflows will be:

Time		*£000*
Immediately	Cost of vans	(150)
1 year's time	Net saving before depreciation	30
2 years' time	Net saving before depreciation	30
3 years' time	Net saving before depreciation	30
4 years' time	Net saving before depreciation	30
5 years' time	Net saving before depreciation	30
6 years' time	Net saving before depreciation	30
6 years' time	Disposal proceeds from the vans (10 × 3)	30

The total annual depreciation expense (assuming a straight-line approach) will be £20,000 (that is, (£150,000 − £30,000)/6). Thus, the average annual saving, after depreciation, is £10,000 (that is, £30,000 − £20,000).

The average investment will be

$$\text{Average investment} = \frac{£150{,}000 + £30{,}000}{2}$$

$$= £90{,}000$$

Thus, the ARR of the investment is

$$\text{ARR} = \frac{£10{,}000}{£90{,}000} \times 100\% = 11.1\%$$

ARR and the return on capital employed (ROCE) ratio take the same approach to performance measurement, in that they both relate accounting profit to the cost of the assets invested to generate that profit. We may recall from Chapter 6 that ROCE is a popular means of assessing the performance of a business, as a whole, *after* it has performed. ARR is an approach that assesses the potential performance of a particular investment, taking the same approach as ROCE, *before* it has performed.

Since private-sector businesses are normally seeking to increase the wealth of their owners, ARR may seem to be a sound method of appraising investment opportunities. Profit can be seen as a net increase in wealth over a period, and relating it to the size of investment made to achieve it seems a logical approach.

A user of ARR would require that any investment undertaken by the business would be able to achieve a minimum ARR. Perhaps the minimum would be the rate that previous investments had actually achieved (as measured by ROCE). Perhaps it would be the industry-average ROCE.

Where there are competing projects that all seem capable of exceeding this minimum rate, the one with the higher or highest ARR would normally be selected.

ARR is said to have a number of advantages as a method of investment appraisal. It was mentioned earlier that ROCE seems a widely used measure of business performance. Shareholders seem to use this ratio to evaluate management performance, and sometimes the financial objective of a business will be expressed in terms of a target ROCE. It therefore seems sensible to use a method of investment appraisal that is consistent with this overall approach to measuring business performance. ARR is also a measure of profitability that many believe is the correct way to evaluate investments, and it gives the result expressed as a percentage. It seems that some managers feel comfortable with using measures expressed in percentage terms.

Activity 10.3

ARR suffers from a very major defect as a means of assessing investment opportunities. Can you reason out what this is? Consider the three competing projects whose cash flows are shown below. All three of these involve investment in a machine that is expected to have no residual value at the end of the five years. Note that all of the projects have the same total net profits over the five years.

Project		A	B	C
Time		*£000*	*£000*	*£000*
Immediately	Cost of machine	(200)	(200)	(200)
1 year's time	Net profit after depreciation	20	10	160
2 years' time	Net profit after depreciation	40	10	10
3 years' time	Net profit after depreciation	60	10	10
4 years' time	Net profit after depreciation	60	10	10
5 years' time	Net profit after depreciation	20	160	10

***Hint*: The defect is not concerned with the ability of the decision maker to forecast future events, though this too can be a problem. Try to remember what was the essential feature of investment decisions that we identified at the beginning of this chapter.**

The problem with ARR is that it almost completely ignores the time factor. In the Billingsgate Battery example, exactly the same ARR would have been computed under any of the three scenarios.

Since the same total profit over the five years arises in all three of these projects (that is, £200,000) and the average investment in each project is £100,000 (that is, £200,000/2), this means that each case will give rise to the same ARR of 40 per cent (that is, £40,000/£100,000).

Given a financial objective of increasing the wealth of the business, any rational decision maker faced with these three scenarios as a choice between the three separate investments, set out in Activity 10.3, would strongly prefer Project C. This is because most of the benefits from the investment come in within 12 months of investing the £200,000 to establish the project. Project A would rank second, and Project B would come a poor third in the rankings. Any appraisal technique that is not capable of distinguishing between these three situations is seriously flawed.

Clearly the use of ARR can easily cause poor decisions to be made. We shall look in more detail at the reason for timing being so important later in this chapter.

There are other defects associated with the ARR method. For investment appraisal purposes, it is cash flows rather than accounting profits that are important. Cash is the ultimate measure of the economic wealth generated. This is because it is cash that is used to acquire resources and for distribution to shareholders. Accounting profit is more appropriate for reporting achievement over the short term. It is a useful measure of productive effort for a relatively short period, such as a year, rather than for a long period. ARR also fails to take account of the fact that pounds received at a later date are worth less than pounds received at an earlier date.

The ARR method can also create problems when considering competing investments of different size.

Activity 10.4

Sinclair Wholesalers plc is currently considering opening a new sales outlet in Coventry. Two possible sites have been identified for the new outlet. Site A has a capacity of 30,000 sq. metres. It will require an average investment of £6 million, and will produce an average profit of £600,000 a year. Site B has a capacity of 20,000 sq. metres. It will require an average investment of £4 million, and will produce an average profit of £500,000 a year.

What is the ARR of each investment opportunity? Which site would you select, and why?

The ARR of Site A is £600,000/£6 million = 10 per cent. The ARR of Site B is £500,000/£4 million = 12.5 per cent. Thus, Site B has the higher ARR. However, in terms of the absolute profit generated, Site A is the more attractive. If the ultimate objective is to maximise the wealth of the shareholders of Sinclair Wholesalers plc, it might be better to choose Site A even though the percentage return is lower. It is the absolute size of the return rather than the relative (percentage) size that is important.

Payback period (PP)

The **payback period** method seems to go some way to overcoming the timing problem of ARR, or at least at first glance it does.

It might be useful to consider PP in the context of the Billingsgate Battery example. We should recall that essentially the project's costs and benefits can be summarised as:

Time		*£000*
Immediately	Cost of machine	(100)
1 year's time	Net profit before depreciation	20
2 years' time	Net profit before depreciation	40
3 years' time	Net profit before depreciation	60
4 years' time	Net profit before depreciation	60
5 years' time	Net profit before depreciation	20
5 years' time	Disposal proceeds	20

Note that all of these figures are amounts of cash to be paid or received (we saw earlier that net profit before depreciation is a rough measure of the cash flows from the project).

The payback period is the length of time it takes for the initial investment to be repaid out of the net cash inflows from the project. In this case, it will be nearly three years before the £100,000 outlay is covered by the inflows, still assuming that the cash flows occur at year ends. The payback period can be derived by calculating the cumulative cash flows as follows:

Time		*Net cash flows*	*Cumulative cash flows*	
		£000	*£000*	
Immediately	Cost of machine	(100)	(100)	
1 year's time	Net profit before depreciation	20	(80)	(–100 + 20)
2 years' time	Net profit before depreciation	40	(40)	(–80 + 40)
3 years' time	Net profit before depreciation	60	20	(–40 + 60)
4 years' time	Net profit before depreciation	60	80	(20 + 60)
5 years' time	Net profit before depreciation	20	100	(80 + 20)
5 years' time	Disposal proceeds	20	120	(100 + 20)

We can see that the cumulative cash flows become positive at the end of the third year. Had we assumed that the cash flows arise evenly over the year, the precise payback period would be:

$$2 \text{ years} + (40/60) = 2\tfrac{2}{3} \text{ years}$$

(where 40 represents the cash flow still required at the beginning of the third year to repay the initial outlay, and 60 is the projected cash flow during the third year). Again we must ask how to decide whether $2\frac{2}{3}$ years is acceptable. A manager using PP would need to have a minimum payback period in mind. For example, if Billingsgate Battery had a minimum payback period of three years it would accept the project, but it would not go ahead if its minimum payback period were two years. If there were two competing projects that both met the minimum payback period requirement, the decision maker should select the project with the shorter payback period.

Activity 10.5

What is the payback period of the Chaotic Industries project from Activity 10.2?

The inflows and outflows are expected to be:

Time		*Net cash flows*	*Cumulative net cash flows*	
		£000	*£000*	
Immediately	Cost of vans	(150)	(150)	
1 year's time	Net saving before depreciation	30	(120)	(–150 + 30)
2 years' time	Net saving before depreciation	30	(90)	(–120 + 30)
3 years' time	Net saving before depreciation	30	(60)	(–90 + 30)
4 years' time	Net saving before depreciation	30	(30)	(–60 + 30)
5 years' time	Net saving before depreciation	30	0	(–30 + 30)
6 years' time	Net saving before depreciation	30	30	(0 + 30)
6 years' time	Disposal proceeds from the machine	30	60	(30 + 30)

The payback period here is five years; that is, it is not until the end of the fifth year that the vans will pay for themselves out of the savings that they are expected to generate.

The PP approach has certain advantages. It is quick and easy to calculate, and can be easily understood by managers. The logic of using PP is that projects that can recoup their cost quickly are economically more attractive than those with longer payback periods, that is, it emphasises liquidity. PP is probably an improvement on ARR in respect of the timing of the cash flows. PP is not, however, the whole answer to the problem.

Activity 10.6

In what respect, in your opinion, is PP not the whole answer as a means of assessing investment opportunities? Consider the cash flows arising from three competing projects:

		Project 1	Project 2	Project 3
Time		*£000*	*£000*	*£000*
Immediately	Cost of machine	(200)	(200)	(200)
1 year's time	Net profit before depreciation	40	10	80
2 years' time	Net profit before depreciation	80	20	100
3 years' time	Net profit before depreciation	80	170	20
4 years' time	Net profit before depreciation	60	20	200
5 years' time	Net profit before depreciation	40	10	500
5 years' time	Disposal proceeds	40	10	20

***Hint*: Again, the defect is not concerned with the ability of the manager to forecast future events. This is a problem, but it is a problem whatever approach we take.**

Any rational manager would prefer Project 3 to either of the other two projects, yet PP sees all three of them as being equally attractive in that they all have a three-year payback period. The method cannot distinguish between those projects that pay back a significant amount before the three-year payback period and those that do not. Project 3 is by far the best bet because the cash flows come in earlier and they are greater in total, yet PP would not identify it as the best.

The cumulative cash flows of each project in Activity 10.6 are set out in Figure 10.1.

Within the payback period, PP ignores the timing of the cash flows. Beyond the payback period, the method totally ignores both the size and the timing of the cash flows. While ignoring cash flows beyond the payback period neatly avoids the practical problems of forecasting cash flows over a long period, it means that relevant information may be ignored.

The PP approach is often seen as a means of dealing with the problem of risk by favouring projects with a short payback period. However, this is a fairly crude approach to the problem. There are more systematic approaches to dealing with risk that can be used.

Figure 10.1 The cumulative cash flows of each project in Activity 10.6

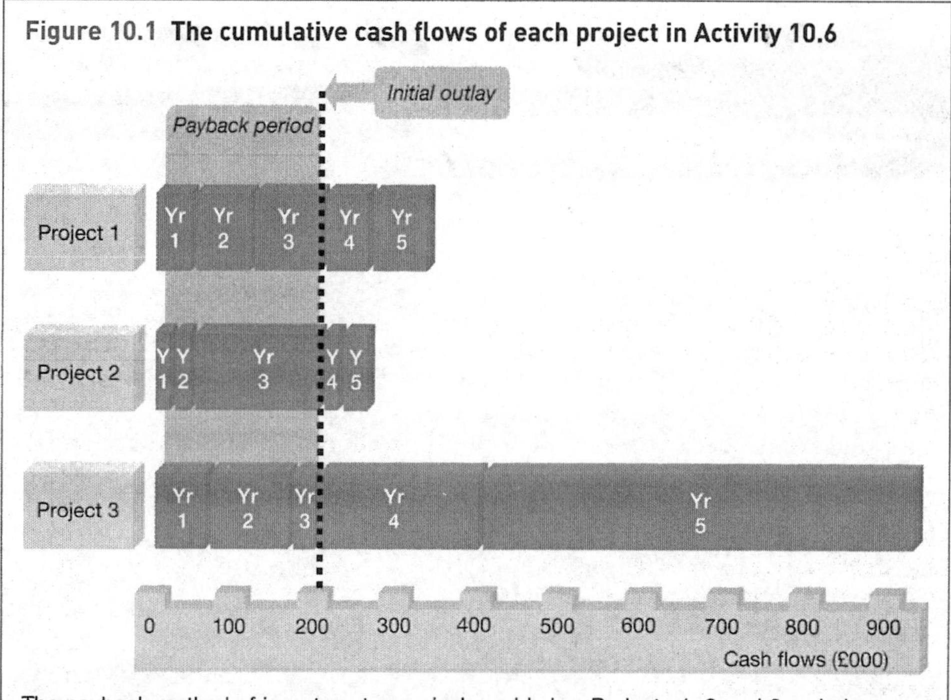

The payback method of investment appraisal would view Projects 1, 2 and 3 as being equally attractive. In doing so, the method completely ignores the fact that Project 3 provides the payback cash earlier in the three-year period and goes on to generate large benefits in later years.

It seems that PP has the advantage of taking some note of the timing of the costs and benefits from the project, but it suffers from the disadvantage of ignoring relevant information. ARR ignores timing to a great extent, but it does take account of all benefits and costs. What we really need to help us to make sensible decisions is a method of appraisal that takes account of all of the costs and benefits of each investment opportunity, but which also makes a logical allowance for the timing of those costs and benefits.

Net present value (NPV)

What we really need to help us to make sensible investment decisions is a method of appraisal that takes account of *all* of the costs and benefits of each investment opportunity and that also makes a logical allowance for the *timing* of those costs and benefits. The **net present value** method provides us with this.

Consider the Billingsgate Battery example, which we should recall can be summarised as follows:

Time		*£000*
Immediately	Cost of machine	(100)
1 year's time	Net profit before depreciation	20
2 years' time	Net profit before depreciation	40
3 years' time	Net profit before depreciation	60
4 years' time	Net profit before depreciation	60
5 years' time	Net profit before depreciation	20
5 years' time	Disposal proceeds	20

Given that the principal financial objective of the business is probably to increase wealth, it would be very easy to assess this investment if all of the cash flows were to occur now (all at the same time). All that we should need to do would be to add up the benefits (total £220,000) and compare them with the cost (£100,000). This would lead us to the conclusion that the project should go ahead, because the business would be better off by £120,000. Of course, it is not as easy as this, because time is involved. The cash outflow (payment) will occur immediately if the project is undertaken. The inflows (receipts) will arise at a range of later times.

The time factor arises because normally people do not see £100 paid out now as equivalent in value to £100 receivable in a year's time. If we were to be offered £100 in 12 months, provided that we paid £100 now, we should not be prepared to do so, unless we wished to do someone (perhaps a friend or relation) a favour.

Activity 10.7

Why would you see £100 to be received in a year's time as unequal in value to £100 to be paid immediately? (There are basically three reasons.)

The reasons are:

- interest lost
- risk
- effects of inflation.

We shall now take a closer look at these three reasons in turn.

Interest lost

If we are to be deprived of the opportunity to spend your money for a year, we could equally well be deprived of its use by placing it on deposit in a bank or building society. In this case, at the end of the year we could have our money back and have interest as well. Thus, unless the opportunity to invest will offer similar returns, we shall be incurring an *opportunity cost.* An opportunity cost occurs where one course of action, for example making an investment in, say, a computer, deprives us of the opportunity to derive some benefit from an alternative action, for example putting the money in the bank.

From this we can see that any investment opportunity must, if it is to make us wealthier by taking it than by ignoring it, do better than the returns that are available from the next best opportunity. Thus, if Billingsgate Battery Company sees putting the money in the bank on deposit as the alternative to investment in the machine, the return from investing in the machine must be better than that from investing in the bank. If the bank offered a better return, the business would become wealthier by putting the money on deposit.

Risk

Buying a machine to manufacture a product to be sold in the market, on the strength of various estimates made in advance of buying the machine, exposes the business to **risk**. Things may not turn out as expected.

Activity 10.8

Can you suggest some areas where things could go other than according to plan in the Billingsgate Battery Company example?

We have come up with the following:

- The machine might not work as well as expected; it might break down, leading to loss of production and to loss of sales.
- Sales of the product may not be as buoyant as expected.
- Labour costs may prove to be higher than was expected.
- The sale proceeds of the machine could prove to be less than was estimated.

It is important to remember that the decision as to whether or not to invest in the machine must be taken *before* any of these things are known. It is only after the machine has been purchased that we could discover that the level of sales that had been estimated before the event is not going to be achieved. It is not possible to wait until we know for certain whether the market will behave as we expected before we buy the machine. We can study reports and analyses of the market. We can commission sophisticated market surveys, and these may give us more confidence in the likely outcome. We can advertise strongly and try to expand sales. Ultimately, however, we have to decide whether or not to jump off into the dark and accept the risk if we want the opportunity to make profitable investments.

Normally, people expect to receive greater returns where they perceive risk to be a factor. Examples of this in real life are not difficult to find. One such example is that banks tend to charge higher rates of interest to borrowers whom the bank perceives as more risky than to those who can offer good security for a loan and who can point to a regular source of income.

Going back to Billingsgate Battery Company's investment opportunity, it is not enough to say that we should not advise making the investment unless the returns from it are higher than those from investing in a bank deposit. Clearly we should want returns above the level of bank deposit interest rates, because the logical equivalent to investing in the machine is not putting the money on deposit but making an alternative investment that seems to have a risk similar to that of the investment in the machine.

In practice, we tend to expect a higher rate of return from investment projects where the risk is perceived as being higher. How risky a particular project is, and therefore how large this **risk premium** should be, are matters that are difficult to handle. In practice, it is necessary to make some judgement on these questions.

Inflation

If we are to be deprived of £100 for a year, when we come to spend that money it will not buy as much in the way of goods and services as it would have done a year earlier. Generally, we shall not be able to buy as many tins of baked beans or loaves of bread or bus tickets for a particular journey as we could have done a year earlier. Clearly, the investor needs this loss of purchasing power to be compensated for if the investment is to be made. This is on top of a return that takes account of the returns that could have been gained from an alternative investment of similar risk.

In practice, interest rates observable in the market tend to take **inflation** into  account. Rates that are offered to potential building society and bank depositors include an allowance for the rate of inflation that is expected in the future.

Actions of a logical investor

To summarise these factors, we can say that the logical investor, who is seeking to increase his or her wealth, will only be prepared to make investments that will compensate for the loss of interest and purchasing power of the money invested and for the fact that the returns expected may not materialise (risk). This is usually assessed by seeing whether the proposed investment will yield a return that is greater than the basic rate of interest (which would include an allowance for inflation) plus a risk premium.

These three factors (interest lost, risk and inflation) are set out in Figure 10.2.

Naturally, investors need at least the minimum returns before they are prepared to invest. However, it is in terms of the effect on their wealth that they should logically assess an investment project. Usually it is the investment with the highest percentage return that will make the investor most wealthy, but we shall see later in this chapter that this is not always the case. For the time being, therefore, we shall concentrate on wealth.

Let us now return to the Billingsgate Battery Company example and assume that instead of making this investment the business could make an alternative investment with similar risk and obtain a return of 20 per cent a year.

We should recall that we have seen that it is not sufficient just to compare the basic figures for the investment. It would therefore be useful if we could express each of these cash flows in similar terms so that we could make a direct comparison between the sum of the inflows over time and the immediate £100,000 investment. In fact, we can do this.

Figure 10.2 The factors influencing the discount rate to be applied to a project

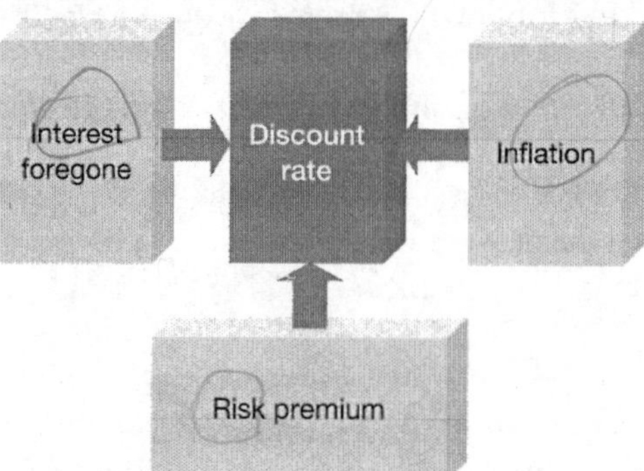

The figure shows the three factors influencing the opportunity cost of finance that were discussed earlier.

Activity 10.9

We know that Billingsgate Battery Company could alternatively invest its money at a rate of 20 per cent a year. How much do you judge the present (immediate) value of the expected first year receipt of £20,000 to be? In other words, if instead of having to wait a year for the £20,000, and being deprived of the opportunity to invest it at 20 per cent, you could have some money now, what sum to be received now would you regard as exactly equivalent to getting £20,000, but having to wait a year for it?

We should obviously be happy to accept a lower amount if we could get it immediately than if we had to wait a year. This is because we could invest it at 20 per cent (in the alternative project). Logically, we should be prepared to accept the amount that with a year's income will grow to £20,000. If we call this amount PV (for present value) we can say:

$$PV + (PV \times 20\%) = £20,000$$

that is, the amount plus income from investing the amount for the year equals the £20,000.

If we rearrange this equation we find:

$$PV \times (1 + 0.2) = £20,000$$

Note that 0.2 is the same as 20 per cent, but expressed as a decimal.

Further rearranging gives:

$$PV = £20,000/(1 + 0.2)$$

$$PV = £16,667$$

Thus, rational investors who have the opportunity to invest at 20 per cent a year would not mind whether they have £16,667 now or £20,000 in a year's time. In this sense we can say that, given a 20 per cent investment opportunity, the present value of £20,000 to be received in one year's time is £16,667.

If we could derive the present value (PV) of each of the cash flows associated with Billingsgate's machine investment, we could easily make the direct comparison between the cost of making the investment (£100,000) and the various benefits that will derive from it in years 1 to 5. Fortunately we can do precisely this.

We can make a more general statement about the PV of a particular cash flow. It is:

PV of the cash flow of year n = Actual cash flow of year n divided by $(1 + r)^n$

where n is the year of the cash flow (that is, how many years into the future) and r is the opportunity investing rate expressed as a decimal (instead of as a percentage).

We have already seen how this works for the £20,000 inflow for year 1. For year 2 the calculation would be:

$$\text{PV of year 2 cash flow (£40,000)} = £40,000/(1 + 0.2)^2$$

$$\text{PV} = £40,000/(1.2)^2 = £40,000/1.44 = £27,778$$

Thus the present value of the £40,000 to be received in two years' time is £27,778.

Activity 10.10

See if you can show that an investor would be indifferent to £27,778 receivable now, or £40,000 receivable in two years' time, assuming that there is a 20 per cent investment opportunity.

The reasoning goes like this:

	£
Amount available for immediate investment	27,778
Add Interest for year 1 (20% × 27,778)	5,556
	33,334
Add Interest for year 2 (20% × 33,334)	6,667
	40,001

(The extra £1 is only a rounding error.)

Thus because the investor can turn £27,778 into £40,000 in two years, these amounts are equivalent, and we can say that £27,778 is the present value of £40,000 receivable after two years (given a 20 per cent rate of return).

Now let us deduce the present values of all of the cash flows associated with the Billingsgate machine project and hence the *net present value* of the project as a whole.

The relevant cash flows and calculations are as follows:

Time	*Cash flow*	*Calculation of PV*	*PV*
	£000		*£000*
Immediately (time 0)	(100)	$(100)/(1 + 0.2)^0$	(100.00)
1 year's time	20	$20/(1 + 0.2)^1$	16.67
2 years' time	40	$40/(1 + 0.2)^2$	27.78
3 years' time	60	$60/(1 + 0.2)^3$	34.72
4 years' time	60	$60/(1 + 0.2)^4$	28.94
5 years' time	20	$20/(1 + 0.2)^5$	8.04
5 years' time	20	$20/(1 + 0.2)^5$	8.04
			24.19

(Note that $(1 + 0.2)^0 = 1$)

Once again, we must ask how we can decide whether the machine project is acceptable to the business. In fact, the decision rule is simple. If the NPV is positive we accept the project; if it is negative we reject the project. In this case, the NPV is positive, so we accept the project and buy the machine.

Investing in the machine will make the business £24,190 better off. What the above is saying is that the benefits from investing in this machine are worth a total of £124,190 today. Since the business can 'buy' these benefits for just £100,000 the investment should be made. If, however, the benefits were below £100,000 they would be less than the cost of 'buying' them.

Activity 10.11

What is the *maximum* the Billingsgate Battery Company would be prepared to pay for the machine, given the potential benefits of owning it?

The business would be prepared to pay up to £124,190 since the wealth of the owners of the business would be increased up to this price – though the business would prefer to pay as little as possible.

Using discount tables

Deducing the present values of the various cash flows is a little laborious using the approach that we have just taken. To deduce each PV we took the relevant cash flow and multiplied it by $1/(1 + r)^n$. Fortunately, there is a quicker way. Tables exist that show values of this **discount factor** for a range of values of r and n. Such a table is appended at the end of this chapter on p. 317. Take a look at it.

Look at the column for 20 per cent and the row for one year. We find that the factor is 0.833. Thus the PV of a cash flow of £1 receivable in one year is £0.833. So a cash flow of £20,000 receivable in one year's time is £16,660 (that is, 0.833 × £20,000), the same result as we found doing it in longhand.

Activity 10.12

What is the NPV of the Chaotic Industries project from Activity 10.2, assuming a 15 per cent opportunity cost of finance (discount rate)? You should use the discount table on p. 317.

Remember that the inflows and outflow are expected to be:

Time		*£000*
Immediately	Cost of vans	(150)
1 year's time	Net saving before depreciation	30
2 years' time	Net saving before depreciation	30
3 years' time	Net saving before depreciation	30
4 years' time	Net saving before depreciation	30
5 years' time	Net saving before depreciation	30
6 years' time	Net saving before depreciation	30
6 years' time	Disposal proceeds from the machine	30

The calculation of the NPV of the project is as follows:

Time	*Cash flows*	*Discount factor (15% – from the table)*	*Present value*
	£000		*£000*
Immediately	(150)	1.000	(150.00)
1 year's time	30	0.870	26.10
2 years' time	30	0.756	22.68
3 years' time	30	0.658	19.74
4 years' time	30	0.572	17.16
5 years' time	30	0.497	14.91
6 years' time	30	0.432	12.96
6 years' time	30	0.432	12.96
		Net present value	(23.49)

Activity 10.13

How would you interpret this result?

The fact that the project has a negative NPV means that the present value of the benefits from the investment are worth less than the cost of entering into it. Any cost up to £126,510 (the present value of the benefits) would be worth paying, but not £150,000.

The discount tables reveal how the value of £1 diminishes as its receipt goes further into the future. Assuming an opportunity cost of finance of 20 per cent a year, £1 to be received immediately, obviously, has a present value of £1. However, as the time before it is to be received extends, the present value diminishes significantly, as is shown in Figure 10.3.

Figure 10.3 Present value of £1 receivable at various times in the future, assuming an annual financing cost of 20 per cent

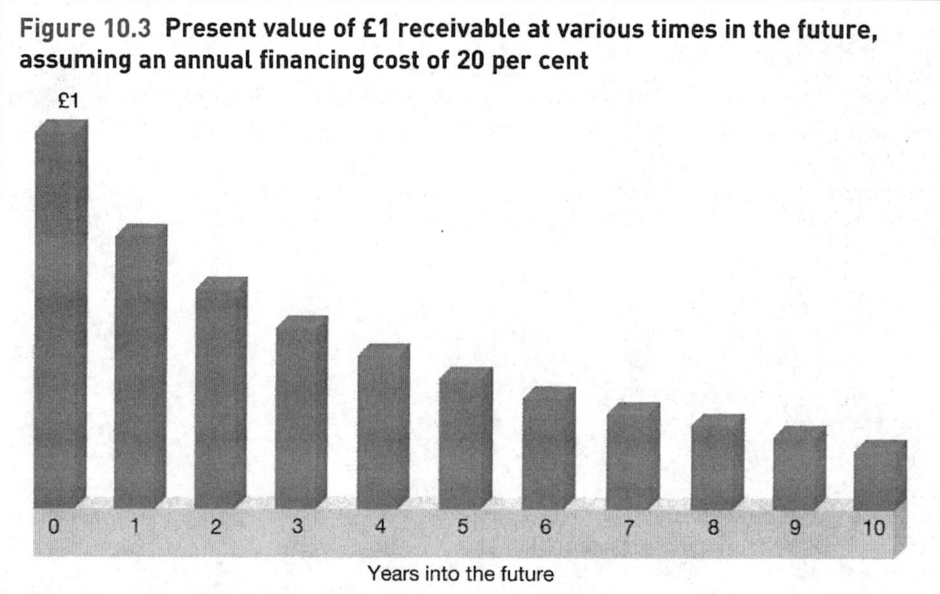

The present value of a future receipt (or payment) of £1 depends on how far in the future it will occur. Those that will occur in the near future will have a larger present value than those whose occurrence is more distant in time.

Why NPV is superior to ARR and PP

From what we have seen, NPV seems to be a better method of appraising investment opportunities than either ARR or PP. This is because it fully addresses each of the following issues:

- *The timing of the cash flows.* By discounting the various cash flows associated with each project according to when it is expected to arise, the fact that cash flows do not all occur simultaneously is taken into account by NPV. Associated with this is the fact that by discounting, using the opportunity cost of finance (that is, the return that the next best alternative opportunity would generate), the net benefit after financing costs have been met is identified (as the NPV of the project).
- *The whole of the relevant cash flows.* NPV includes all of the relevant cash flows, irrespective of when they are expected to occur. It treats them differently according to their date of occurrence, but they are all taken into account in the NPV, and they all have an influence on the decision.
- *The objectives of the business.* NPV is the only method of appraisal in which the output of the analysis has a direct bearing on the wealth of the business. (Positive NPVs enhance wealth; negative ones reduce it.) Since most private-sector businesses seek to maximise shareholders' wealth, NPV is superior to the methods previously discussed.

We saw earlier that a business should take on all projects with positive NPVs, when their cash flows are discounted at the opportunity cost of finance. Where a choice has to be made among projects, a business should normally select the one with the highest NPV.

Internal rate of return (IRR)

This is the last of the four major methods of investment appraisal that are found in practice. It is quite closely related to the NPV method in that, like NPV, it also involves discounting future cash flows. The **internal rate of return** of a particular investment is the discount rate that, when applied to its future cash flows, will produce an NPV of precisely zero. In essence, it represents the yield from the project.

We should recall that when we discounted the cash flows of the Billingsgate Battery Company machine investment opportunity at 20 per cent, we found that the NPV was a positive figure of £24,190 (see p. 298).

Activity 10.14

What does the NPV of the machine project (that is, £24,190 (positive)) tell us about the rate of return that the investment will yield for the business?

The fact that the NPV is positive when discounting at 20 per cent implies that the rate of return that the project generates is more than 20 per cent. The fact that the NPV is a pretty large figure implies that the actual rate of return is quite a lot above 20 per cent. We should expect increasing the size of the discount rate to reduce NPV, because a higher discount rate gives a lower discounted figure. Thus future inflows are more heavily discounted, which will reduce their impact on the NPV.

It is somewhat laborious to deduce the IRR by hand, since it cannot usually be calculated directly. Thus iteration (trial and error) is the only approach.

Let us try a higher rate and see what happens, say, 30 per cent:

Time	*Cash flow*	*Discount factor*	*PV*
	£000	*30%*	*£000*
Immediately (time 0)	(100)	1.000	(100.00)
1 year's time	20	0.769	15.38
2 years' time	40	0.592	23.68
3 years' time	60	0.455	27.30
4 years' time	60	0.350	21.00
5 years' time	20	0.269	5.38
5 years' time	20	0.269	5.38
			(1.88)

Figure 10.4 The relationship between the NPV and IRR methods

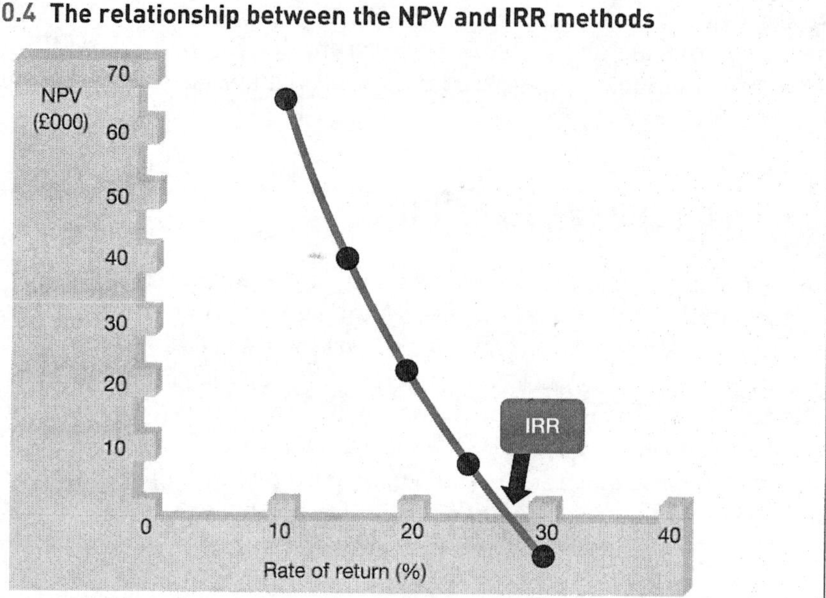

If the discount rate were zero, the NPV would be the sum of the net cash flows. In other words, no account would be taken of the time value of money. However, if we assume increasing discount rates, there is a corresponding decrease in the NPV of the project. When the NPV line crosses the horizontal axis there will be a zero NPV, and the point where it crosses is the IRR.

In increasing the discount rate from 20 per cent to 30 per cent, we have reduced the NPV from £24,190 (positive) to £1,880 (negative). Since the IRR is the discount rate that will give us an NPV of exactly zero, we can conclude that the IRR of Billingsgate Battery Company's machine project is very slightly below 30 per cent. Further trials could lead us to the exact rate, but there is probably not much point, given the likely inaccuracy of the cash flow estimates. It is probably good enough, for practical purposes, to say that the IRR is about 30 per cent.

The relationship between the NPV method discussed earlier and the IRR is shown graphically in Figure 10.4 using the information relating to the Billingsgate Battery Company.

We can see that, where the discount rate is zero, the NPV will be the sum of the net cash flows. In other words, no account is taken of the time value of money. However, as the discount rate increases there is a corresponding decrease in the NPV of the project. When the NPV line touches the horizontal axis there will be a zero NPV, and that will also represent the IRR.

Activity 10.15

What is the internal rate of return of the Chaotic Industries project from Activity 10.2? You should use the discount table at the end of this chapter. *Hint*: Remember that you already know the NPV of this project at 15 per cent.

Since we know (from a previous activity) that, at a 15 per cent discount rate, the NPV is a relatively large negative figure, our next trial is using a lower discount rate, say 10 per cent:

Time	*Cash flows*	*Discount factor*	*Present value*
	£000	*(10% – from the table)*	*£000*
Immediately	(150)	1.000	(150.00)
1 year's time	30	0.909	27.27
2 years' time	30	0.826	24.78
3 years' time	30	0.751	22.53
4 years' time	30	0.683	20.49
5 years' time	30	0.621	18.63
6 years' time	30	0.565	16.95
6 years' time	30	0.565	16.95
		Net present value	(2.40)

We can see that NPV increased by about £21,000 (£23,490 – £2,400) for a 5 per cent drop in the discount rate: that is, about £4,200 for each 1 per cent. We need to know the discount rate for a zero NPV: that is, a fall of a further £2,400. This logically would be roughly 0.6 per cent (that is, 2,400/4,200). Thus the IRR is close to 9.4 per cent. However, to say that the IRR is about 9 per cent is near enough for most purposes.

Users of the IRR approach should apply the following decision rules:

- For any project to be acceptable, it must meet a minimum IRR requirement. Logically, this minimum should be the opportunity cost of finance.
- Where there are competing projects (for example, the business can choose one of the projects only) the one with the higher or highest IRR would be selected.

IRR has certain attributes in common with NPV. All cash flows are taken into account, and their timing is logically handled. The main disadvantage with IRR is the fact that it does not address the question of wealth generation. It could therefore lead to the wrong decision being made. This is because IRR would, for example, always see a return of 25 per cent being preferable to a 20 per cent IRR, assuming an opportunity cost of finance of, say, 15 per cent. Though this may well lead to the project being taken that could most effectively increase wealth, this may not always be the case. This is because IRR completely ignores the *scale of investment*. With a 15 per cent cost of finance, £15 million invested at 20 per cent would make us richer than £5 million invested at 25 per cent. IRR does not recognise this. It should be acknowledged that it is not usual for projects to be competing where there is such a large difference in scale.

Even though the problem may be rare and, typically, IRR will give the same signal as NPV, a method (NPV) that is always reliable must be better to use than IRR.

A further problem with the IRR method is that it has difficulty handling projects with unconventional cash flows. In the examples studied so far, each project has a negative cash flow arising at the start of its life and then positive cash flows thereafter. However, in some cases, a project may have both positive and negative cash flows at future points in its life. Such a pattern of cash flows can result in the IRR method providing more than one solution, or even no solution at all.

Some practical points

When undertaking an investment appraisal, there are several practical points that we should bear in mind:

- *Relevant costs.* As with all decision making, we should only take account of cash flows that vary according to the decision in our analysis. Thus cash flows that will be the same, irrespective of the decision under review, should be ignored. For example, overheads that will be incurred in equal amount whether or not the investment is made should be ignored, despite the fact that the investment could not be made without the infrastructure that the overhead costs create. Similarly, past costs should be ignored as they are not affected by, and do not vary with, the decision.
- *Opportunity costs.* Opportunity costs arising from benefits foregone must be taken into account. Thus, for example, when considering a decision concerning whether or not to continue to use a machine already owned by the business, for producing a new product, the realisable value of the machine may be an important opportunity cost.
- *Taxation.* Tax will usually be affected by an investment decision. The profits will be taxed, the capital investment may attract tax relief, and so on. Tax is levied on these at significant rates. This means that, in real life, unless tax is formally taken into account, the wrong decision could easily be made.
- *Cash flows not profit flows.* We have seen that for the NPV, IRR and PP methods, it is cash flows rather than profit flows that are relevant to the evaluation of investment projects. In a problem requiring the application of any of these methods we may be given details of the profits for the investment period, and will be required to adjust these in order to derive the cash flows. Remember, the net profit before depreciation is an approximation to the cash flows for the period, and so we should work back to this figure.

  When the data are expressed in profit rather than cash flow terms, an adjustment in respect of working capital may also be necessary. Some adjustment should be made to take account of changes to working capital. For example, launching a new product may give rise to an increase in the net cash investment (or divestment) made in trade debtors, stock and creditors, requiring an immediate outlay of cash.

This outlay for additional working capital should be shown in the NPV calculations as part of the initial cost. However, the additional working capital will be released by the end of the life of the project, so the resulting inflow of cash at the end of the life of the project should also be taken into account.

- *Interest payments*. When using discounted cash flow techniques, interest payments should not be taken into account in deriving the cash flows for the period. The discount factor already takes account of the costs of financing, so to take account of interest charges in deriving cash flows for the period would be double counting.
- *Other factors*. Investment decision making must not be viewed as simply a mechanical exercise. The results derived from a particular investment appraisal method will be only one input to the decision-making process. There may be broader issues connected to the decision that have to be taken into account, but which may be difficult or impossible to quantify. The reliability of the forecasts and the validity of the assumptions used in the evaluation will also have a bearing on the final decision.

Activity 10.16

The directors of Manuff (Steel) Ltd have decided to close one of its factories. There has been a reduction in the demand for the products made at the factory in recent years, and the directors are not optimistic about the long-term prospects for these products. The factory is situated in the north of England, in an area where unemployment is high.

The factory is leased, and there are still four years of the lease remaining. The directors are uncertain as to whether the factory should be closed immediately or at the end of the period of the lease. Another business has offered to sublease the premises from Manuff at a rental of £40,000 a year for the remainder of the lease period.

The machinery and equipment at the factory cost £1,500,000, and have a balance sheet value of £400,000. In the event of immediate closure, the machinery and equipment could be sold for £220,000. The working capital at the factory is £420,000, and could be liquidated for that amount immediately, if required. Alternatively, the working capital can be liquidated in full at the end of the lease period. Immediate closure would result in redundancy payments to employees of £180,000.

If the factory continues in operation until the end of the lease period, the following operating profits (losses) are expected:

	Year 1	*Year 2*	*Year 3*	*Year 4*
	£000	*£000*	*£000*	*£000*
Operating profit (loss)	160	(40)	30	20

The above figures include a charge of £90,000 per year for depreciation of machinery and equipment. The residual value of the machinery and equipment at the end of the lease period is estimated at £40,000.

Redundancy payments are expected to be £150,000 at the end of the lease period if the factory continues in operation. The business has an annual cost of capital of 12 per cent. Ignore taxation.

Activity 10.16 continued

Required:

(a) Calculate the relevant cash flows arising from a decision to continue operations until the end of the lease period rather than to close immediately.

(b) Calculate the net present value of continuing operations until the end of the lease period, rather than closing immediately.

(c) What other factors might the directors take into account before making a final decision on the timing of the factory closure?

(d) State, with reasons, whether or not the business should continue to operate the factory until the end of the lease period.

Your answer to this activity should be as follows:

(a) **Relevant cash flows**

			Years		
	0	*1*	*2*	*3*	*4*
	£000	*£000*	*£000*	*£000*	*£000*
Operating cash flows (Note 1)		250	50	120	110
Sale of machinery (Note 2)	(220)				40
Redundancy costs (Note 3)	180				(150)
Sublease rentals (Note 4)		(40)	(40)	(40)	(40)
Working capital invested (Note 5)	(420)				420
	(460)	210	10	80	380

Notes:

1 Each year's operating cash flows are calculated by adding back the depreciation charge for the year to the operating profit for the year. In the case of the operating loss, the depreciation charge is deducted.

2 In the event of closure, machinery could be sold immediately. Thus an opportunity cost of £220,000 is incurred if operations continue.

3 By continuing operations, there will be a saving in immediate redundancy costs of £180,000. However, redundancy costs of £150,000 will be paid in four years' time.

4 By continuing operations, the opportunity to sublease the factory will be foregone.

5 Immediate closure would mean that working capital could be liquidated. By continuing operations this opportunity is foregone. However, working capital can be liquidated in four years' time.

(b)					
Discount rate 12 per cent	1.000	0.893	0.797	0.712	0.636
Present value	(460)	187.5	8.0	57.0	241.7
Net present value	34.2				

(c) Other factors that may influence the decision include:

- *The overall strategy of the business.* The business may need to set the decision within a broader context. It may be necessary to manufacture the products made at the factory because they are an integral part of the business's product range. The business may wish to avoid redundancies in an area of high unemployment for as long as possible.

Activity 10.16 continued

- *Flexibility*. A decision to close the factory is probably irreversible. If the factory continues, however, there may be a chance that the prospects for the factory will brighten in the future.
- *Creditworthiness of sublessee*. The business should investigate the creditworthiness of the sublessee. Failure to receive the expected sublease payments would make the closure option far less attractive.
- *Accuracy of forecasts*. The forecasts made by the business should be examined carefully. Inaccuracies in the forecasts or any underlying assumptions may change the expected outcomes.

(d) The NPV of the decision to continue operations rather than close immediately is positive. Hence, shareholders would be better off if the directors took this course of action. The factory should therefore continue in operation rather than close down. This decision is likely to be welcomed by employees, as unemployment is high in the area.

? Self-assessment question 10.1

Beacon Chemicals plc is considering buying some equipment to produce a chemical named X14. The new equipment's capital cost is estimated at £100,000, and if its purchase is approved now, the equipment can be bought and commence production by the end of this year. £50,000 has already been spent on research and development work. Estimates of revenues and costs arising from the operation of the new equipment appear below:

	Year 1	*Year 2*	*Year 3*	*Year 4*	*Year 5*
Sales price (£ per unit)	100	120	120	100	80
Sales volume (units)	800	1,000	1,200	1,000	800
Variable costs (£ per unit)	50	50	40	30	40
Fixed costs (£000)	30	30	30	30	30

If the equipment is bought, sales of some existing products will be lost, and this will result in a loss of contribution of £15,000 a year over its life.

The accountant has informed you that the fixed costs include depreciation of £20,000 a year on the new equipment. They also include an allocation of £10,000 for fixed overheads. A separate study has indicated that if the new equipment were bought, additional overheads, excluding depreciation, arising from producing the chemical would be £8,000 a year. Production would require additional working capital of £30,000.

For the purposes of your initial calculations ignore taxation.

Required:

(a) Deduce the relevant annual cash flows associated with buying the equipment.
(b) Deduce the payback period.
(c) Calculate the net present value using a discount rate of 8 per cent.

Hint: You should deal with the investment in working capital by treating it as a cash outflow at the start of the project and an inflow at the end.

Suggested Answers to Text Questions for Topics 2, 3, 4 and 6

The profit and loss account (Chapter 4)

1. Accounting period.
2. Income and expenditure account.
3. The accounting concepts, accounting standards, and relevant legislation.
4. The correct answer is (a).
   Directors' fees and debenture interest should have already been deducted in computing the net profit or loss. They are considered to be charges which should be dealt with in the profit and loss account. They are **not** considered to be appropriations.
5.

	£000	£000
Sales		150
Less **Cost of sales**		
Opening stock	12	
Add Purchases	100	
	112	
Less Closing stock	18	94
Gross profit (or gross margin)		56

(The cost of sales is £94,000.)

6. A manufacturing account.

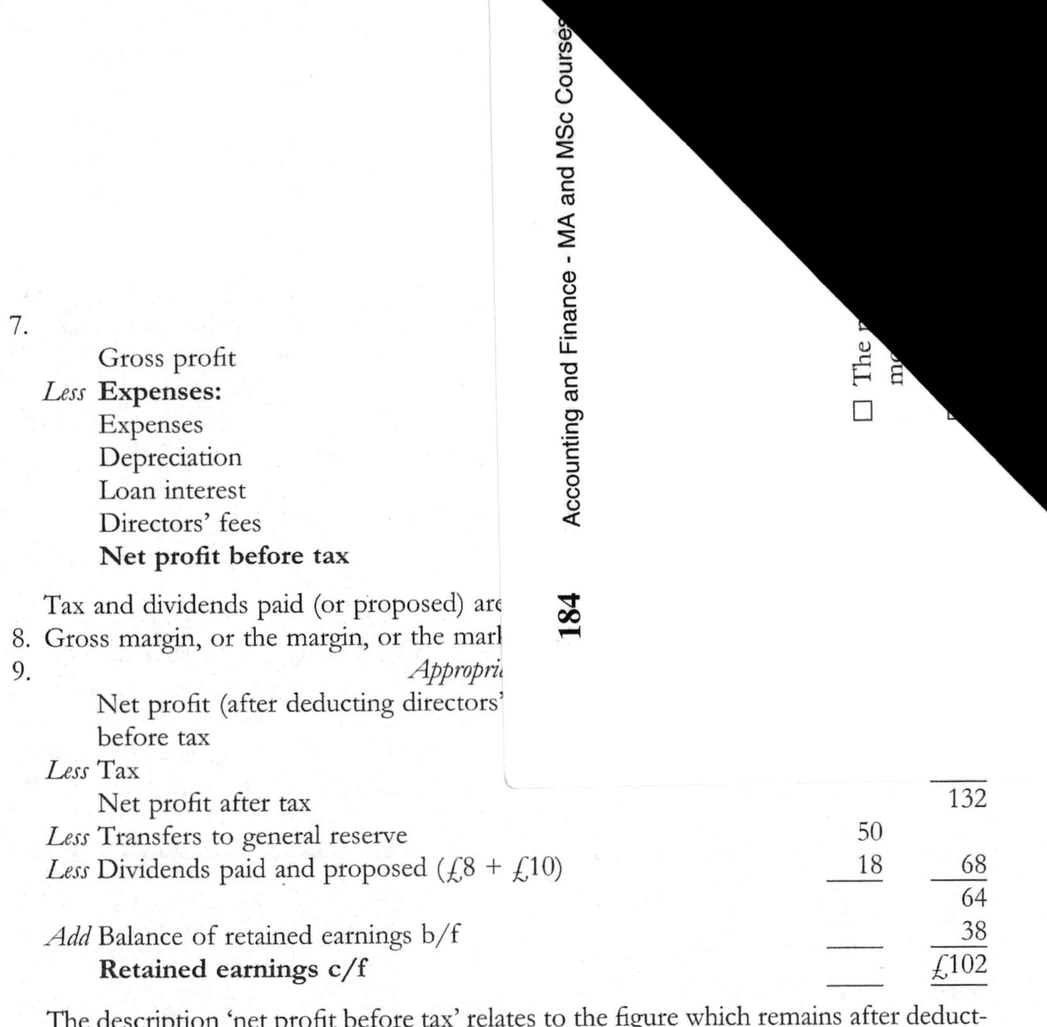

7.

Gross profit
Less **Expenses:**
Expenses
Depreciation
Loan interest
Directors' fees
Net profit before tax

Tax and dividends paid (or proposed) ar

8. Gross margin, or the margin, or the mar

9. *Appropri*

Net profit (after deducting directors' before tax		
Less Tax		
Net profit after tax		132
Less Transfers to general reserve	50	
Less Dividends paid and proposed (£8 + £10)	18	68
		64
Add Balance of retained earnings b/f		38
Retained earnings c/f		£102

The description 'net profit before tax' relates to the figure which remains after deducting all of the relevant expenses for the period, including the directors' fees and loan interest, i.e. before appropriations.

10. P&L account balance and ploughed-back profits.
You may come across other descriptions, such as undistributed profits or unappropriated profits.

The balance sheet 1 (Chapter 5)

1. (a) statement
   (b) capital = assets less liabilities
   (c) has come from
   has gone to
   (d) as at
   frozen
2. Any three limitations from the following:
   - ☐ The photograph, i.e. it only shows the position at a particular point in time.
   - ☐ The materiality concept could mean that certain fixed assets which are low in value may simply be charged as an expense (written off) in the profit and loss account, and will not, therefore, appear in the balance sheet.
   - ☐ The cost concept. It shows many of the assets at their historic cost or cost less depreciation. These book values can be significantly different from their re-sale values.

…money measurement concept. Important factors which cannot be measured in monetary terms are not shown in a balance sheet, for example morale, industrial relations, etc.

- ☐ Window dressing (creative accounting) may be responsible for the production of figures which are totally unrepresentative of the situation which existed throughout the year.

3. The £400,000 is simply the historic cost of the equipment less the depreciation. This value, i.e. the book value, may be way out of line with the amount which could be received if the equipment were sold.
4. The stock figure shown in the balance sheet could have been subjected to window dressing. It could have been allowed to run down to a level which is so low, that it is not a true representation of the position which existed throughout the accounting period.

   Note that the debtors and creditors could have also been subject to window dressing, for example, by understating or overstating them (when compared with their levels throughout the accounting period). This could significantly affect the picture portrayed by the accounts.
5. The concepts mentioned in the chapter which affect the figures which are disclosed in a balance sheet, were:
   - materiality;
   - the money measurement concept;
   - the cost concept.

The balance sheet 2 (Chapter 5)

1. Capital represents an amount owing to whosoever invested it in the business, e.g. the shareholders.
2. Ordinary share capital *plus* reserves *plus* long-term debt (long-term liabilities) equals the capital employed.

   Note that some writers also include the current liabilities in their definition of capital employed.
3. Long-term debt (or long-term liability).

   Note, however, that if debentures or long-term loans are to be repaid within the next twelve months they would be shown as a current liability.
4. The authorized share capital should be shown as a note on the face of the balance sheet. It is there for reference/information purposes. It is not added to the issued share capital.
5. The ordinary shares.

   Note, however, that companies sometimes issue 'A' ordinary shares which do not have voting rights, and preference shareholders may have voting rights if their dividends are in arrear. The class rights do vary and to find out exactly what they are you must refer to the company's Memorandum and Articles of Association.
6. The ordinary shareholders. They are paid out last if their company has to be wound up.
7. The preference shares receive a fixed dividend.

Note, however, that some preference shares may also have a right to participate in a distribution of profits (participating preference shares).

8. The nominal value of a share may also be referred to as the par value or the face value.
9. Share premium.

   Note that it is shown as a reserve in the balance sheet. It tends to be described as being a statutory reserve, because its use in the United Kingdom is governed/ restricted by company law.
10. Revenue reserves represent ploughed-back profits, i.e. retained or undistributed profits, which have accumulated since the formation of the company.
11. Revenue reserves are shown as liabilities because they are in effect amounts owing to the ordinary shareholders. They comprise amounts earned which could have been distributed to the ordinary shareholders.
12. The equity shareholders' interest in a company consists of the issued ordinary share capital paid up *plus* all the reserves, i.e. both capital and revenue reserves.
13. Long-term debts consist of long-term loans, debentures and, if appropriate, the bank overdraft.
14. No, it is sometimes used as a long-term source of funds. For example, £5m secured on the fixed assets of a small company, which the company does not intend to repay for some considerable time, is perhaps better classified as long-term debt. It is most certainly not a current liability, which is a point worthy of further debate.
15. Fixed assets (and leasehold property) which we buy outright are shown in the balance sheet. Those which are rented are simply treated as an expense of the accounting period to which they relate, i.e. the rent is charged as an expense in the profit and loss account.
16. Working capital equals current assets less current liabilities.

    Note that it is sometimes described as the circulating capital of the business.
17. Current liabilities.

    Note that the dividend proposed is an amount owing to the shareholders which will be paid within, say, the next six months.
18. A prepaid expense will be shown as a current asset.

    Note that it is, in fact, a type of deferred expense, i.e. something that was paid out during the current period, the benefit of which extends into the next accounting period.
19. Calls are instalments of the balance of the amount owing from ordinary shareholders to the company on the shares which they hold. For example, £1 shares issued for £2.40, payable £1 now, the balance by two instalments of 70p each. Until the first of the 70p instalments is received the amount paid up is £1 per share and the calls amount to £1.40 per share. All of the calls received will be classed as share premium i.e. £1.40 per share in excess of the normal (or par) value.
20. Capital reserves may be caused by:
    - share premium;
    - a revaluation of fixed assets;
    - the acquisition of shares in a subsidiary company;
    - the redemption of own shares.

Festiclyn plc (Chapter 6)

CASH FLOW STATEMENT FOR THE YEAR ENDED (FRS 1)
31 DECEMBER 20X8

		£000	£000
Net cash flow from operating activities	(W1)		77
Returns on investments, and the servicing of finance			
Dividends received		—	
Dividends paid	(W2)	(16)	
Interest paid	(given)	(5)	(21)
			56
Taxation			
Tax paid	(W3)		(58)
			(2)
Investing activities			
Purchase of tangible fixed assets	(W4)	(97)	
Sale of tangible fixed assets	(W5)	17	
Proceeds from sale of trade investments		—	(80)
			(82)
Financing			
Proceeds from new ordinary share capital (350 – 200)		150	
New bank loan		60	
Repayment of preference shares		(120)	90
Increase in cash and cash equivalents (19 – 11)			8

Workings

Festiclyn plc

W1 The net cash flow from operating activities:

	£000	£000
Net profit before tax (given)		109
Add loan interest (given)		5
= Net profit before interest and tax		114
Plus Depreciation (W4)	18	
Loss on sale of plant (W5)	3	21
Less		135
Increase in stock	(54)	
Increase in debtors	(8)	
Increase in creditors	4	
		(58)
		77

W2 Dividends paid:	£000
20X7 b/f	16
Add appropriation	22
	38
Less 20X8 c/f	22
Paid	16

W3 Tax paid:	£000
20X7 b/f	64
Add appropriation	72
	136
Less 20X8 c/f	78
Paid	58

W4 New plant and machinery purchased and the depreciation charge:

	Cost	Depreciation
	£000	£000
20X7 b/f	490	76
Less asset sold	24	4
Balance 20X8 c/f (excluding new P&M)	466	72
20X8 c/f (including new P&M)	563	90
NEW PLANT & MACHINERY	= 97	= 18

W5 Sale of plant and machinery

	£000	£000
Sale proceeds		17
Less Cost of plant sold	24	
Less depreciation to date	4	20
LOSS ON SALE		(3)

Woodcroft plc (Chapter 7)

Ratio analysis work sheet

Ratio	20X7	20X8	Brief comments
Liquidity:			
Current ratio			
$\frac{500}{400}:\frac{520}{380}$	1.25	1.37	Slight improvement. However could be on the low side when compared to industry figures.
Acid test (quick ratio)			
$\frac{300}{400}:\frac{340}{380}$	0.75	0.90	Improved in 20X8 to possibly around the industry average.

Ratio	20X7	20X8	Brief comments
Profitability:			
Net profit to sales			
$\frac{120}{1200} \times 100 : \frac{180}{1600} \times 100$	10%	11.25%	Better margins, better control of overhead expenses = a better performance in 20X8.
Return on investment (return on assets)			
$\frac{120}{200} \times 100 : \frac{180}{260} \times 100$	60%	69.24%	Looks like a very good return indeed. Especially when compared to investing in a bank or building society.
Efficiency:			
Average collection period			
$\frac{260 + 300}{2} = \frac{280}{1200} \times 365$: $\frac{300 + 340}{2} = \frac{320}{1600} \times 365$	86 days	73 days	An improvement in 20X8 in the credit control, i.e. collecting debts more speedily. However, if the industry average is say 60 days there is room for improvement.
Credit period taken			
$\frac{120 + 160}{2} = \frac{140}{1200} \times 365$: $\frac{160 + 180}{2} = \frac{170}{1600} \times 365$	43 days	39 days	Could be in the habit of paying off creditors too quickly. Many companies may take around 60 days or longer to pay their debts. They are paying the debts they owe in about half the time they allow their customers!
(The purchases figure was not available so the sales figure was used.)			
Stock turnover			
$\frac{160 + 200}{2} = 180$ Average stock $\frac{200 + 180}{2} = 190$ Average stock			Rate improved in 20X8 due to carrying a lower level of stock even though sales volume had increased.
$\frac{1200}{180} : \frac{1600}{190}$	6.67 times	8.43 times	

Ratio	20X7	20X8	Brief comments
Investment:			
Earnings/shareholders' equity $\frac{80}{200} \times 100 : \frac{130}{260} \times 100$	40%	50%	Looks like a high return.
Dividend cover $\frac{80}{60} : \frac{130}{70}$	1.34	1.86	Improving, but high payout could be a problem if the company has a bad year.
Earnings per ordinary share (EPS) $\frac{80}{100} : \frac{130}{100}$	0.80	1.30	A high rate of return.

Points to note (not part of the answer)

Without industry figures, it is quite difficult to make sound judgements. However, reasonable comments can be made by using the following general rules:

- ☐ The current ratio ought to be around 2.00.
- ☐ The acid test, ought to be around 1.00, i.e. one to one.
- ☐ The average collection period and period of credit ought to be around 60 days, which is quite typical.
- ☐ The profitability ratios can be compared to the cost of borrowing and/or the interest rates paid by banks and building societies.
- ☐ However, remember that ordinary shareholders received a two-fold return:
  - The earnings on their shares, some of which may be distributed to them as dividends, with the remainder being retained within the company, i.e. reinvested in the company.
  - The capital growth (or capital loss) on the shares which they hold.

However, to calculate just what return they are really getting is a difficult task, because of the fluctuations in share prices.

Nether Ltd and Thong Ltd (Chapter 7)

Ratio analysis work sheet for year 20X8

Ratio	Nether Ltd	Thong Ltd	Industry average	Comments
Liquidity:				
Current ratio				
$\frac{60}{40}:\frac{90}{60}$	1.5	1.5	2.00	Both below industry average, indicating possible liquidity problems.
Acid test (quick ratio)				
$\frac{60-25}{40}:\frac{90-60}{60}$	0.88	0.50	0.90	Thong Ltd does have liquidity problems, i.e. only 50p worth of liquid assets for every £1 owing in current liabilities.
Profitability:				
Net profit before tax to sales				
$\frac{25}{125}\times 100:\frac{40}{250}\times 100$	20%	16%	20%	Thong Ltd has a lower than average net profit margin. Possibly using the lower margin to attract a higher volume of sales.
Return on investment (return on assets)				
$\frac{25}{120}\times 100:$ $\frac{40}{150}\times 100$	20.84%	26.67%	24%	Thong Ltd making more efficient use of its capital, i.e. making a better return on investment.
Efficiency:				
Average collection period				
$\frac{20}{125}\times 365:\frac{30}{250}\times 365$	59 days	44 days	60 days	Thong Ltd collecting its debts more quickly, i.e. more efficient credit control. Probably because it is desperate for the cash.
(No average available – current year's figures used.)				
Credit period taken				
$\frac{40}{125}\times 365:\frac{35}{250}\times 365$	117 days	52 days	70 days	Nether Ltd taking too long to pay its creditors and Thong Ltd paying them too quickly. They are a source of short-term finance.

Ratio	Nether Ltd	Thong Ltd	Industry average	Comments
(The purchases figure was not available so the sales figure had to be used; also no average available so current year's figures used.)				
Stock turnover				
$\frac{125}{25}:\frac{250}{60}$	5 times	4.17 times	7 times	Both on the low side possibly because they could be carrying too high levels of stock. Indicates the need for better inventory control.
Investment:				
Earnings/shareholders' equity				
$\frac{20}{120}\times 100:\frac{32}{150}\times 100$	16.67%	21.34%	20%	Nether Ltd not performing too well on these measures. This could have an effect on its share price.
Earnings per ordinary share				
$\frac{20}{100}:\frac{32}{100}$	0.20	0.32	£0.30	

The stock turnover position for both companies suggests that stocks are moving too slowly through each company and that they may be carrying stock levels which are too high. This means that capital which could be available for other purposes is being tied up in stocks of raw materials, fuels, finished goods and work-in-progress.

It is recommended that the companies could adopt the following courses of action to improve their performance:

	Nether Ltd	Thong Ltd
Liquidity and efficiency	Reduce the stock level.	Reduce the stock level.
	(i.e. both to improve their inventory management, e.g. concentrate on reducing slow-moving, low-margin lines)	
	Improve credit control (if Thong Ltd can do it, why can't Nether Ltd?).	Try to keep the credit control at this level, provided it does not involve giving hefty cash discounts for prompt payment.
	Reduce the time taken in paying creditors to around the industry average.	Take a little longer time to pay creditors, unless this means the loss of generous cash discounts for prompt payment.

	Nether Ltd	Thong Ltd
Profitability and investment	Manage overheads more efficiently and increase gross margins (if possible).	Manage overheads more efficiently and improve gross margins (if possible).

Conclusions and recommendations

Nether Ltd is performing better than Thong Ltd when it comes to liquidity. However, Nether Ltd could experience some difficulty in meeting its obligations as they arise because it is working at a level which is below the industry average. Thong Ltd does have quite serious liquidity problems, as indicated by the acid test ratio. It has only 50p's worth of liquid assets for every £1 it owes to its current liabilities.

It would appear that Thong Ltd is achieving its higher volume of sales by working on a lower net profit to sales margin. Thong Ltd's profitability and investment performance are superior to Nether Ltd's, i.e. it is getting better returns on its capital employed and better returns for its shareholders.

Thong's very good performance on the average collection period is an indication that it has an efficient and effective system of credit control. However, when it comes to the period of credit taken from creditors, the figure (52 days) suggests that it could be paying its creditors too promptly. Nether Ltd appears to be taking far too long to pay its creditors, i.e. 117 days, compared to an industry average of 70 days. Thus, there is a possibility that creditors who feel that they are having to wait too long may take them to court. This could damage the company's reputation in the market place.

Comment (not part of the answer): You should be able to observe from your study of the figures that profitability and liquidity do not go hand in hand. Although Thong Ltd is the more profitable, it does have liquidity problems.

Even where a ratio is satisfactory, i.e. around the industry average, this is no reason for inaction. If action can be taken to improve the performance, then it should be.

The problems of interfirm comparison (Chapter 7)

A comparison of the textile companies listed is difficult because:

- Some of them may be highly diversified and others may not be.
- Their product ranges could be significantly different.
- Of the way in which the source data were arrived at, e.g. the application of the accounting concepts.

- Of off-balance-sheet financing, e.g. some companies may be renting some of their plant, machinery and equipment.
- Their year ends are different, i.e. the comparison does not cover the same accounting period/trading conditions!
- As indicated by the turnover, the companies are different in size.
- Some companies may have had certain fixed assets revalued, e.g. buildings recently, years ago, or never!
- Some could be highly automated and others more labour intensive.
- The net profit could be affected by location, e.g. the overheads of a company in South-East England compared to a company in North Wales could be significantly different.
- The stock figures of certain companies could have been affected by window dressing (creative accounting), e.g. run down to a very low year-end level. This would enable them to show a higher rate of stock turnover.

Suggested Answers to Text Questions for Topics 7, 8, 9 and 10

APPENDIX 1

Suggested answers to self-assessment questions

Self-assessment 4.1: Throngfirth Manufacturing

See Table A.1.1 for answer to Question 1.
See Table A.1.2 for answers to Questions 2 and 3.

Points to note (not part of the answer)

Relating to Tables A.1.1 and A.1.2.

- ☐ First, notice that we have lumped together those overheads which are shared out according to the same method of apportionment, e.g. buildings insurance and lighting are both shared out according to floor area.
- ☐ The total column provides a cross-add which acts as a check on the arithmetic accuracy of the figures.
- ☐ We have used the word 'allocate' to mean an overhead which can be directly associated with a department/cost centre, and 'apportionment' to denote those overheads which cannot be identified with a specific department/cost centre. You should note that other authors do not attempt to draw such a fine distinction between these words.
- ☐ Also, even though we know the direct labour hours for the machine department, we do not use them to work out the overhead absorption rate. Why? Because the machine department overheads are being recovered using a rate per machine hour.
- ☐ Again, note that we use the 15 machine hours to compute the machine department overheads applicable to product PQ.
- ☐ Finally, when you select a basis of apportionment, e.g. floor area, you have to select the basis which is most appropriate for sharing out the particular item of overhead expenditure concerned.

Table A.1.1 Throngfirth Manufacturing: departmental overhead summary/analysis

Overheads	Total	Production departments Machine	Paint	Assembly	Service departments Stores	Power
	£	£	£	£	£	£
Indirect materials & labour (allocated)	91,700	36,730	11,270	11,900	16,680	15,120
Fuel (allocated)	74,000	–	–	–	–	74,000
Buildings insurance & lighting (floor area)	9,600	4,800 (8/16)	1,200 (2/16)	2,400 (4/16)	600 (1/16)	600 (1/16)
Supervision & canteen (No. of employees)	43,200	12,960 (6/20)	4,320 (2/20)	17,280 (8/20)	4,320 (2/20)	4,320 (2/20)
Machinery insurance (value of machines)	4,800	2,880 (3/5)	960 (1/5)	–	–	960 (1/5)
Depreciation (allocated)	25,700	12,400	6,300	2,100	1,400	3,500
	249,000	69,770	24,050	33,680	23,000	98,500
Stores (technical estimates)		5,750	5,750	9,200	–23,000	2,300
						100,800
Power (technical estimates)		60,480	25,200	15,120		–100,800
	£249,000	£136,000	£55,000	£58,000		
Overhead absorption rates						
Machine hours		20,000 = £6.80				
Direct labour hours			5,000 = £11.00	8,000 = £7.25		

Table A.1.2 Throngfirth Manufacturing: calculation of the proposed selling price of product PQ

		£	£
Direct materials			1,277
Direct labour			
(4 hrs × £9)	Machine dept	36	
(3 hrs × £8)	Paint dept	24	
(16 hrs × £7)	Assembly dept	112	172
Overheads			
(15 hrs × £6.80)	Machine dept	102	
(3 hrs × £11)	Paint dept	33	
(16 hrs × £7.25)	Assembly dept	116	251
	Product cost		1,700
add Mark-up (40% × £1,700) =			680
	Proposed selling price		2,380

Self-assessment 5.2: Pawilkes & Co. Ltd

Activity cost pools

Dept 1 (£000)	Dept 2 (£000)	Setting-up (£000)	Computing (£000)	Purchasing (£000)	Total (£000)
680	410	40	200	100	1430
Cost drivers (000)					
340 Machine hrs	410 Direct lab. hrs	10 Set-ups	40 Computer hrs	50 Orders	
£2 per machine hour	£1 per direct lab. hr	£4 per set-up	£5 per computer hour	£2 per order	

Activity-based costing profit statement

	Product D		Product E	
Sales/production (units) (£000)	200,000		120,000	
	£	£	£	£
Sales		2,400		3,360
Less prime cost		1,600		2,160
		800		1,200
Cost pools:				
Dept. 1 @ £2 per machine hour	200		480	
Dept. 2 @ £1 per direct lab. hour	50		360	
Setting up @ £4 per set-up	24		16	
Computing @ £5 per computer hour	100		100	
Purchasing @ £2 per order	80	454	20	976
Profit		346		224

Total profit = £570,000

Self-assessment 6.1: Heaton Postex plc

See Table A.1.3 for the answer to Question 1.

See Table A.1.4 for Question 2.

The contribution needed to produce a profit of £796 in Table A.1.3 would be as shown in Table A.1.5 (Question 3).

The answer to Question 4 is in Table A.1.6.

Table A.1.3 Heaton Postex plc: marginal costing statement

		Current position 20X8		Next year 20X9	
		Per unit	40,000 units	Per unit	50,000 units
		£	£000	£	£000
	Selling price	120	4,800	125	6,250
less	variable cost	96	3,840	100	5,000
	Contribution	24	960	25(20%)	1,250
	(Proof £24 × 40,000)			(proof £25 × 50,000)	
less	Fixed costs		164		186
	Profit		796		1,064

Table A.1.4 Heaton Postex plc: breakeven points

	20X8 £000		20X9 £000
Fixed costs	164		186
Profit volume ratio (as above)	20%		20%
Breakeven point	£000		£000
(Fixed cost ÷ PV ratio) =	820	=	930

Table A.1.5 Heaton Postex plc: sales needed to achieve profit target

		£000
	Fixed costs 20X9	186
add	Profit	796
	Contribution required	982

The number of units which must be sold to produce the contribution required is therefore

$$\frac{\text{contribution required}}{\text{contribution per unit}} = \frac{£982{,}000}{£25} = 39{,}280 \text{ units}$$

This has a sales value of 39,280 units × £125 = £000 4,910 (Question 3)

Table A.1.6 Heaton Postex plc: amount available for additional fixed costs

		£000
The total contribution from the sale of 56,000 units @ £25 per unit would be		1,400
	£000	
less Fixed costs	186	
Profit target	1,200	1,386
Amount available for additional fixed costs		14

Points to note (not part of the answer)

Relating to Tables A.1.3 to A.1.6 inclusive.

- ☐ Good layout and presentation should make the information produced more understandable.
- ☐ The contributions in (1) of £960,000 and £1,250,000 and (4) of £1,400,000 could be calculated quickly by multiplying the units sold by the contribution per unit.
- ☐ The profit volume ratio, i.e. the contribution as a percentage of sales, can be used to calculate the breakeven point. However, other methods are quite acceptable.

- ☐ Both parts (3) and (4) involve the use of the technique designed to help with profit target problems, i.e. the knowledge that the contribution required equals the fixed costs plus the profit target.
- ☐ In (4) a comparison is made between the contribution which is expected to be generated and the contribution which is needed to cover fixed costs and the profit target, the difference being the amount which is available to spend on additional fixed costs.

Self-assessment 6.2: Scoubado Manufacturing

See Tables A.1.7 and A.1.8.

The ranking in terms of the highest contribution per hour is:

1. L up to 60 units £60.
2. J up to 30 units £50.
3. J over 30 units £44.
4. K up to 24 units £32.
5. L over 60 units £30.
6. K over 24 units £28.

The maximum contribution per day is as shown in Table A.1.9.

Points to note (not part of the answer)

- ☐ The reductions in the selling prices for J, K and L respectively are matched by a reduction in their contribution per unit of the same amount.
- ☐ The key factor (limiting factor) in this problem was the productive time available.
- ☐ The above solution therefore answered the question, 'Which combination of products will maximize the contribution per day if there are only 42 hours of production time available?'

Table A.1.7 Scoubado Manufacturing: marginal costing/limiting factor analysis (first output level)

Output level (first)	J up to 30 units £	K up to 24 units £	L up to 60 units £
Selling price	75	108	59
less Variable cost	50	84	39
Contribution	25	24	20
Production per hour (units)	×	×	×
	2	1.33	3
	=	=	=
Contribution per hour	£50	£32	£60

Table A.1.8 Scoubado Manufacturing: marginal costing/limiting factor analysis (second output level)

Output level (second)	J over 30 units £	K over 24 units £	L over 60 units £
Selling price	72	105	49
less Variable cost	50	84	39
Contribution	£22	£21	£10
Production per hour (units)	× 2 =	× 1.33 =	× 3 =
Contribution per hour	£44	£28	£30

Table A.1.9 Scoubado Manufacturing: maximum contribution per day

Product	Quantity	Time per unit	Total time (hours)	Contribution per hour	Total
	units	mins		£	£
L	60	20	20	60	1,200
J	30	30	15	50	750
			35		
J	14	30	7	44	308
			42 hours		2,258

- ☐ When the total hours needed reached 35 hours, the final question which had to be answered was, 'With the seven hours left and using the third ranked contribution, how many units can be produced?' (Seven hours at half an hour per unit = 14 units.)

Self-assessment 6.3: Holme Honley Products plc

The breakeven chart (Question 1) is shown in Figure A.1.1, which also indicates the margin of safety. Table A.1.10 answers Question 2.

Points to note (not part of the answer)

- ☐ The horizontal scale of the breakeven chart can be expressed in terms of output or level of activity.
- ☐ The breakeven point can be worked out mathematically, in terms of value and output/ level of activity.
- ☐ To read off the position for a particular level of activity from the breakeven chart, all you have to do is project a vertical line upwards (e.g. at 60%) to see where it crosses the fixed cost line, the total cost line and the sales line. The gap between the £1,800 total cost and the sales revenue of £1,500 represents the loss of £300.

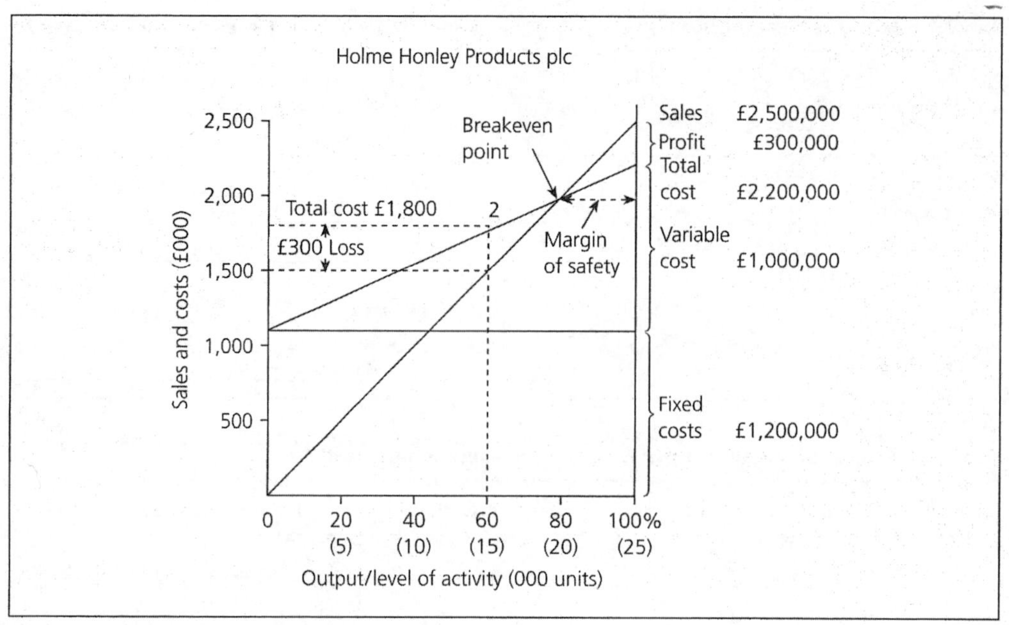

Figure A.1.1 Holme Honley Products plc: breakeven chart

Table A.1.10 Holme Honley Products plc: calculation of the breakeven point

		Per unit £		25,000 units £000		15,000 units £000
	Selling price	100		2,500		1,500
less	Variable cost	40		1,000		600
	Contribution	60	(60% PV ratio)	1,500		900
less	Fixed costs			1,200		1,200
		Profit		300	(Loss)	(300)

Breakeven point (£000)

= fixed cost ÷ PV ratio

$$= £1{,}200 \times \frac{100}{60} = £2{,}000$$

Breakeven point (in 000 units)

$$= \frac{\text{fixed cost}}{\text{contribution per unit}} = \frac{£1{,}200}{£60} = 20$$

Self-assessment 7.1: Budgetary control self-check

Budget

A budget has been defined by the CIMA (The Chartered Institute of Management Accountants) as:

> A plan expressed in money. It is prepared and approved prior to the budget period and may show income, expenditure, and the capital to be employed. May be drawn up showing incremental effects on former budgeted or actual figures, or be compiled by zero base budgeting.

Additional notes

You should note that a budget can be prepared in terms of quantity and/or value. For example, in practice, the production budget will first of all be drawn up in terms of quantity only. When it is clear that it coheres with the other budgets, e.g. sales, material requirements, labour requirements, etc., it will then be costed.

The keywords which you could have included in your own definition could include the following:

- ☐ It needs to be *predetermined/prepared in advance* of the period to which it relates.
- ☐ It aims at achieving specific *objectives.*
- ☐ It lays down the *policy* to be followed so that the objectives can be attained.
- ☐ In addition to budgeting income and expenditure it can also be used to budget the capital employed.

Budgetary control

Budgetary control has been defined by CIMA as:

> The establishment of budgets relating the responsibilities of executives to the requirements of a policy, and by continuous comparison of actual with budgeted results, either to secure by individual action the objectives of that policy or to provide a basis for its revision.

Additional notes

The keywords which you should have included in your definition are as follows:

- ☐ *Control by responsibility.*
- ☐ The *policy* to be followed.
- ☐ The *continuous comparison* of actual/budgeted figures, i.e. monitor at frequent intervals.
- ☐ *Management action* relating to the significant adverse variances, i.e. *management by exception.*
- ☐ The *attainment of the objectives.*
- ☐ The *revision* of the budget, if necessary, e.g. where basic assumptions change.

For both budgets and budgetary control you could also include:

- ☐ The involvement/participation of certain employees, e.g. supervisors.
- ☐ A common-sense approach, e.g. the setting of realistic and attainable targets.
- ☐ Consideration of the interrelationships between budgets.
- ☐ The importance of taking behavioural factors into account.

The principal budget factor

The principal budget factor (also known as the 'key factor' or 'limiting factor') is the factor which must be taken into account first when budgeting, because it places a constraint upon the activities of a company/organization. For example, if production capacity was limited in a certain period to 45,000 units it would be stupid to have a sales budget of 75,000 units. You cannot sell what you have not got! However, the principal budget factor (key factor/limiting factor) is not a fixed state of affairs and managers can, by their actions, eliminate it or reduce its effect. For example, if production capacity was the limiting factor, it could be increased by working shifts, buying more machines, using subcontractors, etc.

Control by responsibility

Control by responsibility in budgeting takes place when the responsibility for a budget/part of a budget is **delegated** to a particular person who then becomes responsible for the achievement of the targets set. He or she has to explain to management the reasons why targets are not being achieved and the reasons for significant adverse variances. For example, a sales area manager will be responsible for the achievement of monthly sales targets in his/her area. In turn, each individual sales person would be responsible for their own monthly sales target.

Management by exception

This is a system which is designed to enable managers to use their time in a more productive/effective way. Reports and statements should highlight those items of significance which are *not* going according to plan. Managers will, therefore, devote a lot of time and effort into carefully reviewing such items and putting into place any necessary corrective action. They can devote their time and talents to those tasks which really need their undivided attention. It in effect directs and in some ways forces managers to manage!

Self-assessment 7.2: The difference between profit and cash

The cash budget deals only with the actual cash which comes in or goes out during the period, i.e. the actual physical movement of cash. However, the profit and loss account deals with items which are not included in the cash budget, which in the case of Brendug Co. Ltd are as follows:

- ☐ The sales figure of £88,000 represents the total sales made during the period irrespective of whether or not the cash has been received.
- ☐ £66,000 is the total purchases figure for the period, i.e. it includes those which have been paid for in cash of £54,000 and those which have not yet been paid for of £12,000.
- ☐ The closing stock of materials of £6,000. This is deducted in computing the cost of sales but does not affect the cash budget at all.
- ☐ The charge for the use of plant and machinery, i.e. depreciation, charges a proportion of the cost in computing the loss.

Other comments

It must also be remembered that when profit is generated it is used to finance the purchase of fixed assets such as plant and machinery, fixtures and fittings, and to finance increases in the working capital, e.g. stocks and debtors. Thus, profit does not tend to stay cash for long, because the business spends it. Accrued and prepaid items will also be adjusted for in the profit and loss account but will not be adjusted for in the cash budget.

Self-assessment 7.3: Jeanles Ltd

See Tables A.1.11–A.1.13.

Table A.1.11 Jeanles Ltd: cash budget

	Inflows		Outflows					
	Opening balance	Sales	Purchases	Rent	Wages & salaries	General expenses	Fixed assets	Closing balance
	£000	£000	£000	£000	£000	£000	£000	£000
Jan	60 Share capital	–	–	1.4	1	0.5	59	(1.9)
Feb	(1.9)	8	–		1	0.5		4.6
Mar	4.6	20	10		1	0.5	16	(2.9)
Apr	(2.9)	28	15	1.4	1	0.5		7.2
May	7.2	28	21		1	0.5		12.7
Jun	12.7	28	21		1	0.5		18.2
		112	67	2.8	6.0	3.0	75	
+ debtors (1 month)		28						
		140						
+ creditors (2 months)			42					
			109					

Table A.1.12 Jeanles Ltd: budgeted profit and loss account

		£000	£000
	Sales		140
less	Cost of sales:		
	Opening stock	–	
add	Purchases	109	
		109	
less	Closing stock	4	105
	Gross profit (25% of sales)		35
less	Expenses:		
	Rent	2.8	
	Wages and salaries	6.0	
	General expenses	3.0	
	Depreciation (75 × 20%) for half-year	7.5	19.3
	Net profit		15.7

Table A.1.13 Jeanles Ltd: budgeted balance sheet

		£000	£000
	Capital employed:		
	Issued ordinary share capital	60	
	Retained profit	15.7	75.7
	Employment of capital:		
	Fixed assets	75	
less	Depreciation	7.5	67.5
	Working capital:		
	Current assets		
	Stock	4	
	Debtors (one month)	28	
	Cash & bank (per cash budget)	18.2	
		50.2	
	Current liabilities:		
	Creditors (two months)	42	8.2
			75.7

Comments (not part of the answer)

Note that during January and March the cash budget reveals an overdraft but this is covered by the current overdraft limit negotiated with the bank. Note also that the depreciation of £7,500 is for half a year. It was assumed that all the cash from the issue of the ordinary share capital would be received before January 20X4. Note also that the internal balance sheet format used started with the capital employed, it could have used the format which we used in Table 7.10 on page 65.

Suggested Answers to Text Questions for Topic 11

Chapter 10

10.1 (a) Relevant cash flows:

Year	0	1	2	3	4	5
	£000	£000	£000	£000	£000	£000
Sales revenue	–	80	120	144	100	64
Loss of contribution		(15)	(15)	(15)	(15)	(15)
Variable costs		(40)	(50)	(48)	(30)	(32)
Fixed costs (see Note 1)		(8)	(8)	(8)	(8)	(8)
Operating cash flows		17	47	73	47	9
Working capital	(30)					30
Capital cost	(100)					
Net relevant cash flows	(130)	17	47	73	47	39

Notes

1 Only the fixed costs that are incremental to the project (only existing because of the project) are relevant. Depreciation is irrelevant because it is not a cash flow.

2 The research and development cost is irrelevant since it has been spent irrespective of the decision on X14 production.

(b) Payback period:

Cumulative cash flows	(130)	(113)	(66)	7

Thus, the equipment will have repaid the initial investment by the end of the third year of operations.

(c) Net present value:

Discount factor	1.00	0.926	0.857	0.794	0.735	0.681
Present value	(130)	15.74	40.28	57.96	34.55	26.56
Net present value	45.09 (that is, the sum of the present values for years 0 to 5)					

APPENDIX 2

Present value tables and annuity tables

Table A.2.1 Present value of £1 due at end of *n* years

n	1%	2%	3%	4%	5%	6%	7%	8%	9%	10%	*n*
1	0.99010	0.98039	0.97007	0.96154	0.95238	0.94340	0.93458	0.92593	0.91743	0.90909	1
2	0.98030	0.96117	0.94260	0.92456	0.90703	0.89000	0.87344	0.85734	0.84168	0.82645	2
3	0.97059	0.94232	0.91514	0.88900	0.86384	0.83962	0.81630	0.79383	0.77218	0.75131	3
4	0.96098	0.92385	0.88849	0.85480	0.82270	0.79209	0.76290	0.73503	0.70843	0.68301	4
5	0.95147	0.90573	0.86261	0.82193	0.78353	0.74726	0.71299	0.68058	0.64993	0.62092	5
6	0.94204	0.88797	0.83748	0.79031	0.74622	0.70496	0.66634	0.63017	0.59627	0.56447	6
7	0.93272	0.87056	0.81309	0.75992	0.71068	0.66506	0.62275	0.58349	0.54703	0.51316	7
8	0.92348	0.85349	0.78941	0.73069	0.67684	0.62741	0.58201	0.54027	0.50187	0.46651	8
9	0.91434	0.83675	0.76642	0.70259	0.64461	0.59190	0.54393	0.50025	0.46043	0.42410	9
10	0.90529	0.82035	0.74409	0.67556	0.61391	0.55839	0.50835	0.46319	0.42241	0.38554	10
11	0.89632	0.80426	0.72242	0.64958	0.58468	0.52679	0.47509	0.42888	0.38753	0.35049	11
12	0.88745	0.78849	0.70138	0.62460	0.55684	0.49697	0.44401	0.39711	0.35553	0.31863	12
13	0.87866	0.77303	0.68095	0.60057	0.53032	0.46884	0.41496	0.36770	0.32618	0.28966	13
14	0.86996	0.75787	0.66112	0.57747	0.50507	0.44230	0.38782	0.34046	0.29925	0.26333	14
15	0.86135	0.74301	0.64186	0.55526	0.48102	0.41726	0.36245	0.31524	0.27454	0.23939	15
16	0.85282	0.72845	0.62317	0.53391	0.45811	0.39365	0.33873	0.29189	0.25187	0.21763	16
17	0.84438	0.71416	0.60502	0.51337	0.43630	0.37136	0.31657	0.27027	0.23107	0.19784	17
18	0.83602	0.70016	0.58739	0.49363	0.41552	0.35034	0.29586	0.25025	0.21199	0.17986	18
19	0.82774	0.68643	0.57029	0.47464	0.39573	0.33051	0.27651	0.23171	0.19449	0.16351	19
20	0.81954	0.67297	0.55367	0.45639	0.37689	0.31180	0.25842	0.21455	0.17843	0.14864	20
21	0.81143	0.65978	0.53755	0.43883	0.35894	0.29415	0.24151	0.19866	0.16370	0.13513	21
22	0.80340	0.64684	0.52189	0.42195	0.34185	0.27750	0.22571	0.18394	0.15018	0.12285	22
23	0.79544	0.63414	0.50669	0.40573	0.32557	0.26180	0.21095	0.17031	0.13778	0.11168	23
24	0.78757	0.62172	0.49193	0.39012	0.31007	0.24698	0.19715	0.15770	0.12640	0.10153	24
25	0.77977	0.60953	0.47760	0.37512	0.29530	0.23300	0.18425	0.14602	0.11597	0.09230	25

Note: $PV = £1/(1+r)^n$

Table A.2.1 continued

n	11%	12%	13%	14%	15%	16%	17%	18%	19%	20%	n
1	0.90090	0.89286	0.88496	0.87719	0.86957	0.86207	0.85470	0.84746	0.84034	0.83333	1
2	0.81162	0.79719	0.78315	0.76947	0.75614	0.74316	0.73051	0.71818	0.70616	0.69444	2
3	0.73119	0.71178	0.69305	0.67497	0.65752	0.64066	0.62437	0.60863	0.59342	0.57870	3
4	0.65873	0.63552	0.61332	0.59208	0.57175	0.55229	0.53365	0.51579	0.49867	0.48225	4
5	0.59345	0.56743	0.54276	0.51937	0.49718	0.47611	0.45611	0.43711	0.41905	0.40188	5
6	0.53464	0.50663	0.48032	0.45559	0.43233	0.41044	0.38984	0.37043	0.35214	0.33490	6
7	0.48166	0.45235	0.42506	0.39964	0.37594	0.35383	0.33320	0.31392	0.29592	0.27908	7
8	0.43393	0.40388	0.37616	0.35056	0.32690	0.30503	0.28487	0.26604	0.24867	0.23257	8
9	0.39092	0.36061	0.33288	0.30751	0.28426	0.26295	0.24340	0.22546	0.20897	0.19381	9
10	0.35218	0.32197	0.29459	0.26974	0.24718	0.22668	0.20804	0.19106	0.17560	0.16151	10
11	0.31728	0.28748	0.26070	0.23662	0.21494	0.19542	0.17781	0.16192	0.14756	0.13459	11
12	0.28584	0.25667	0.23071	0.20756	0.18691	0.16846	0.15197	0.13722	0.12400	0.11216	12
13	0.25751	0.22917	0.20416	0.18207	0.16253	0.14523	0.12989	0.11629	0.10420	0.09346	13
14	0.23199	0.20462	0.18068	0.15971	0.14133	0.12520	0.11102	0.09855	0.08757	0.07789	14
15	0.20900	0.18270	0.15989	0.14010	0.12289	0.10793	0.09489	0.08352	0.07359	0.06491	15
16	0.18829	0.16312	0.14150	0.12289	0.10686	0.09304	0.08110	0.07078	0.06184	0.05409	16
17	0.16963	0.14564	0.12522	0.10780	0.09393	0.08021	0.06932	0.05998	0.05196	0.04507	17
18	0.15282	0.13004	0.11081	0.09456	0.08080	0.06914	0.05925	0.05083	0.04367	0.03756	18
19	0.13768	0.11611	0.09806	0.08295	0.07026	0.05961	0.05064	0.04308	0.03669	0.03130	19
20	0.12403	0.10367	0.08678	0.07276	0.06110	0.05139	0.04328	0.03651	0.03084	0.02608	20
21	0.11174	0.09256	0.07680	0.06383	0.05313	0.04430	0.03699	0.03094	0.02591	0.02174	21
22	0.10067	0.08264	0.06796	0.05599	0.04620	0.03819	0.03162	0.02622	0.02178	0.01811	22
23	0.09069	0.07379	0.06014	0.04911	0.04017	0.03292	0.02702	0.02222	0.01830	0.01509	23
24	0.08170	0.06588	0.05322	0.04308	0.03493	0.02838	0.02310	0.01883	0.01538	0.01258	24
25	0.07361	0.05882	0.04710	0.03779	0.03038	0.02447	0.01974	0.01596	0.01292	0.01048	25

Table A.2.1 continued

n	21%	22%	23%	24%	25%	26%	27%	28%	29%	30%	*n*
1	0.82645	0.81967	0.81301	0.80645	0.80000	0.79365	0.78740	0.78125	0.77519	0.76923	1
2	0.68301	0.67186	0.66098	0.65036	0.64000	0.62988	0.62000	0.61035	0.60093	0.59172	2
3	0.56447	0.55071	0.53738	0.52449	0.51200	0.49991	0.48819	0.47684	0.46583	0.45517	3
4	0.46651	0.45140	0.43690	0.42297	0.40960	0.39675	0.38440	0.37253	0.36111	0.35013	4
5	0.38554	0.37000	0.35520	0.34111	0.32768	0.31488	0.30268	0.29104	0.27993	0.26933	5
6	0.31863	0.30328	0.28878	0.27509	0.26214	0.24991	0.23833	0.22737	0.21700	0.20718	6
7	0.26333	0.24859	0.23478	0.22184	0.20972	0.19834	0.18766	0.17764	0.16822	0.15937	7
8	0.21763	0.20376	0.19088	0.17891	0.16777	0.15741	0.14776	0.13878	0.13040	0.12259	8
9	0.17986	0.16702	0.15519	0.14428	0.13422	0.12493	0.11635	0.10842	0.10109	0.09430	9
10	0.14864	0.13690	0.12617	0.11635	0.10737	0.09915	0.09161	0.08470	0.07836	0.07254	10
11	0.12285	0.11221	0.10258	0.09383	0.08590	0.07869	0.07214	0.06617	0.06075	0.05580	11
12	0.10153	0.09198	0.08339	0.07567	0.06872	0.06245	0.05680	0.05170	0.04709	0.04292	12
13	0.08391	0.17539	0.06780	0.06103	0.05498	0.04957	0.04472	0.04039	0.03650	0.03302	13
14	0.06934	0.06180	0.05512	0.04921	0.04398	0.03934	0.03522	0.03155	0.02830	0.02540	14
15	0.05731	0.05065	0.04481	0.03969	0.03518	0.03122	0.02773	0.02465	0.02194	0.01954	15
16	0.04736	0.04152	0.03643	0.03201	0.02815	0.02478	0.02183	0.01926	0.01700	0.01503	16
17	0.03914	0.03403	0.02962	0.02581	0.02252	0.01967	0.01719	0.01505	0.01318	0.01156	17
18	0.03235	0.27289	0.02408	0.02082	0.01801	0.01561	0.01354	0.01175	0.01022	0.00889	18
19	0.02673	0.02286	0.01958	0.01679	0.01441	0.01239	0.01066	0.00918	0.00792	0.00684	19
20	0.02209	0.01874	0.01592	0.01354	0.01153	0.00983	0.00839	0.00717	0.00614	0.00526	20
21	0.01826	0.01536	0.01294	0.01092	0.00922	0.00780	0.00661	0.00561	0.00476	0.00405	21
22	0.01509	0.01259	0.01052	0.00880	0.00738	0.00619	0.00520	0.00438	0.00369	0.00311	22
23	0.01247	0.01032	0.00855	0.00710	0.00590	0.00491	0.00410	0.00342	0.00286	0.00239	23
24	0.01031	0.00846	0.00695	0.00573	0.00472	0.00390	0.00323	0.00267	0.00222	0.00184	24
25	0.00852	0.00693	0.00565	0.00462	0.00378	0.00310	0.00254	0.00209	0.00172	0.00152	25

Table A.2.1 continued

n	31%	32%	33%	34%	35%	36%	37%	38%	39%	40%	n
1	0.76336	0.75758	0.75188	0.74627	0.74074	0.73529	0.72993	0.72464	0.71942	0.71429	1
2	0.58272	0.57392	0.56532	0.55692	0.54870	0.54066	0.53279	0.52510	0.51757	0.51020	2
3	0.44482	0.43479	0.42505	0.41561	0.40644	0.39754	0.38890	0.38051	0.37235	0.36443	3
4	0.33956	0.32939	0.31959	0.31016	0.30107	0.29231	0.28387	0.27573	0.26788	0.26031	4
5	0.25920	0.24953	0.24029	0.23146	0.22301	0.21493	0.20720	0.19980	0.19272	0.18593	5
6	0.19787	0.18904	0.18067	0.17273	0.16520	0.15804	0.15124	0.14479	0.13865	0.13281	6
7	0.15104	0.14321	0.13584	0.12890	0.12237	0.11621	0.11040	0.10492	0.09975	0.09486	7
8	0.11530	0.10849	0.10214	0.09620	0.09064	0.08545	0.08058	0.07603	0.07176	0.06776	8
9	0.08802	0.08219	0.07680	0.07179	0.06714	0.06283	0.05882	0.05509	0.05163	0.04840	9
10	0.06719	0.06227	0.05774	0.05357	0.04973	0.04620	0.04293	0.03992	0.03714	0.03457	10
11	0.05129	0.04717	0.04341	0.03998	0.03684	0.03397	0.03134	0.02893	0.02672	0.02469	11
12	0.03915	0.03574	0.03264	0.02984	0.02729	0.02498	0.02287	0.02096	0.01922	0.01764	12
13	0.02989	0.02707	0.02454	0.02227	0.02021	0.01837	0.01670	0.01519	0.01383	0.01260	13
14	0.02281	0.02051	0.01845	0.01662	0.01497	0.01350	0.01219	0.01101	0.00995	0.00900	14
15	0.01742	0.01554	0.01387	0.01240	0.01109	0.00993	0.00890	0.00798	0.00716	0.00643	15
16	0.01329	0.01177	0.01043	0.00925	0.00822	0.00730	0.00649	0.00578	0.00515	0.00459	16
17	0.01015	0.00892	0.00784	0.00691	0.00609	0.00537	0.00474	0.00419	0.00370	0.00328	17
18	0.00775	0.00676	0.00590	0.00515	0.00451	0.00395	0.00346	0.00304	0.00267	0.00234	18
19	0.00591	0.00512	0.00443	0.00385	0.00334	0.00290	0.00253	0.00220	0.00192	0.00167	19
20	0.00451	0.00388	0.00333	0.00287	0.00247	0.00213	0.00184	0.00159	0.00138	0.00120	20
21	0.00345	0.00294	0.00251	0.00214	0.00183	0.00157	0.00135	0.00115	0.00099	0.00085	21
22	0.00263	0.00223	0.00188	0.00160	0.00136	0.00115	0.00098	0.00084	0.00071	0.00061	22
23	0.00201	0.00169	0.00142	0.00119	0.00101	0300085	0.00072	0.00061	0.00051	0.00044	23
24	0.00153	0.00128	0.00107	0.00089	0.00074	0.00062	0.00052	0.00044	0.00037	0.00031	24
25	0.00117	0.00097	0.00080	0.00066	0.00055	0.00046	0.00038	0.00032	0.00027	0.00022	25

Table A.2.2 Present value of an annuity of £1 for *n* years

n	1%	2%	3%	4%	5%	6%	7%	8%	9%	10%	*n*
1	0.9901	0.9804	0.9709	0.9615	0.9524	0.9434	0.9346	0.9259	0.9174	0.9091	1
2	1.9704	1.9416	1.9135	1.8861	1.8594	1.8334	1.8080	1.7833	1.7591	1.7355	2
3	2.9410	2.8839	2.8286	2.7751	2.7232	2.6730	2.6243	2.5771	2.5313	2.4868	3
4	3.9020	3.8077	3.7171	3.6299	3.5459	3.4651	3.3872	3.3121	3.2397	3.1699	4
5	4.8535	4.7134	4.5797	4.4518	4.3295	4.2124	4.1002	3.9927	3.8896	3.7908	5
6	5.7955	5.6014	5.4172	5.2421	5.0757	4.9173	4.7665	4.6229	4.4859	4.3553	6
7	6.7282	6.4720	6.2302	6.0020	5.7863	5.5824	5.3893	5.2064	5.0329	4.8684	7
8	7.6517	7.3254	7.0196	6.7327	6.4632	6.2098	5.9713	5.7466	5.5348	5.3349	8
9	8.5661	8.1622	7.7861	7.4353	7.1078	6.8017	6.5152	6.2469	5.9852	5.7590	9
10	9.4714	8.9825	8.5302	8.1109	7.7217	7.3601	7.0236	6.7101	6.4176	6.1446	10
11	10.3677	9.7868	9.2526	8.7604	8.3064	7.8868	7.4987	7.1389	6.8052	6.4951	11
12	11.2552	10.5753	9.9539	9.3850	8.8632	8.3838	7.9427	7.5361	7.1607	6.8137	12
13	12.1338	11.3483	10.6349	9.9856	9.3935	8.8527	8.3576	7.9038	7.4869	7.1034	13
14	13.0038	12.1062	11.2960	10.5631	9.8986	9.2950	8.7454	8.2442	7.7861	7.3667	14
15	13.8651	12.8492	11.9379	11.1183	10.3796	9.7122	9.1079	8.5595	8.0607	7.6061	15
16	14.7180	13.5777	12.5610	11.6522	10.8377	10.1059	9.4466	8.8514	8.3125	7.8237	16
17	15.5624	14.2918	13.1660	12.1656	11.2740	10.4772	9.7632	9.1216	8.5436	8.0215	17
18	16.3984	14.9920	13.7534	12.6592	11.6895	10.8276	10.0591	9.3719	8.7556	8.2014	18
19	17.2261	15.6784	14.3237	13.1339	12.0853	11.1581	10.3356	9.6036	8.9501	8.3649	19
20	18.0457	16.3514	14.8774	13.5903	12.4622	11.4699	10.5940	9.8181	9.1285	8.5136	20
21	18.8571	17.0111	15.4149	14.0291	12.8211	11.7640	10.8355	10.0168	9.2922	8.6487	21
22	19.6605	17.6580	15.9368	14.4511	13.1630	12.0416	11.0612	10.2007	9.4424	8.7715	22
23	20.4559	18.2921	16.4435	14.8568	13.4885	12.3033	11.2722	10.3710	9.5802	8.8832	23
24	21.2435	18.9139	16.9355	15.2469	13.7986	12.5503	11.4693	10.5287	9.7066	8.9847	24
25	22.0233	19.5234	17.4131	15.6220	14.0939	12.7833	11.6536	10.6748	9.8226	9.0770	25

Table A.2.2 continued

n	11%	12%	13%	14%	15%	16%	17%	18%	19%	20%	*n*
1	0.0009	0.8929	0.8850	0.3772	0.8696	0.8621	0.8547	0.8475	0.8403	0.8333	1
2	1.7125	1.6901	1.6681	1.6467	1.6257	1.6052	1.5852	1.5656	1.5465	1.5278	2
3	2.4437	2.4018	2.3612	2.3216	2.2832	2.2459	2.2096	2.1743	2.1399	2.1065	3
4	3.1024	3.0373	2.9745	2.9137	2.8550	2.7982	2.7432	2.6901	2.6386	2.5887	4
5	3.6959	3.6048	3.5172	3.4331	3.3522	3.2743	3.1993	3.1272	3.0576	2.9906	5
6	4.2305	4.1114	3.9976	3.8887	3.7845	3.6847	3.5892	3.4976	3.4098	3.3255	6
7	4.7122	4.5638	4.4226	4.2883	4.1604	4.0386	3.9224	3.8115	3.7057	3.6046	7
8	5.1461	4.9676	4.7988	4.6389	4.4873	4.3436	3.2072	4.0776	3.9544	3.8372	8
9	5.5370	5.3282	5.1317	4.9464	4.7716	4.6065	4.4506	4.3030	4.1633	4.0310	9
10	5.8892	5.6502	5.4262	5.2161	5.0188	4.8332	4.6586	4.4941	4.3389	4.1925	10
11	6.2065	5.9377	5.6869	5.4527	5.2337	5.0286	4.8364	4.6560	4.4865	4.3271	11
12	6.4924	6.1944	5.9176	5.6603	5.4206	5.1971	4.9884	4.7932	4.6105	4.4392	12
13	6.7499	6.4235	6.1218	5.8424	5.5931	5.3423	5.1183	4.9095	4.7147	4.5327	13
14	6.9819	6.6282	6.3025	6.0021	5.7245	5.4675	5.2293	5.0081	4.8023	4.6106	14
15	7.1909	6.8109	6.4624	6.1422	5.8474	5.5755	5.3242	5.0916	4.8759	4.6755	15
16	7.3792	6.9740	6.6039	6.2651	5.9542	5.6685	5.4053	5.1624	4.9377	4.7296	16
17	7.5488	7.1196	6.7291	6.3729	6.0472	5.7487	5.4746	5.2223	4.9897	4.7746	17
18	7.7016	7.2497	6.8399	6.4674	6.1280	5.8178	5.5339	5.2732	5.0333	4.8122	18
19	7.8393	7.3658	6.9380	6.5504	6.1982	5.8775	5.5845	5.3162	5.0700	4.8435	19
20	7.9633	7.4694	7.0248	6.6231	6.2593	5.9288	5.6278	5.3527	5.1009	4.8696	20
21	8.0751	7.5620	7.1016	6.6870	6.3125	5.9731	5.6648	5.3837	5.1268	4.8913	21
22	8.1757	7.6446	7.1695	6.7429	6.3587	6.0113	5.6964	5.4099	5.1486	4.9094	22
23	8.2664	7.7184	7.2297	6.7921	6.3988	6.0442	5.7234	5.4321	5.1668	4.9245	23
24	8.3481	7.7843	7.2829	6.8351	6.4338	6.0726	5.7465	5.4509	5.1822	4.9371	24
25	8.4217	7.8431	7.3300	6.8729	6.4641	6.0971	5.7662	5.4669	5.1951	4.9476	25

Table A.2.2 continued

n	21%	22%	23%	24%	25%	26%	27%	28%	29%	30%	*n*
1	0.8264	0.8197	0.8130	0.8065	0.8000	0.7937	0.7874	0.7813	0.7752	0.7592	1
2	1.5095	1.4915	1.4740	1.4568	1.4400	1.4235	1.4074	1.3916	1.3761	1.3609	2
3	2.0738	2.0422	2.0114	1.9813	1.9520	1.9234	1.8956	1.8684	1.8420	1.8161	3
4	2.5404	2.4936	2.4483	2.4043	2.3616	2.3202	2.2800	2.2410	2.2031	2.1662	4
5	2.9260	2.8636	2.8035	2.7454	2.6893	2.6351	2.5827	2.5320	2.4830	2.4356	5
6	3.2446	3.1669	3.0923	3.0205	2.9514	2.8850	2.8210	2.7594	2.7000	2.6427	6
7	3.5079	3.4155	3.3270	3.2423	3.1611	3.0833	3.0087	2.9370	2.8682	2.8021	7
8	3.7256	3.6193	3.5179	3.4212	3.3289	3.2407	3.1564	3.0758	2.9986	2.9247	8
9	3.9054	3.7863	3.6731	3.5655	3.4631	3.3657	3.2728	3.1842	3.0997	3.1090	9
10	4.0541	3.9232	3.7993	3.6819	3.5705	3.4648	3.3644	3.2689	3.1781	3.0915	10
11	4.1769	4.0354	3.9018	3.7757	3.6564	3.5435	3.4365	3.3351	3.2388	3.1473	11
12	4.2785	4.1274	3.9852	3.8514	3.7251	3.6060	3.4933	3.3868	3.2859	3.1903	12
13	4.3624	4.2028	4.0530	3.9124	3.7801	3.6555	3.6381	3.4272	3.3224	3.2233	13
14	4.4317	4.2646	4.1082	3.9616	3.8241	3.6949	3.5733	3.4587	3.3507	3.2487	14
15	4.4890	4.3152	4.1530	4.0013	3.8593	3.7261	3.6010	3.4834	3.3726	3.2682	15
16	4.5364	4.3567	4.1894	4.0333	3.8874	3.7509	3.6228	3.5026	3.3896	3.2832	16
17	4.5755	4.3908	4.2190	4.0591	3.9099	3.7705	3.6400	3.5177	3.4028	3.2948	17
18	4.6079	4.4187	4.2431	4.0799	3.9279	3.7861	3.6536	3.5294	3.4130	3.3037	18
19	4.6346	4.4415	4.2627	4.0967	3.9424	3.7985	3.6642	3.5386	3.4210	3.3105	19
20	4.6567	4.4603	4.2786	4.1103	3.9539	3.8083	3.6726	3.5458	3.4271	3.3158	20
21	4.6750	4.4756	4.2916	4.1212	3.9631	3.8161	3.6792	3.5514	3.4319	3.3198	21
22	4.6900	4.4882	4.3021	4.1300	3.9705	3.8223	3.6844	3.5558	3.4356	3.3230	22
23	4.7025	4.4985	4.3106	4.1371	3.9764	3.8273	3.6885	3.5592	3.4384	3.3254	23
24	4.7128	4.5070	4.3176	4.1428	3.9811	3.8312	3.6918	3.5619	3.4406	3.3272	24
25	4.7213	4.5139	4.3232	4.1474	3.9849	3.8342	3.6943	3.5640	3.4423	3.3286	25

Table A.2.2 continued

n	31%	32%	33%	34%	35%	36%	37%	38%	39%	40%	*n*
1	0.7634	0.7576	0.7519	0.7463	0.7407	0.7353	0.7299	0.7246	0.7194	0.7143	1
2	1.3461	1.3315	1.3172	1.3032	1.2894	1.2760	1.2627	1.2497	1.2370	1.2245	2
3	1.7909	1.7663	1.7423	1.7188	1.6959	1.6735	1.6516	1.6302	1.6093	1.5889	3
4	2.1305	2.0957	2.0618	2.0290	1.9969	1.9658	1.9355	1.9060	1.8772	1.8492	4
5	2.3897	2.3452	2.3021	2.2604	2.2200	2.1807	2.1427	2.1058	2.0699	1.9352	5
6	2.5875	2.5342	2.4828	2.4331	2.3852	2.3388	2.2936	2.2506	2.2086	2.1680	6
7	2.7386	2.6775	2.6187	2.5620	2.5075	2.4550	2.4043	2.3555	2.3083	2.2628	7
8	2.8539	2.7860	2.7208	2.6582	2.5982	2.5404	2.4849	2.4315	2.3801	2.3306	8
9	2.9419	2.8681	2.7976	2.7300	2.6653	2.6033	2.5437	2.4866	2.4317	2.3790	9
10	3.0091	2.9304	2.8553	2.7836	2.7150	2.6495	2.5867	2.5265	2.4689	2.4136	10
11	3.0604	2.9776	2.8987	2.8236	2.7519	2.6834	2.6180	2.5555	2.4956	2.4383	11
12	3.0995	3.0133	2.9314	2.8534	2.7792	2.7084	2.6409	2.5764	2.5148	2.4559	12
13	3.1294	3.0404	2.9559	2.8757	2.7994	2.7268	2.6576	2.5916	2.5286	2.4685	13
14	3.1522	3.0609	2.9744	2.8923	2.8144	2.7403	2.6698	2.6026	2.5386	2.4775	14
15	3.1696	3.0764	2.9883	2.9047	2.8255	2.7502	2.6787	2.6106	2.5457	2.4839	15
16	3.1829	3.0882	2.9987	2.9140	2.8337	2.7575	2.6852	2.6164	2.5509	2.4885	16
17	3.1931	3.0971	3.0065	2.9209	2.8398	2.7629	2.6899	2.6202	2.5546	2.4918	17
18	3.2008	3.1039	3.0124	2.9260	2.8443	2.7668	2.6934	2.6236	2.5573	2.4941	18
19	3.2067	3.1090	3.0169	2.9299	2.8476	2.7697	2.6959	2.6258	2.5592	2.4958	19
20	3.2112	3.1129	3.0202	2.9327	2.8501	2.7718	2.6977	2.6274	2.5606	2.4970	20
21	3.2174	3.1158	3.0227	2.9349	2.8519	2.7734	2.6991	2.6285	2.5616	2.4979	21
22	3.2173	3.1180	3.0246	2.9365	2.8533	2.7746	2.7000	2.6294	2.5623	2.4985	22
23	3.2193	3.1197	3.0260	2.9377	2.8543	2.7754	2.7008	2.6300	2.5628	2.4989	23
24	3.2209	3.1210	3.0271	2.9386	2.8550	2.7760	2.7013	2.6304	2.5632	2.4992	24
25	3.2220	3.1220	3.0279	2.9392	2.8556	2.7765	2.7017	2.6307	2.5634	2.4994	25

INDEX

Notes

Notes

Notes

Notes